**Loss of faith in a given religion
does not by any means
imply the eradication of
the religious instinct.
It merely means that
the instinct,
temporarily repressed,
will seek an object elsewhere.**

R. C. Zaehner, Oxford University, 1959

Hungry *for* Heaven

Rock 'n' Roll & the Search for Redemption

Steve Turner

InterVarsity Press
Downers Grove, Illinois

InterVarsity Press® is the book-publishing division of InterVarsity Christian Fellowship®, a student movement active on campus at hundreds of universities, colleges and schools of nursing in the United States of America, and a member movement of the International Fellowship of Evangelical Students. For information about local and regional activities, write Public Relations Dept., InterVarsity Christian Fellowship, 6400 Schroeder Rd., P.O. Box 7895, Madison, WI 53707-7895.

Cover photographs: Carlos Vergara

ISBN 0-8308-1382-9

Printed in the United States of America ∞

Library of Congress Cataloging-in-Publication Data

Turner, Steve.
   Hungry for heaven: rock 'n' roll and the search for redemption/
Steve Turner.
     p.   cm.
   Includes bibliographical references (p.   ).
   ISBN 0-8308-1382-9
   1. Rock music—Religious aspects—Christianity.   I. Title.
ML3534.T87   1995
781.66'09—dc20   95-6426
                                         CIP
                                         MN

17	16	15	14	13	12	11	10	9	8	7	6	5	4	3	2	1
09	08	07	06	05	04	03	02	01	00	99	98	97	96	95		

Preface _____ 7

Acknowledgments _____ 9

Introduction: I Believe in the Promised Land _____ 11

1 Crying in the Chapel _____ 17

2 Hallelujah, I Love Her So _____ 37

3 Heaven Is in Your Mind _____ 52

4 My Sweet Lord _____ 66

5 Sympathy for the Devil _____ 85

6 The Dream Is Over _____ 103

7 Into the Mystic _____ 114

8 Rivers of Babylon _____ 127

9 No Future _____ 138

10 New Gold Dream _____ 147

11 Knockin' on Heaven's Door _____ 159

12 Mysterious Ways _____ 175

13 Like a Prayer _____ 187

14 Countdown to Armageddon _____ 197

15 Techno Tribal & Positively Primal _____ 209

Sources _____ 221

Index _____ 229

Preface

Hungry for Heaven was first published in Britain in 1988 by Virgin Books. The original idea was contained in a twelve-part radio series that I conceived, researched and wrote; this was titled *The History of Rock and Religion* and was broadcast in America in 1980.

For this edition the text has been revised and expanded. I have dropped the old introduction and first chapter to permit a crisper beginning, and have added three further chapters to chronicle developments between 1988 and 1994. I also had to update material in chapters one through twelve, either because of new information or because the artists covered had released further albums that affected my conclusions. This was particularly true of the chapter on U2. When I completed the first edition of this book, *The Joshua Tree* was U2's latest release.

I'm conscious of not having been able to cover every musician who has had a dalliance with religion. This is because my main task has been to build my argument and to stick to the general belief systems and periods that each chapter was designed to deal with.

Hungry for Heaven is not an encyclopedia or a book of lists. Nor is it a guide to world religions. I realize that the teachings of a historical religion can't be judged solely by their representation in the works of a handful of rock musicians. What the book does do, though, is enable you to judge how consistently the devotees have lived within their chosen beliefs, and how those beliefs, as communicated by them in song and interview, square with reality.

I speak throughout the book of "rock 'n' roll" and use the term generically to include everything from rockabilly and reggae to rap and house. It's far too confusing to switch from *rock 'n' roll* to *beat* to *metal* to *folk*. Van Morrison says he doesn't play rock and isn't a star, but everyone knows what you mean when you describe him as a rock star.

When one deals with spiritual aspirations, as this book does, one finds that there is a paucity of vocabulary available to communicate to the religious and the nonreligious person alike. Even phrases like "spiritual aspiration" and "religious person" are fraught with dangers. I've therefore used the word *spiritual* to describe a search for meaning that acknowledges the nonmaterial dimension. In doing so I'm not making moral claims for the searchers. Likewise, "hungry for heaven" and "the search for redemption" in the title and subtitle are not meant to suggest the hungering and thirsting after righteousness that Jesus spoke of, but the feeling, however inadequately expressed, that we need to break free from this fallen world.

In the fourth century St. Augustine wrote, "Man was made for God, and his heart is forever restless until it finds its rest in him." Some fifteen centuries later, Bruce Springsteen sang, "Everybody's got a hungry heart." *Hungry for Heaven* attempts to build a link between those two statements.

Acknowledgments

The original version of *Hungry for Heaven* was edited by Cat Ledger for Virgin Books, London, with help from Alastair Dougall. Alison Taylor obtained permissions, and Robert Devereux commissioned the book. This revised and expanded edition was edited by James Catford for Hodder & Stoughton, London, and was recommissioned by Andrew Le Peau of InterVarsity Press, Illinois, U.S.A.

The radio series *The History of Rock and Religion* was commissioned by Mary Neely of The Warehouse in Sacramento, California, and broadcast on 168 radio stations throughout America in 1980.

I would like to thank fellow writers who have allowed me to pick their brains: Dave Marsh, Neil Spencer, Mick Watts, Mick Brown, Chris Welch, Cliff White, Harry Shapiro, Roy Carr, Martin Wroe, Barry Miles, David Toop and David Rodigan.

Many of the quotes in the book are from my own interviews with the following people: Jerry Lee Lewis, Don Butler, Roy Orbison, the Reverend James E. Hamill, J. D. Sumner, Carl Perkins, the Reverend W. Herbert Brewster, Ray Charles, Lamont Dozier, the late Thomas

Dorsey, Al Green, Jessy Dixon, Andrae Crouch, Robin Williamson, Chet Helms, Mike Pinder, Yusef Islam, Eric Clapton, Pete Townshend, John Lennon, Prabhu Guptara, Ravi Shankar, Mick Jagger, Kenneth Anger, Christopher Gibbs, John Michell, Roger McGuinn, George Martin, Arthur Brown, Kip Trevor, Jim Gannon, William Burroughs, Allen Ginsberg, Ozzy Osborne, Tommy Lee, Wilfrid Mellers, I. M. Lewis, Jackson Browne, Bernie Leadon, Van Morrison, Jon Anderson, Dave Davies, Nik Turner, Bob Geldof, Winston Rodney (Burning Spear), Norman Grant, Linton Kwesi Johnson, Brian Eno, David Byrne, the late Stiv Bators, Larry Norman, Gordon Gano, Bono, Sting, Hammer, Mixmaster Morris and Moby.

Thanks to John Pearce for persuading Jerry Lee Lewis to speak to me, to Bill E. Burk for showing me Memphis, to Bill Ferris of the University of Mississippi, Twyla Dixon of Graceland, Ronnie Pugh of the Country Music Foundation in Nashville, Nicola Joss from Pete Townshend's office, and Keith Altham.

Above all, I have to thank those special people who have helped shape my views of rock 'n' roll and religion through years of friendship—Larry Norman, T-Bone Burnett, Mike Roe, Malcolm Doney, Steve Scott and the late David G. Rees.

I Believe in the Promised Land

Introduction

I don't know which will go first: rock 'n' roll or Christianity.
John Lennon

Pop is the perfect religious vehicle.
Donovan

Rock 'n' roll has its feet down in the mud and its head up in the clouds.
Bono

*I*t was interesting to watch people's responses when I told them I was writing a book about rock music and religion. Some were clearly nonplussed—as if I had announced I was researching the subject of deep-sea fishing in outer space—and muttered a polite "That must be interesting." Others showed a bit more understanding but assumed I was referring to either the influence of evangelical singers Pat Boone and Cliff Richard or the burning of supposedly Satanic records in the Bible Belt.

Many people assume that rock 'n' roll is irreligious, if not completely antireligious, and that it meets religion only in combat—or because a particular religious group has decided to "use" rock 'n' roll as a "tool" to "reach young people." Either way, the result is not considered very edifying. Rock 'n' roll, such people agree, is best left to its secular self.

The fact is that religion has had a profound effect on almost all of rock 'n' roll's innovators and has helped to shape the music at key stages in its development. Even avowedly secular rock 'n' roll often has at its heart a quest for transcendence that uses the language of religion.

Early rock 'n' rollers like Elvis Presley and Little Richard were affected by the passions of Pentecostalism, and soul music grew directly out of black American gospel music. As the church lost its grip on young people in the 1960s, the appeal of the religiously primitive, the pagan and the exotic grew. The Beatles looked east toward India, the Rolling Stones became fascinated with occultism, Van Morrison sang of nature mysticism, and Jim Morrison of the Doors flirted with shamanism.

In more recent years Islam has had an impact on rap, as seen in the records of acts such as Public Enemy and Brand Nubian, while various forms of New Age ideas have filtered into the dance scene through gurus like Terence McKenna and musicians like the Shamen. It's now no longer a surprise when Boy George calls his act "Jesus Loves You" and makes a pop record in praise of the Hindu god Krishna, or when Michael Jackson writes, as he did in the sleeve notes of his album *Dangerous,* "On many an occasion when I am dancing, I have felt touched by something sacred. In those moments, I felt my spirit soar, and become one with everything that exists."

If these were purely private beliefs, they wouldn't warrant a book like this; but as I've illustrated, they have become integrated with the music and publicized by the artists. When the Beatles began investigating Hinduism, the results were immediately evident in their songs; and when Bob Dylan turned to Christianity in 1979, he began lecturing his audiences on their lack of faith. Bob Marley openly preached the virtues of Rastafarianism, just as Public Enemy have worked to promote the Nation of Islam.

When I remind people of facts like these, the relevance of religion to rock 'n' roll becomes clear. Thus my first task with this book has been to pile on the evidence of this still largely unexplored subject, so that the pattern becomes clear.

My main sources have been the albums themselves, backed up by contemporary accounts drawn from books, newspapers and magazines. I've also been able to draw on my own interviews with many of the main participants, including John Lennon, Mick Jagger, Al Green, Roy Orbison, David Byrne and Bono. Musicians such as Jerry Lee Lewis, Van Morrison, Jon Anderson, Pete Townshend, Brian Eno, Moby and Sting spoke to me specifically for the book.

I've arranged the material chronologically rather than under subject headings because I felt I was uncovering a secret history of rock 'n' roll and that only in sequence does the development become clear. Although I could equally well have started with country music, gospel or blues, I decided to begin with the rock 'n' roll revolution ushered in by Elvis and to end with the techno dance scene, which is still mutating as I write.

Each chapter concentrates on a single influence over a particular period. The drawback in structuring the book in this way was that some artists either had careers that spanned several time periods or had beliefs that didn't fit my categories. Where could I fit Michael Jackson, who was raised a Jehovah's Witness, now appears to believe in a form of pantheism and had his first hit, with the Jackson Five, in 1970? Where would Boy George fit? At the peak of his fame with Culture Club, he was best known as a gay ex-Catholic. Now that he is no longer an international star, he has become a devotee of Krishna and follows a form of religion that had its major impact on rock 'n' roll at the end of the 1960s.

Some people with long careers and a multitude of faiths had to be fitted in where I considered they'd made their most significant contribution. Bob Dylan has drawn from his knowledge of Judaism, Christianity, Zen Buddhism, the Cabala, numerology, the tarot and various arcane philosophies, but I decided to encapsulate his journey in the chapter on born-again Christian belief. Likewise Van Morrison, who has been interested in nature mysticism, Christianity, Scientology and Native American religions, is dealt with fully in the chapter on New Age.

So many musicians have now embraced religious ideas that in dealing with the 1990s I had to be selective, choosing to focus on the rap and dance scenes. This meant not being able to discuss Sinead O'Connor, who—although she tore up a photo of the pope on television—claims to be on a mission from God, and bands like Crash Test Dummies ("God Shuffled His Feet") and Jah Wobble's Invaders of the Heart ("Take Me to God"). Eventually I had to limit myself to dealing with those who were responsible for bringing about major changes in the treatment of redemption in rock 'n' roll in the hope that, having gotten a glimpse of the overall picture, readers will be able to see where their favorite musician fits in.

I came to believe that there is something in the essence of rock 'n' roll that mirrors the religious search, and my second task is to try to distill that essence. It is for this reason that *Hungry for Heaven* is subtitled *Rock 'n' Roll and the Search for Redemption.* I became convinced that one of the reasons so many rock 'n' rollers eventually embrace a religious worldview is that the best rock 'n' roll is itself a crying out for an experience of transcendence that the modern secular world doesn't offer.

Redemption, a word that came into rock 'n' roll usage through the songs of Bob Marley and Bruce Springsteen, means to be "ransomed" or "bought back," implying that we are naturally imprisoned and in need of release. In Christian theology the explanation for this is that we are imprisoned by the power, guilt and consequence of sin and need to be released in order to enjoy a fuller life on earth and eternal life thereafter. The price paid for the ransom was the death of Christ. Other religions suggest we're in bondage to ego or suffering or illusion and need to redeem ourselves by becoming enlightened.

Secular rock 'n' roll is not specific about either the problem or the solution, but there is an underlying feeling that we are in the wrong place and, as Jim Morrison once put it when he was with the Doors, we needed to "break on through to the other side." It was a small step from the screaming and thrashing of the Who's "Anyway Anyhow Anywhere" ("Nothing gets in my way / Not even locked doors") to the spiritual solutions offered to the same problems in its rock operas *Tommy* and *Quadrophenia.*

I wanted to show ways in which religion had affected not only the ideas in the lyrics of rock 'n' roll but also the music itself. Elements of gospel were present in the earliest rock, but as more esoteric religions have been investigated, so new forms of music have made their presence felt, from the ragas of India to the trance music of Africa and Siberia.

Finally, I wanted to discover why rock 'n' roll stars appear to be more open to religion than, for example, actors, ballet dancers or architects. Is it simply the result of having too much too soon? Is it faddishness? Is it a necessary support after drugs and drink have done their damage? Or is there something within music that makes musicians more attracted to the numinous?

My own interest in rock music and religion stems from an upbringing immersed in evangelicalism—what we British call "nonconformist Christianity"—and a love affair with rock 'n' roll that began in the late 1950s, when I could hear the music only on Radio Luxembourg or on a café jukebox. At that time rock n' roll seemed like an alternative to the drabness of formal worship, but in the 1960s, particularly through Bob Dylan and the Beatles, I saw them come together. Around the same time that I became committed as a writer, seeing my first article published in *The Beatles Book* in 1969, I became committed as a Christian.

It's been a long and interesting journey. Over the years religion has become more and more acceptable as a topic of debate within rock 'n' roll. A statement made by Bono sums up my feelings and sets the stage for what is to come in this book. "Once I thought that rock 'n' roll didn't have a place for spiritual concerns," he said. "But I've since discovered that a lot of the artists who have inspired me—Bob Dylan, Van Morrison, Patti Smith, Al Green and Marvin Gaye—were in a similar position. . . . That's why I'm more at ease."

Crying in the Chapel

1

My first love would be spiritual music.
Elvis Presley

I was a preacher one time. Scared the pants off every congregation.
Jerry Lee Lewis

I don't think there's much question that "rhythm and blues" is a term which I coined when I was working at *Billboard*. If I understood then what I know now, I would have called it "rhythm and gospel."
Jerry Wexler

*R*ock 'n' roll, as a commercial form of music aimed at white teenagers, was born in the Southern states of America, where the predominant religion was fundamentalist/evangelical Protestantism and the musical heritage a mixture of Celtic folk, English hymns and West African rhythm. People born in the immediate prewar years (the founding fathers of rock 'n' roll) were touched by each of these.

Although there were many denominations, each distinguished by a different doctrinal emphasis, there was a shared belief that people are exiled from God by virtue of our sinful nature and can be redeemed only by a personal act of repentance based on a faith that Jesus Christ, in his crucifixion, took our deserved punishment. Only on making this decision could you say you were "saved," that you were truly a Christian. Usually this would be followed by a baptism in which you'd be plunged beneath the waters in a symbolic act of death (the old sinful self) and rebirth (the new life of the Spirit).

However, a Christian wasn't just someone who assented to the Bible's teachings. It was someone who had participated in a supernatural transaction. Christianity teaches that redemption is complete only after death, but it starts here with God's gift of the Holy Spirit, who comes inside a person to give strength, guidance, wisdom and comfort. At this point denominations diverge.

The Pentecostals—named after the Day of Pentecost on which the first Christians were empowered with the Holy Spirit, who appeared as tongues of fire—believe that specific evidence of the Spirit should be displayed by all true believers. Pentecostals like to hear "speaking in tongues"—that is, when a convert begins to talk in an unknown language, a heavenly tongue. They like to see people lay hands on the sick and disabled and produce immediate healing. Some of them believe in being "slain in the Spirit," when a worshiper will collapse on the floor in an ecstatic spasm, apparently overwhelmed by the divine encounter.

In 1955, when rock 'n' roll was showing its first stirrings, church attendance was at an all-time high in the United States. Between 1940 and 1958 there was an increase from 64.5 million worshipers to 109.6 million. Social status was attached to being a church member; middle-class morality and respectability were framed by it; and with the post-war baby boom in full swing, parents were anxious to get their children into Sunday school.

One observer of the time wrote that churchgoing appeared to give Americans self-confidence, and even self-righteousness. "It appeared to guarantee success for the individual in his professional career and victory for the nation in its struggle against atheistic, materialistic communism. Religious affiliation seemed to provide a means by which Americans could define themselves in their community and their society. Religion became a part of 'belonging,' a quick way to establish social identity."

And so it was that the Assemblies of God were blessed with Elvis Presley and Jerry Lee Lewis, and the Baptists with Chuck Berry, Little Richard and Buddy Holly. Holly made a "decision for Christ" when he was seventeen years old and was baptized at Tabernacle Baptist Church, Lubbock, Texas. Little Richard mostly attended the New Hope Baptist Church in Macon, Georgia, but he liked to sneak down to the Holiness Church, where the people danced and he could imitate them speaking in tongues.

Yet churchgoing didn't necessarily indicate personal faith—it was often no more than the conventional behavior of the time. Says Ray Charles, "In certain areas of America there are things that just happen. In the Southern part of the United States, which is quite conservative, children went to church. All kids went to church when I was coming up. You just did. There was no such thing as not going to church."

Lamont Dozier, of the legendary Motown songwriting team Holland-Dozier-Holland, had the same experience growing up in Michigan. "We all went to church," he said. "That was one of the things we had to do, like going to school. It was something you didn't say no to. There was no rock 'n' roll on a Sunday. No foolishness."

Elvis Presley

Elvis Presley is on record as saying that his was "a religious family" that regularly attended camp meetings and revivals. The family went to the First Assembly of God Church, initially in East Tupelo, Mississippi, and then in Memphis, Tennessee, after moving there in 1948. However, recollections of the pastors from these churches show that Presley's parents were not among those who totally committed themselves to the life and work of the church.

"I might straighten your thinking out on Elvis before he became a singer," said the Reverend James E. Hamill, once the pastor of the Memphis church. He was tired of hearing how Presley got his start in some sort of family group at the First Assembly of God. "He never sang in church, and never had a part in the musical program. The fact of the matter is, I never knew he sang until he hit the big time.

"There's something else that needs to be straightened out too," Hamill continued. "Elvis never joined the church. He was never part of the church officially. He attended in his teens, he attended quite regularly, but he never became a member."

Hamill's point is that religious though Elvis was, he never went through the procedure of repentance, baptism and church member-ship. He watched and listened, but he never contributed. "We believe that a person accepts Jesus Christ as Savior and then he joins the church, becomes part of the church and supports the church with his efforts, time and talent," Hamill says. "Elvis never did that."

There are parallels between Elvis and Jerry Lee Lewis. Both grew up touched by gospel music, inspired by preaching and respectful of the Christian gospel, but neither of them felt able to give himself totally to what, in his heart of hearts, he believed to be right. The drunkenness and fornication they'd been taught to shun had too great an attraction for them.

Hamill told me how in the late 1950s, when Elvis was already a legendary American figure and at the height of his powers, he came into Hamill's vestry at the close of a Sunday-night service. "I had been concerned about Elvis, concerned about the fact that he grew up in our church under my preaching and teaching, yet he was doing this kind of entertainment. Anyway, he came to me, and the first thing he said was, 'Pastor, I'm the most miserable young man you've ever seen.'

"He said, 'I've got all the money I'll ever need to spend. I've got millions of fans. I've got friends. But I'm doing what you taught me not to do, and I'm not doing the things you taught me to do.' That night gave me an insight into Elvis."

At the end of his life Elvis was still beset by doubts about his career. Vocalist J. D. Sumner, one of his childhood gospel-singing heroes, remembers that once in Las Vegas Elvis met backstage with the TV evangelist Rex Humbard and seriously asked whether he should devote his show to gospel music.

"Humbard told him that he shouldn't," recalled Sumner. "He said that by drawing in the multitudes and singing songs like 'Why Me?' and 'How Great Thou Art' he was tilling more soil for ministers like himself than anyone else in the world. He told him that he really would be doing wrong if he sang only gospel."

The Assemblies of God, founded in Hot Springs, Arkansas, in 1914, is a Pentecostal denomination, the second largest in America by the time of World War II. Its emphasis on holy living and being Spirit-filled was to make an unusual contribution to rock 'n' roll, one that would not be approved by the church. It's possible to see the spontaneity of being "moved by the Spirit"—when a worshiper might speak, sing, dance, wail or prophesy at the urging of the Spirit—being reinterpreted secularly by Presley, Little Richard and Jerry Lee Lewis.

Little Richard, with his frenzied piano style and nonsense language in songs like "Tutti Frutti," was quite clearly imitating what he saw and heard in church. "My music is the healing music that makes the dumb and deaf hear and talk," he would say.

Elvis, too, attached great importance to being "moved." When he cut "Milkcow Blues Boogie" in 1954, during one of his first sessions for Sun Records, he started with a slow version and then stopped his musicians. On the recording you hear him say, "Hold it, fellows. That don't move me. Let's get real, real gone." Always, when asked about his uninhibited stage gyrations, he would disclaim responsibility. "It's the beat that gets you," he would explain. "If you like it and you feel it, you can't help but move to it. That's what happens to me. I can't help it." Doesn't this sound remarkably like the Pentecostal injunction to "resist not the Holy Spirit" or to "let go and let God"?

Jerry Lee Lewis

Holy living in the Assemblies of God embraced, but went beyond, the prescriptions of the Bible. Besides fornication, adultery and drunken-

ness, it frowned on anything it deemed "worldly," and that included
tobacco, makeup, television, films and dancing. For teenagers like
Elvis and Jerry Lee this caused almost unbearable tensions. The cost
of becoming "worldly" appeared to include not just social disgrace but
the possibility of damnation.

Rock 'n' roll, with its acceptance of drinking and dancing and its
then-implicit approval of fornication, was clearly unacceptable. "I
didn't approve of rock 'n' roll," the Reverend Hamill told me. "And I
still don't for that matter." To play rock 'n' roll, to hang out in sleazy
joints where people got drunk and danced, to celebrate animal lust, was
to make a choice for unholy living. It wasn't something you could be
halfhearted about. If this was sin, you were going to have to sin boldly.

Roy Orbison, raised in the Church of Christ in Wink, Texas, recalls
his own point of crisis as a teenager. "They were against dancing at
my church, and I was trying to play at dances. I wasn't old enough
to figure out anything for myself. So I just didn't go to church. I didn't
want to attend and feel uncomfortable. I went and played the dances."

The forbiddenness of their music supplied those young musicians
with an air of danger they wouldn't otherwise have had. Whether it
was true, as the Alabama White Citizens Council believed, that rock
'n' roll rhythms appealed "to the base in man, [bringing out] the an-
imalism and vulgarity," mattered less than the fact that the musicians
themselves had a strong suspicion that rock 'n' roll was the devil's
music. The music critic Robert Palmer has remarked that Jerry Lee
Lewis's authority and tension resulted from the fact that he "knew
from the first that he was going to hell for playing rock 'n' roll, and
he went ahead and rocked anyway."

In the case of Jerry Lee, the tension has been deep and long-lasting.
Raised in an Assembly of God church in Ferriday, Louisiana, he has
lived with the conviction that he's not strong enough to be a Christian.
In his early life he vacillated between repentance and drunkenness,
preaching and playing in local blues clubs. As a teenager he enrolled
at Southwestern Bible Institute in Waxahachie, Texas, but was ex-

pelled after three months when he played a boogie-woogie version of
the hymn "My God Is Real" for morning assembly.

For years his prodigality was set in sharp relief by the career of his
cousin Jimmy Lee Swaggart, who was America's top television evangelist and a keen opponent of rock 'n' roll until his demise in the 1980s.
The story, as told by Swaggart, is that the two boys grew up together,
sat with each other in church and were both blessed with the gift of
piano playing. The difference is that whereas Swaggart dediated his
gift to God, Lewis didn't or couldn't.

In his autobiography, *To Cross a River,* Swaggart recalls how at a
local talent competition he went back on his word and played a song
taught him by a local blues musician. He claims that as he touched
the keys to pound out that song, a "strange feeling" came over him.

I was able to do runs on that piano I had never been able to do
before. It seemed like a force beyond me had gripped and charged
my body. My fingers literally flew over the keys.

For the first time in my life, I sensed what it felt like to be
anointed by the Devil. I don't know any other way to describe it.
It was unlike anything I had ever experienced in my life. I knew it
wasn't from God. . . . After I finished, Jerry Lee sang and played,
drawing the identical response from the crowd. The same demonic
anointing I experienced was also on him.

Whatever happened, Lewis was cursed with this explanation and has
been unable to shake off the belief that musical inspiration must pro-
ceed from either God or the devil. The thought was very much on his
mind in 1957, when he came to record his best-known hit, "Great Balls
of Fire." The double-entendre song full of hot sex and the vaguely
Pentecostal imagery of "balls of fire" caused him to fall into one of
his frequent bouts of remorse, which, thanks to a vigilant tape engi-
neer, was recorded for posterity, leaving us with a vivid insight into
the spiritual tensions Lewis lived with.

He kicked off the session by claiming that rock 'n' roll was "worldly
music" and that to approach God you have to be untainted by the

world. Producer Sam Phillips, who had also produced Presley, was as acquainted with the Bible as any other Southern boy, and tried to reason with Lewis by suggesting that by arousing good feelings, rock 'n' roll was injecting good into the world. He pointed out that Jesus Christ not only preached but also healed and did good works.

"You can do good, Mr. Phillips," acknowledged Lewis. "Don't get me wrong. You can have a kind heart . . . you can help people . . ."

Thinking he was winning his argument, Phillips moved in with his clincher. "You can save people," he said with authority.

At this Lewis erupted with all the godly zeal he could muster. This was heresy. "No. No. NO! No! No!" he began. "How can the Devil save souls? What are you talkin' about?"

Phillips immediately tried to calm him down, but Lewis wasn't buying it. He knew rock 'n' roll couldn't save souls, because he was the living example. "I have the Devil in me," he shouted. "If I didn't, I'd be a Christian."

This conviction of his own damnation has never left him. In his life of drunkenness, drug-taking, violence, divorce and the deaths of two wives and a son, it's been as if instead of living a life "worthy of his calling," as the New Testament commands, he has lived a life worthy of the damnation he has felt to be his due. "I know the right way," he told *Rolling Stone* during the 1970s. "I was raised a good Christian. But I couldn't make it. Too weak I guess."

This attitude brings to mind novelist Flannery O'Connor's observation, made in 1960, that "while the South is hardly Christ-centered, it is most certainly Christ-haunted. The Southerner, who isn't convinced of it, is very much afraid that he may have been formed in the image and likeness of God. Ghosts can be very instructive."

Lewis's career, with its headline-grabbing upsets—his expulsion from Britain in 1958 for traveling with an underage wife; the suspicious death of a later wife—has seemed like a headlong flight away from God. "Salvation bears down on me," he told *People* magazine in 1980. "I don't wanna die and go to hell. But I don't think I'm heading in the right direction. . . . I'm lost and undone, without God or son. I should've been a Christian, but I was too weak for the gospel. I'm a rock 'n' roll cat. We all have to answer to God on Judgment Day."

With all of this in mind, I went to meet Lewis on Easter Sunday 1982. Dressed in a black velvet jacket over blue jeans and brandishing a large cigar, he started by telling me, with a concerned look on his pallid face, that things back at the church in Ferriday weren't what they used to be. "They've fallen short of the glory of God, for one thing," he said, drawing a cloud of smoke into his mouth. "The Pentecostal Assembly of God Church has got more like the Baptist Church used to be. We didn't used to believe in that because the Baptists didn't preach the full gospel. Still don't."

This concern for the doctrinal purity of his denomination is part of his inherent contradiction. He never denies the gospel, just says he's too weak to live it. He said that if he had to preach the gospel again, as he once did, his message would be "that if a man's not saved, sanctified and filled with the Holy Ghost, reborn with the blood of Jesus Christ, he will not go to heaven." To be saved, he clarified, you need to repent of your sins "and, behold, you become a new person. All sins are wiped away! All things are new! Pretty hard to live that way, I would think. But I've seen people do it."

On the subject of the devil's music he was slippery. Hadn't he said he was heading in the wrong direction? "I don't feel I'm doing the wrong thing," he said. "I didn't say that. That remains to be seen." Hadn't he told one journalist that he was "dragging the audience to hell" with him? "If I really thought that, I wouldn't do it. I ain't never met the devil. I might have married a couple of 'em, but . . ."

Of the "Great Balls of Fire" tape he commented, "I was twenty years old . . . straight from church. We were talkin' about the Bible. I backed [Sam Phillips] into a corner. He couldn't quote the Scripture, but I could."

It seemed that he was presenting a new case. He was not living the wrong life. Rock 'n' roll was not of the devil. So could he now envisage rock 'n' roll in a Christian setting? Suddenly we were transported back to 1957. I was Phillips. He was still Lewis.

"How do you see 'A Whole Lotta Shakin' and 'Great Balls of Fire' done in church?" he asked incredulously. "Can you picture Jesus Christ singin' it? On Easter Sunday . . . can you picture that?"

Could *he* picture it? "No, I couldn't," he said flatly. I asked why he couldn't, and he looked slowly around the room and tapped his cigar on the edge of an ashtray. "Why do you think he would?" he said steadily. "Everything he preached was against it."

Surely then, I reasoned, Lewis thought he was disobeying God by playing rock 'n' roll. The argument hadn't changed a jot in twenty-five years. "You're doin' the talkin' now," he retorted accusingly. "I'm just answerin' the questions. You'll not back the Killer into no corner. As far as bein' the devil's music—don't believe that. No. It's God's music. Everything belongs to God, don't it? Now Satan has power next to God, don't he? He has more power than Jesus Christ. People don't realize the power Satan has."

He appeared to accept Swaggart's judgment of all those years ago. He didn't accept that the emotions aroused at a revival meeting have any common root with those kicked up at a rock 'n' roll concert. "It's the devil's excitement and God's excitement," he said. "It's just which one you want. You can't go back and forth. I'm not a hypocrite now. I don't run back and forth to church."

Which power falls on Jerry Lee Lewis? "Power of voodoo," he said, working his way out of a corner. "I know what you're talkin' about. Power of God can fall on a congregation. Power of Satan can fall on a congregation."

I asked the question again. "*My* power," he said, and then broke into a satisfied laugh. "Got you on that one! There's power in the blood, there's also power in Jerry Lee Lewis! God gimme the power. I probably missed it, but that's left to me."

It was clear that on this day at least, he wasn't going to pursue his own logic. He wasn't going to name his demon. "I wasn't avoiding your questions," he said afterward. "I just didn't want to get into the religious aspect." As he left the room he turned to his road manager and said, "He just asked me what power, and I said my power. Those questions really get to me, man!"

Little Richard

Little Richard has had similar battles. The first came in 1957, when, during an Australian tour, he quit rock 'n' roll in order to enter Bible college. Like Presley and Lewis, he recorded hymns but was eventually drawn back to rock 'n' roll. Then again in 1977 he gave up to become a Bible salesman. Now, as an evangelist for the Universal Remnant Church of God, he walks a path somewhere between the two, cutting rock 'n' roll tracks and denouncing rock 'n' roll, preaching on the importance of the Ten Commandments while recounting the most explicit descriptions of his sinful past with what appears to be a certain amount of relish.

The message of his church is certainly unorthodox, and the persona of Little Richard obscures whatever repentance and humility there may be in his heart. His view of rock 'n' roll today is that it's "demonic." He says, "A lot of the beats in music today are taken from voodoo, from the voodoo drums. If you study music in rhythms, like I have, you'll see that is true. I believe that kind of music is driving people from Christ. It is contagious. I believe that God wants people to turn from rock 'n' roll to the Rock of Ages, to get ready for eternal life."

Yet the gap between rock 'n' roll and the Rock of Ages is not as great as Richard believes. He himself took his style almost wholesale from the church, having grown up singing gospel and admiring gospel stars Brother Joe May and Sister Rosetta Tharpe. Indeed, his first recordings were for a gospel label whose agents were looking for a "churchy sound" they could use to get a foothold in the rhythm and blues market.

When Richard yelped and screamed on stage, he was drawing on his childhood reminiscences of preachers and the Spirit-slain. Of course, as an unrepentant sinner, he was not bringing the ecstasy of the Spirit but the ecstasy of the flesh. His songs were clearly about raunchy, uncommitted sex. But the power he brought was a facsimile of black Pentecostalism. "It's hypnotic," said Mick Jagger after seeing him in concert. "It's like an evangelistic meeting where, for want of a better phrase, Richard is the disciple and the audience the flock that follows."

Gospel Roots

Although the sentiments of early rock 'n' roll songs owed more to country and blues, where salvation lay in orgasm or true love, their harmonies, vocal coloring, stage movements and emotional orchestration drew heavily on gospel, both black and white. Presley and Lewis were inspired to play by performing preachers—in Lewis's case, a visiting speaker who managed to hammer out a tune on the piano with one hand while balancing a Bible on the other; in Presley's case, the pastor of the church in East Tupelo, who used an acoustic guitar during his sermons.

Buddy Holly, an admirer of Mahalia Jackson, modeled the sound of the Crickets' harmonies on his church choir and the country spirituals of the Louvin Brothers. Before he died he was planning an album of gospel songs, and "True Love Ways," one of his last singles, was based on the Angelic Gospel Singers' version of the hymn "It'll Be All Right." "His own religious faith remained a strong force in his life," wrote his biographer John Goldrosen. "In truth, it is by no means stretching matters to see a strong Christian strain in the attitude of faith and patience that color his songs."

Presley consciously drew on blues, country, black gospel and quartet singing. Precocious teenager that he was, he would travel down to the blues clubs on Beale Street, listen to the local country radio station, check out the gospel acts at East Trigg Baptist Church and attend all-night "gospel sings" at the Ellis Auditorium. From blues and country he got a certain amount of sentiment, swing and style, but gospel, as he would often remind people, remained his first love.

Quartet Fever

The white gospel quartets of the 1950s, when Presley started to study them, were every bit as exciting as their black counterparts, using show-biz hype, whipping up crowds and creating stars. Reporting on an all-night sing in Atlanta, Georgia, for *The Saturday Evening Post* (June 1956), Furman Bisher compared the audience response to the Oak Ridge Quartet to bobby soxers' swooning for Frank Sinatra. "Women out there shrieked, and a couple of young girls rushed to the stage edge to snap pictures of the tenor who was holding that high note the way a trumpet player prolongs a 'ride,' " wrote Bisher. "Even grown men—and there were a good many present—cheered and whistled. The crowd soon was stamping its feet. It was more like the cross between an emotional peak at a soul-saving camp meeting and late in the evening at Stan Kenton."

Presley idolized such gospel stars for the rest of his life. His particular favorites were J. D. Sumner, the tall, stringy bass vocalist with the Blackwood Brothers, who also went to the First Assembly of God Church in Memphis, and Jake Hess and Hovie Lister of the Statesmen Quartet (which actually had five members). An ordained minister, Lister is often credited with bringing show business to quartet singing. At the time he said, "If it takes shaking my hair down, beating a piano like Liberace or Piano Red to keep these young people out of beer joints and the rear seats of cars, I'll do it. The Devil's got his kind of entertainment. We've got ours. They criticize me, say I'm too lively for religion, but I get results. That's what counts."

White quartet singing had developed in the 1920s, created by publishing houses such as J. D. Vaughan, V. O. Stamps and J. R. Baxter, to sell Christian songs printed in sixty-cent songbooks. The groups, composed of alto, tenor, bass and soprano, would often tackle the most difficult songs in the catalog to show their prowess. Just before

World War II, aware of their own drawing power, they began to loosen their connections with publishing houses and seek work as performers in their own right.

That was how they began to develop showmanship and gimmicks during the 1940s. The Rangers Quartet set the pace by dressing as Texas Rangers and cycling to their performances. The group boasted an Irish tenor in Denver Crumpler and "the world's lowest bass singer" in Arnold Hyles. Later they grew thin mustaches and wore pinstriped double-breasted suits, looking more like Chicago gangsters than messengers of the Word in song. They also broke ground by having commercial sponsors for their fifteen-minute CBS radio shows—Vicks Chemical Company and B. C. Headache Powders.

While the Blackwood Brothers and the Harmoneers were restrained in appearance, Hovie Lister, a dashing young man with long, dark wavy hair and an Errol Flynn mustache, loved to shake it all up for the Lord. He joined with Crumpler and Jake Hess to form the Statesmen Quartet, which was to become one of the first supergroups of white gospel, catapulting the music to commercial acceptability and setting the style for emergent rock 'n' rollers bred on holy music.

Although much was made of the evils of dancing, show business, jukeboxes and television, the success of the gospel quartets was largely due to their presenting much of the same gloss and excitement in an acceptable context. The songs were about loving your neighbor, being holy and not giving in to "modern religion," but the performances drew from pop, blues, country, ragtime and jazz. For those with a conscience about visiting dance halls and cinemas, this was an opportunity for guilt-free celebration and self-expression.

"God didn't intend for religion to wear a long face," declared Lister at the time. "I don't think anybody found anything wrong with the good old hearty shouting of a man or woman filled with the Spirit of the Lord at a revival meeting. That's how we sing. We give them the Spirit."

Don Butler, now director of archives for the Nashville-based Gospel

Music Association, was the Statesmen Quartet's manager during the 1950s. "They were sensational," he remembers. "Hovie Lister had no peer in showmanship. He created a tremendous rapport with the audience. He could turn their emotions on and off just like that.

"They also had highly polished harmonies and arrangements. Hovie would jump onto a piano and shake his long black hair into his face while the rest of the group danced on stage. They were the first quartet to use four individual microphones. Before that everyone had gathered around one mike."

Elvis Gospel

The Statesmen Quartet's main competitors, the Blackwood Brothers, suffered a double tragedy in June 1954, when R. W. Blackwood (baritone) and Bill Lyles (bass) were killed as the group's two-engined plane crashed on landing. The young Presley, who knew them as performers and fellow church members, grieved at the news. He was a Sunday-school friend of Cecil Blackwood, R. W.'s son and a member of a junior gospel quartet, the Songfellows. Cecil now stepped into his father's place, and Presley was offered his vacancy in the Songfellows. But it was too late. Four days after the funeral he was cutting "That's All Right" at Sun Studios.

The replacement for Lyles was Presley's hero J. D. Sumner, a musician who was to be with him until the end, backing him in Las Vegas along with his group, the Stamps. "Gospel music was about all he listened to," Sumner has said of Elvis. "In Las Vegas he'd have us come to his suite after each show and we'd sing gospel. He'd especially have it done for other stars like Frank Sinatra, Charlton Heston, Red Skelton and Sammy Davis Jr. He'd have us sing for them because they'd be amazed at the perfection of gospel music and what it said."

This love of gospel was shared by the other young Sun recording artists. One carefree afternoon, captured on tape and released as an album many years later, Elvis, Jerry Lee, Johnny Cash and Carl Perkins, visiting the studios at the same time, gathered around a piano to sing. They sang not pop songs or rock 'n' roll but gospel—"Just a Little Talk with Jesus," "Peace in the Valley," "Blessed Jesus Hold My Hand," "Down by the Riverside."

Carl Perkins, composer of "Blue Suede Shoes," later explained, "In those early days, gospel music had as much to do with rock 'n' roll as anything else. We were all definitely inspired by gospel. That handclapping, deep Southern style of singing goes right along with 'Don't you step on my blue suede shoes.' Gospel had a great input into rockabilly."

Scotty Moore, Elvis's guitarist on the early Sun recordings, had said as much at the time. Telling the *Memphis Press-Scimitar* that the group was playing "Elvis music" rather than "rock 'n' roll," he explained the difference by reminding the reporter: "You know, religious music has had a strong effect on our style." Bass player Bill Black agreed, adding, "Just about every time we have a rehearsal we end up doing religious songs with Elvis and the Jordanaires."

The Influence of Black Gospel

Besides his exposure to the quartets, Presley had frequently visited East Trigg Baptist Church, where the Reverend W. Herbert Brewster, an educated and politically radical minister, attracted some of America's top black gospel soloists. Born in 1901, Brewster was a songwriter himself, having composed classic songs for Mahalia Jackson such as "Just over the Hill," "How I Got Over" and "Move on up a Little Higher," the million-seller that established her as the queen of gospel in the 1940s.

When I spoke to Brewster in 1982, he dismissed any patronizing notions that East Trigg Baptist was a Sunday madhouse where poor ignorant blacks went into temporary spasms. "This church is an educational institution," he said. "We have a theological seminary here, and we're not the type of people for rollicking and rolling. They clap their hands rhythmically. It's a Baptist church from that old Southern Baptist tradition. This church isn't Pentecostal. It's Bible-based and

Christ-centered."

Brewster worked out a radio program that he called *The Old Time Camp Meeting of the Air,* where old spirituals and new songs were mixed together. "There was something for everyone, and groups of young people used to flock here. Elvis was among them, with another black boy from around here—B. B. King. That period was called the Golden Age of Gospel." Here Elvis saw some of the great female vocalists—Queen C. Anderson, Marion Williams and Mahalia Jackson among them. Years later, explaining that "spiritual music" was his first love, he said, "I mean some of the old colored spirituals from years back. I know practically every religious song that's been written."

Undoubtedly rock 'n' roll benefited from the style and presentation of the gospel music of this era. The emotional structure of Presley's performances, the phrasing of his vocals and the reaching toward the point of ecstasy all betray his love of spiritual music. He even claimed that his notorious "wiggle" was borrowed from revivalist preachers. "We used to go to these religious singin's all the time," he said. "There were these singers, perfectly fine singers, but nobody responded to them. Then there were the preachers and they cut up all over the place, jumpin' on the piano, movin' every which way. The audience liked 'em. I guess I learned from them."

Brewster unhesitatingly agreed that the imprint of black gospel was discernible in Elvis's music. "It was evidenced in the rhythm, and there were certain plaintive lines and certain slurs that were characteristic of early gospel. His version of 'Peace in the Valley' was one of the best gospel recordings I've ever heard. Also, the kind of excitement when he was singing his songs was the same as the youngsters would do in the church when we had our songs."

The Gospel-Rock Synthesis
Ultimately it was the redemption *feel* rather than the redemptive *message* that Southern rock 'n' rollers took to the world. Confused, tor-

tured and unsure of their own salvation, they vacillated between God-fearing repentance and outright debauchery, drugs and violence. Their music, too, alternated between secular and sacred. Both Presley and Lewis recorded albums of gospel songs, but they could never envisage a marriage of rock 'n' roll with religion. To them that would have been like fornicating on an altar.

Elvis would sing hymns in his Vegas stage shows, and he would even read portions of the Bible out between numbers, but he could never rock out with the gospel. Sumner recalls being with him one day when he was sent an album by the Imperials, who, since leaving him as a backing group, had gone on to record what was being called "contemporary Christian music"—gospel lyrics to a beat group instrumentation. "After listening to a couple of songs," says Sumner, "he broke the album across his knee. He said, 'If they're gonna sing rock, why don't they sing rock? If they're gonna sing gospel, why don't they sing gospel?' The songs he wanted to hear really did say something."

When W. J. Cash published his classic study *The Mind of the South,* Elvis was only six years old, but Cash's description of the Southern male as a romantic hedonist who "likes to expand his ego, his senses, his emotions, accept what pleases him and reject what does not, and in general prefers the extravagant, the flashing, and the brightly colored" could have been written about Elvis. So could Cash's following summary of the child-man who, despite his desire for self-gratification, assents to a stern form of evangelicalism.

His Puritanism was no mere task put on from cold calculation, but as essential a part of him as the hedonism. And his combination of the two was without conscious imposture. One might say with much truth that it proceeded from a fundamental split in his psyche, from a sort of social schizophrenia. One might say more simply and more safely that it was all part and parcel of the naive capacity for unreality which was characteristic of him.

Of the Million Dollar Quartet—Elvis, Jerry Lee Lewis, Johnny Cash

and Carl Perkins—Cash and Perkins went on to commit themselves
as Christians (both wrote spiritual autobiographies in the 1970s). A
close friend of evangelist Billy Graham, Cash records country-gospel
songs and has written a biography of St. Paul.

Elvis, used to tailor-made costumes and custom-made cars, went on
to construct a personalized religion out of what he'd read of Hinduism, Judaism, numerology, Theosophy, mind control, positive thinking and Christianity—a spiritual concoction that was every bit as extravagant and fantastic as the jewel-studded outfits he wore in Las
Vegas. As a child in Tupelo he had fallen under the spell of Captain
Marvel Junior, "the most powerful boy in the world." As an adult he
saw himself in a similar role, put on earth for a special mission, able
to heal the sick and move clouds. His interest in Christ in his latter
days seems to have had more to do with his perception of himself as
a modern Christ-figure than with humble adoration.

"To say that he is simple is to say in effect that he necessarily lacks
the complexity of mind, the knowledge and, above all, the habit of
skepticism essential to any generally realistic attitude," observed W. J.
Cash of the Southerner. "It is to say that he is inevitably driven back
upon imagination, that his world-construction is bound to be mainly
a product of fantasy, and that his credulity is limited only by his
capacity for conjuring up the unbelievable."

But what Elvis, Jerry Lee, Little Richard and Carl Perkins took
from the church, from the revival meetings and all-night sings, was a
feeling of transcendence. There was something in those early passionate songs that "spat in the face of those badlands," to borrow the
words of Bruce Springsteen, and suggested a strength and a faith that
would get you through to a place where things would be better. Teenagers feeling trapped by the sterility of the decade, social repression,
school, parents or adults in general drew power and confidence from
the songs, just as churchgoers drew power from the authority and
sentiments of gospel music.

Greil Marcus, writing of Presley in *Mystery Train,* his highly respected study of American images in rock 'n' roll, sums up this inheritance well.

Church music caught moments of unearthly peace and desire, and the strength of religion was in its intensity. . . . It was a faith meant to transcend the grimy world that called it up. Like Saturday night, the impulses to dream, the need to escape, the romance and the contradictions of the land, this was a source of energy, tension and power. Elvis inherited these tensions, but more than that, gave them his own shape.

Hallelujah, I Love Her So

2

To have played jazz in a church would have been an abomination.
If I go into a church I'm deadly serious. Everybody has to stand alone
at the time of judgment.
Ray Charles

I don't think that the Tamla sound would have come about
without gospel music. They knew how to take a gospel feeling
and add legitimate chord changes to create a pop flavor.
Abdul Fakir, the Four Tops

Without God . . . you can't have no music or no soul or no nothin'.
Thomas A. Dorsey, the "father of gospel"

*F*our months after Elvis Presley had turned down the Songfellows for Sun Records, a twenty-four-year-old black musician, blind from early childhood, walked into a borrowed radio studio in Atlanta, Georgia, and cut a record that would in its way be every bit as revolutionary as "That's All Right."

"I've Got a Woman," recorded by Ray Charles, did what had not been dared before. It took the music of the black Baptists—the churchy piano, the worshipful moans—and secularized it for the commercial market. You could think you were hearing gospel, but this was no song about the sweet by-and-by or the streets paved with gold. These soulful yearnings were for a woman, not for the Lord.

Hearing the result, producer Jerry Wexler confessed that it was like listening to gospel for the first time in an educated way. This is what Charles had wanted. For years he'd trailed the cocktail and nightclub circuit singing like Nat King Cole, but in private he dreamed of a synthesis of the church music he'd heard growing up in Greenville, Florida, and the blues. He wanted to harness the emotional power of gospel to earthbound stories of what he would later call "love heartaches, money heartaches, pleasure of the flesh and pleasures of the soul."

Spiritual and Blues

As a teenager in the 1940s, Charles had witnessed firsthand what is now recognized as the golden age of gospel, a time when busloads of quartets were touring the United States and "wrecking churches" while developing a music of passion, intensity and glamour. From this era came the groups that dominate the history of black gospel—the Swan Silvertones, the Dixie Hummingbirds, the Soul Stirrers, the Five Blind Boys of Alabama and the Golden Gate Quartet.

Charles particularly fixed on the voices of Mahalia Jackson, Ira Tucker, Claude Jeter, Jess Whitaker and Archie Brownlee. Jeter, lead vocalist for the Swan Silvertones, had a smooth, swooping falsetto that has since inspired generations of singers, white and black. Tucker, of the Dixie Hummingbirds, brought a new breath of show-biz pizzazz to the music. During the war years he developed tricks—such as running down the aisle during a song and then repentantly dropping to his knees—that would later sustain James Brown.

The dream of Charles was to take this music of a few and bring it to a wider public, but to do it without lyrics that said the Lord is there to help us and heaven is the destination of the redeemed. He called it his "spiritual and blues combination" and later commented, "I'd always thought that the blues and spirituals were close musically and emotionally. I was happy to hook 'em up. I was determined to go all out and just be natural."

Not everyone thought it was natural. Black Christians accused Charles of desecrating a music founded to express the glory of God and of making people dance to church music in nightclubs. Blues singer Big Bill Broonzy, who doubled as a weekend preacher, attacked Charles, saying, "He's mixing the blues with spirituals. I know that's wrong. He should be singing in church."

But Charles, who'd developed some idiosyncratic religious views since his childhood days at Shiloh Baptist Church, stayed true to his vision. He never went back to the church and out of principle has resisted recording the obvious album—"Ray Charles Sings Gospel." "Since I play jazz music I won't record a religious album, because I was brought up to believe that you don't serve two gods," he told me in 1981. "If you're gonna play the blues, then you play the blues. If you're gonna do religious music, then you do religious music. It may be antiquated. I don't know. But I still feel that same way today. You can't do both."

By showing that Baptist music could be sold in the marketplace if it spoke of human urges rather than divine intervention, Charles laid the foundations of soul music in nightclubs. As Peter Guralnick said of his classic 1959 hit "What'd I Say," it was "a kind of secular evocation of an actual church service, complete with moans, groans, and a congregation talking in tongues."

The door dividing black gospel music from the white record-buying public had been blown open, and through the gap came a generation of teenage Baptists and Pentecostals who wanted fame beyond the pulpits and pews. They were restless, in love with the new consumerism, and the first generation of young black Americans to question automatic churchgoing.

Some of them—Sam Cooke, Wilson Pickett, Clyde McPhatter, James Brown, Curtis Mayfield, Lou Rawls, David Ruffin—had been part of gospel groups. Others—Otis Redding, Aretha Franklin, Marvin Gaye—had been born into the families of preachers. The African-American church experience had made them who they were, and even when they left their inheritance behind there remained a deep emotional bond. "You can leave the church," the saying goes, "but the church don't never leave you." When Aretha Franklin got together with the Southern California Community Choir in 1972 to record a gospel album, *Amazing Grace,* her father, the Reverend C. L. Franklin, said of the woman who was by now a soul superstar, "Some people say Aretha's come back to the church. The truth is she ain't never left it."

Soul pioneers took the church experience with them in the way they "worked" audiences and in the pleading tones of their voices. They preached and exhorted, they called for congregational responses, they orchestrated their shows to take audiences down to the depths of sorrow and up to peaks of ecstasy. Church phrases like "have mercy," "oh Lord," "I wanna testify" and "can I get a witness?" turned up, with new meanings, in songs by James Brown, Johnnie Taylor and Marvin Gaye.

The African-American Church Experience

For centuries the church had been the one place where American blacks were free to develop their own culture without white interference. Becoming a preacher was the highest a black could rise on the leadership ladder, which is why black preachers such as Martin Luther King Jr. and Jesse Jackson were able to exercise political as well as religious authority. Church was not just a place to visit on a Sunday, but the heart of the community. And at the heart of the church was music.

African-Americans had no place for liturgy or eloquently delivered religious lectures. They relied not on the text but on the promptings of the Spirit. Truth had to be felt as well as heard. "Many of the blacks look upon white people as merely taught by the book," reported a clergyman from Virginia in 1832. "They consider themselves instructed by the inspiration of the Spirit." A slave of the time commented (cited in *Roll, Jordan, Roll* by historian Eugene D. Genovese), "I stays independent of what white folks tells me when I shouts. De Spirit moves me every day. Dat's how I stays in. White folks don't feel sech as I does, so dey stays out."

Indeed, descriptions of black church services show that white folks were astonished and impressed at the dancing, singing, clapping and shouting. One missionary, writing to his sponsors in 1755 to ask for Bibles and copies of Isaac Watts's hymns, remarked, "The negroes, above all the human species that I ever knew, have an ear for musick, and a kind of ecstatic delight in Psalmody." Harriet Beecher Stowe, author of *Uncle Tom's Cabin,* saw a slave woman singing the hymn "There Is a Holy City" and wrote that she "seemed to impersonate the fervor of Ethiopia, wild, savage, hunted of all nations, but burning after God in her tropic heart and stretching her scarred hands towards the glory to be revealed."

The slaves had English hymns but also made up their own songs, drawing from the rich language of the King James Bible and the colorful Old Testament stories of ordinary people who triumphed over worldly power with the help of God.

> Didn't my Lord deliver Daniel
> Didn't my Lord deliver Daniel
> Didn't my Lord deliver Daniel
> An' why not every man? . . .

> He delivered Daniel from de lion's den
> Jonah from de belly of de whale
> An' de Hebrew chillun from de fiery furnace
> An' why not every man?

The Negro spirituals confronted the depths of human loneliness, fear and pain, but with a triumphant faith in Jesus. They never hid their blues beneath a born-again smile, but neither were they ashamed of

their glorious hope. These were truly redemption songs, always looking ahead beyond present pain and beyond the present life.

Nobody knows de trouble I see

Nobody knows but Jesus

Nobody knows de trouble I see

Glory hallelujah!

But following Emancipation many newly educated blacks wanted to
forget the spirituals with their simple, repetitive lyrics of childlike
trust, along with their associations of slavery. It wasn't until the 1920s,
when white people were appreciating jazz, ragtime and African art,
that blacks began to consider that spirituals might be worth preserv-
ing. These were the first stirrings of what would later be termed Black
Pride, a reassessment of the Afro-American heritage.

Thomas Dorsey

It was in the 1920s also that Thomas Dorsey, a blues pianist who had
led Ma Rainey's band, was converted in Philadelphia after hearing a
challenging hymn, "I Do, Don't You?" A born entrepreneur and a
lover of jazz and ragtime, he began writing religious songs with a beat
and a popular appeal. Jazz and blues had been secular developments
from the spirituals (hand claps becoming drums, sorrow becoming
blues), and now Dorsey was taking them back, reuniting them with
the message of Christian gospel.

Born in 1899 and raised in Atlanta, Georgia, he concentrated on
religious music from 1929 onward, organizing choirs to promote his
songbooks and becoming known as the father of gospel. "I started it,"
he proudly told me when I visited him at his Chicago home in 1976.
"I named them gospel songs. They used to call them hymns or church
songs. But *gospel* means 'good news,' and if it's good news it's good
for everybody, whichever way it's delivered. My songs had a beat, a
tempo and a simple good news. It's not in flowery English so that the
ignorant man can't understand. It was time for a change."

Just as Ray Charles was attacked for taking gospel out of the church, in the 1920s Dorsey was accused of bringing the blues and jazz into the church. "I went into a church once and they almost threw me out because I sang one of my gospel songs," he remembered. "After I'd sung it, the people accepted it in such a way that the preacher denounced it, saying, 'You can't sing no gospel. You can only preach it.' I wanted to tell him that was a lie, but I didn't."

Almost every gospel singer has recorded a Dorsey song at some time. "Precious Lord" and "Peace in the Valley" have endured as classic American songs. Gospel music historian Anthony Heilbut comments, "Everything contemporary music aims for, Dorsey accomplished, welding gospel, blues, jazz and country music into a distinctive musical style." He never forgot what it was like to have the blues, "through the storm, through the night," but he also never forgot his hope of redemption: "precious Lord, take my hand, lead me home."

Sam Cooke

Early songwriters and singers plundered this gospel heritage. In many cases Ray Charles literally substituted a woman for God in public domain spirituals. "None of them had copyrights," he explained later. "Black folk had been singing them through the hollow logs as far back as one could remember. And often my tunes would be based on three or four gospel numbers, not just one." Thus "You Better Leave That Liar Alone" became "You Better Leave That Woman Alone," "This Little Light of Mine" was transformed into "This Little Girl of Mine." Even "I've Got a Woman" has been traced back to gospel models, but by now Charles has forgotten exactly how it came about. "It possibly came from a particular song," he said. "I know that chord structure is done in a lot of old spiritual tunes."

Charles had never been a gospel singer, so he never felt the shame of selling a birthright. With the great star Sam Cooke things were different. From 1951 to 1957 Cooke had been the lead vocalist for the legendary Soul Stirrers, a group founded before World War II. With his sweet semiyodel and fine looks, he'd brought yet another change to gospel. He became an icon to the young girls of the black church. Because of this it occurred to him and his manager, J. W. Alexander, that there could be rich pickings in the pop market. As biographer Joe McEwen notes, "If Cooke was having this kind of effect on the sequestered gospel audience, then there was a whole world out there, more openly sexual and sinful, that had to be right for Sam's physical and vocal appeal."

Cooke hesitated. He took a Soul Stirrers favorite, "Wonderful" ("Wonderful / my God, he's so wonderful"), and recorded it as "Lovable" ("Lovable / my girl, she's so lovable"), but the guilt he obviously felt is clearly perceptible in his insincere vocals. So as not to offend his gospel followers, he stayed with the Stirrers for a year while planning his pop breakout, and the song was released under the name Dale Cooke.

It wasn't a hit, and those who heard it weren't fooled by the pseudonym. Cooke's problem was that if he quit but then failed as a pop singer, he knew gospel music would be barred to him forever. "To exploit the lessons of gospel in the pop world was to risk the wrath of the sizable gospel audience," wrote McEwen. "Once the decision was made, there would be no turning back."

Cooke decided to make the break, and he became a black pop celebrity with a string of hits in the late 1950s and early 1960s. The songs, like "Only Sixteen," "Wonderful World," "Cupid" and "Twistin' the Night Away," were often fairly lightweight, but his voice, with its rich yet wispy charm, drew on his gospel heritage. Cooke was responsible for drawing other gospel artists into the pop world. He discovered Bobby Womack, Johnnie Taylor (who replaced him in the Soul Stirrers before becoming a soul star) and Billy Preston (a member of the COGICS with Gloria Jones and gospel star Andrae Crouch).

For those who love parables, there can be none more ironic than the story of Sam Cooke. Riding on the crest of pop stardom in 1964 and married to his childhood sweetheart, he checked into a Los

Angeles motel with a twenty-two-year-old woman named Elisa Boyer. According to testimony she wanted to leave, and she departed with Cooke's clothes. Cooke pursued her, seminaked, and when he couldn't find her he battered down the door of the manager's office. The manager, fifty-five-year-old Bertha Franklin, responded by pumping three bullets into him from a .22-caliber pistol. He died instantly.

Shortly before his death Cooke had been attending Soul Stirrers concerts. At an anniversary gathering in the group's hometown, Chicago, he was invited up to do a guest spot, but instead of the expected rapturous applause for the return of the superstar, there was a deadly hush. The emcee, R. H. Harris, whom Cooke had replaced in 1951, recalled hearing people saying, "Get that blues singer down," and protesting, "This is a Christian program." There was no way that gospel people were going to let him come back after he had defied the message of his own songs.

His last great song, "A Change Is Gonna Come," revealed a current of sorrow and spiritual uncertainty. He appeared despairing of living, yet afraid to die. It's impossible not to compare this with the earlier conviction expressed in the Soul Stirrers' song "On the Firing Line":

> The world with its allurements
> May try to sway my soul
> But it can never sway me
> I've given him control.

James Brown

James Brown, who formed his Famous Flames as a gospel group, was the black preacher come to pop. With his flashy suits, his shrieks and gasps that were a secular form of "agonizing in the Spirit," he became adept at taking charge of an audience's emotions.

Black American preaching is musical in its presentation. A typical sermon starts in serious, soft tones, maybe even quoting a Bible verse or two, but a third of the way through it will build in passion until it ends in pure hysteria. Reverend Johnny "the Hurricane" Jones of

Atlanta, who incidentally takes many of his sermon titles from pop songs and later releases them as albums, refers to this style as "the whoopin' and the hollerin' " and explained to me, "It's what black ministers call 'changing gears.' When you been on the road then you know how to control your voice. You gotta have that voice control to be a commercial preacher, to reach the masses."

Brown followed this pattern, singing sermon-songs like "You've Got the Power," "Say It Loud—I'm Black and I'm Proud" and "Cold Sweat," with guttural gasps and inarticulate groans. On "Give It Up or Turn It Loose" he breaks into a long passage consisting of "aaah," "huh" and "wow," which finally climaxes with a "Lord, have mercy." After he cut his first hit, "Please, Please, Please," in 1956, the owner of the record company was driven to exasperation when he heard it. "This man sounds like he's stoned," he complained to the employee who had signed him. "All he's saying is one word."

Yet the art of the black preacher, who in the days of slavery had most often preached to illiterates, was to go beyond the literal meanings of words and peel back layers of emotion that could be evoked by variant soulful expressions. Explains Genovese in *Roll, Jordan, Roll,* "The preachers relied heavily on tone, gesture, and rhythm and combined an adequate verbal message with a deep emotional appeal that transcended the words themselves." One white woman observed after listening to a plantation preacher, "The words had no meaning at all. It was the devotional passion of voice and manner which was so magnetic."

When these gospel-educated blacks came into pop, the redemptive message beloved of the slaves who had created the spirituals was the first casualty. The name of God had always been considered a commercial turnoff in pop. God had to be sent packing, ideally to be exchanged for the perfect woman. There could still be a religious spirit, but it had to be directed toward something more tangible. When Charles sang "Hallelujah," paused, and then added, "I love her so," it was a brilliant illustration of the secularizing process.

Love as Salvation

The soul music universe, like that of the blues, was one of hardship relieved by good love. Solomon Burke, who began recording secular material in 1959 after a childhood spent as "the Wonder Boy Preacher," encapsulated it in 1964 as "Everybody Needs Somebody to Love." Kip Anderson was even more theological in his understanding. In "Without a Woman" he observed, "A sweet woman's love is a man's salvation."

James Brown preached the same message. In "It's a Man's Man's Man's World," a song deliberately constructed as a sermon, he listed man's life-enhancing inventions—the train, the boat, the electric light—but admitted that he would be nothing "without a woman or a girl." At times the redemptive view of love was made explicit. Johnnie Taylor, when no longer a Soul Stirrer, sang "I've Been Born Again" about his feelings of renewal upon discovering the ideal woman.

For Marvin Gaye it wasn't just love that constituted salvation; it was orgasm. Having been brought up under a particularly stern and eccentric brand of Pentecostalism that hated even the most committed sexual expression, he spent the rest of his life trying to reconcile his strong sex drive with his belief that he'd been ordained by God to sing. His way of doing this was to imagine any orgasm as a religious act.

In songs like "Get It On" he wrestled with the problem of holy sex. On his album *Sexual Healing* he recited a list of credits, including one for "our Lord and Savior Jesus Christ," and then glided straight into a song about wanting a woman's body. That was the way Gaye would have liked it to be. He wanted to purify himself by obeying his darkest passions.

Most of the time soul is less obscene. The lover is viewed as someone who will, like God, come into your life and be dependable and comforting, always ready to lend a helping hand. Songs like Bill Withers's "Lean on Me" and Ben E. King's "Stand by Me" convey the mood of hymns; King's song was strongly influenced by a Soul Stirrers number,

"Be with Me, Jesus." Simon and Garfunkel's "Bridge over Troubled Water," a massive worldwide hit, played on the same notion of lover as savior and, appropriately enough, was based on an ad-lib Claude Jeter made as he sang "Mary Don't You Weep" with the Swan Silvertones.

Ray Charles accepts that just such a transition took place when gospel became processed into soul. "Both blues and gospel are looking for love, hope and faith," he says. "Gospel looks for it in God, and blues looks for love, hope, faith and durability in a woman."

Yet the soul singer, like a preacher with a flock, wants to offer his people more. He may not want to bring God into it or suggest a real eternity, but there's the impulse to provide hope and guidance through his gift. James Brown, besides mimicking the performance of a preacher, uses his songs to instill pride and self-respect. There's a lot of what Mick Jagger once called "do-good jive" in soul music: commonsense advice on how we should all love each other delivered in the authoritative tones of the preacher, but lacking any of the authority. This was typical of Harold Melvin, who in "Wake Up Everybody" cataloged humankind's miseries, concluding that the world won't get better if left alone and we have to change it.

Melvin and his Bluenotes recorded for the influential Philadelphia International Records, better known as the Philly label, owned by Kenneth Gamble and Leon Huff, joint producers of *Wake Up Everybody.* In the album sleeve notes Gamble asserted that the "kingdom of God" is already on earth and all we need to do is open our hearts and minds to it, otherwise we won't "grow into the God-like condition we need so much." Interviewed by *Rolling Stone,* he explained that the label's philosophy was that "instead of giving [the public] a beat we try and deliver a message that will uplift their minds and will get them away from all the evil that's installed in the world."

Years later Cecil Womack explained that Womack and Womack's *Love Wars* album was "religious" because it advocated love. "Everybody seems to think that a religious song is rolling around on the floor, screaming and calling Jesus," he said. "But really the whole statement of the Bible is that people need to love one another and understand one another. We've got to stop limiting ourselves in communicating with other people. That's the only answer to the problems of this world."

Ian Hoare, writing in *The Soul Book,* summarized well the deficiencies of this type of song: "While the catch-phrases obviously derive from gospel, they no longer refer unequivocally to the specific social meaning of the gospel. It becomes a series of limp, moralistic cliches: the world is in a desperate situation and mankind is on the eve of destruction, so we've all got to learn to live with each other—get on board, shake a hand, make a friend."

Even Curtis Mayfield, grandson of a traveling preacher, who began in the 1960s to write songs of social encouragement with a lyrical power borrowed from gospel, deftly shifted the emphasis from faith in God to faith in a nebulously defined faith. Although the word still carried a great spiritual resonance, especially among the black constituency to whom he was singing, what was being promoted in songs like "Keep On Pushing" and "Move On Up" was positive thinking and self-respect, not repentance and union with God.

Redemption language without a real message of redemption raises false hopes. It may well boost spirits, revive pride and unite communities, but the majestic message the words were intended to convey has been lost. When I suggested to Thomas Dorsey that soul music was gospel music without God, he snorted contemptuously: "Without God you can do nothing. You can't have no music or no soul or no nothin'. If we were to put God in all of our plans it wouldn't be such a hard world to live in."

Al Green

One man who'd say "Amen!" to that is Al Green, initially a gospel singer with his brothers, then a soul superstar in the 1970s, and now a gospel singer again as well as minister of the Full Gospel Tabernacle in Memphis, Tennessee. As a boy he swore that, given success, he would devote his life to God. But in 1971, when he scored a million-seller with "Tired of Being Alone," he went back on his pledge. Like his hero Sam Cooke before him, he wallowed in worldly trappings and delayed his Christian service indefinitely.

In 1974, in what came terrifyingly close to a replay of Cooke's sad end, Green was trapped in a motel room with a spurned lover who scalded him with hot food and then shot herself. The tragedy prompted a total reevaluation. In particular Green remembered his childhood promise. Two years later I met him in New York, just as he was about to release the album *Full of Fire,* and a change was obviously under way. "It's been coming for some time," he said. "But now it's here, and I am projected to be a minister of God for the people. I don't want to try and save the church folks. Go and save the sinners! Save the people definitely outside your field. On the new album you'll find three spiritual tunes. They're not gospel, but the love for a lady is translated into everlasting love."

This he in fact did most convincingly on his next release, *The Belle Album* (1977), redirecting soul back to its spiritual roots, but with subtlety because he wasn't playing to a gospel crowd. Instead of substituting a woman for God, Green brought God into the love song, without introducing him by name. "Belle, it's you that I want," he sang on the title track. "But it's him that I need." Greil Marcus, reviewing for *Rolling Stone,* said the album carried "a sense of liberation and purpose deep enough to make the sinner envy the saved." Green himself later said that the record had worked because "it channeled both religion and rock 'n' roll, and it channeled them so well."

Subsequent albums have not always been so accomplished; often they have played straight along the gospel groove instead of developing the implicit spirituality that made *The Belle Album* so powerful. Yet Green appears to have no regrets at returning to the church. "I started from being noplace to being a millionaire," he told me in 1976. "But I'm closer to having nothing now than I've ever been, because

I've found that all the things I worked for so long don't mean a thing. A man's labor is so that he may have food and clothing and acquire some things he wants. Now, when you're in that position, what's the sense in working unless you're working for a divine purpose or reason?"

Healing Power

"I know this is the best over here," Thomas Dorsey had said of his role as a gospel musician. "You see, I'm working for myself and God. I listen to all kinds of music on the radio, and I compare it, and I still think I have the best for the world. Not my music, but gospel singing. It's good news for the world."

Soul music? He wasn't sure it existed. "They just needed a name to touch the people. All they mean is that it's something that gets deeper down inside of you than the ordinary."

Yet Dorsey, the father of gospel, the grandfather of soul, remained a firm believer in the healing power of music. "It has something that will draw. It has something that will soothe. It has something that will attract. It was something that will get inside of a person quicker than anything else. It can do you or me more good than a dose of medicine."

Heaven Is in Your Mind

3

My experience of God came from acid. It's the most important thing that ever happened to me.
Brian Wilson, the Beach Boys

Christ said he would return, and he has. Love is being expounded on the airwaves.
Marty Balin, Jefferson Airplane

God isn't in a pill, but LSD explained the mystery of life. It was a religious experience.
Paul McCartney

I n 1964, when the Beatles were at their "scream-age" peak, no one would have believed that before the decade was out they would be tinkering with religious texts, undergoing spiritual instruction and making pronouncements on world peace. It would have appeared inconceivable that these "wacky" and "irreverent" youths, part of whose charm lay in deflecting serious questions with wisecracks, would get entangled in issues of redemption and the hereafter.

The Beatles were typical second-generation rock 'n' rollers in that none of them suffered any anxiety over a secular-sacred split in their lives. All they knew of gospel was what came through their favorite

American singers. Their connections with church had been notably weak. McCartney's mother was a Catholic, but his father was an agnostic who didn't believe in imposing religion on children. Harrison also had a Catholic mother. The most religiously influenced was Lennon, whose Aunt Mimi sent him to a Church of England Sunday school (he later joined the choir).

By 1964 even these vague childhood influences had worn off. The Beatles were part of a generation that had no sentimental attachment to church and wanted to face life without the aid of a faith in the supernatural. "None of us believe in God," Paul McCartney jauntily announced to an interviewer that year. "But we're more agnostic than atheistic," qualified John Lennon. Another day McCartney admitted that religion was something he didn't even think of. "It doesn't fit into my life."

Lennon could be brutally blasphemous. Perhaps he was angry at a God who allowed his mother to be killed by a drunken driver when he was a teenager; perhaps he was unable to conceive of a reliable heavenly Father, since his earthly father had deserted him shortly after birth. In his Hamburg days he would write letters in the persona of John the Baptist, hang condoms on religious statues and ridicule passing nuns. Some of the venom seeped through in his stories, where vicars, lepers, the crippled and Jesus Christ were subjected to his cruel humor.

The group's press officer, Derek Taylor, told *The Saturday Evening Post* in 1964, "It's incredible, absolutely incredible. Here are these four boys from Liverpool. They're rude, they're profane, they're vulgar, and they've taken over the world. It's as if they'd founded a new religion. They're completely anti-Christ. I mean, I'm anti-Christ as well, but they're so anti-Christ they shock me, which isn't an easy thing."

Spiritual Shift

Two years later Lennon was in the studio with producer George Mar-

tin, singing a lyric made up of lines from Timothy Leary's version of
the Tibetan Book of the Dead. He asked Martin to make him sound
like an Eastern holy man praying from the top of a mountain. By the
summer of 1967 McCartney was telling *The People* that his eyes had
been opened to the existence of God and that "a similar experience
would probably do some of our clergy some good."

The experience of Lennon and McCartney was to be repeated in the
lives of most of the influential rock 'n' roll musicians of the decade.
Apathetic agnostics became passionate seekers after "truth," rock 'n'
roll was perceived as tribal ritual, and the gates were thrown open to
every religion, cult and heresy that humanity has ever known. The
generation that the church was trying to attract by introducing acoustic guitars and priests in open-neck shirts who blessed motorcycles was
suddenly perusing incomprehensible esoteric texts and railing against
the evils of the consumer society.

Throughout the second half of the 1960s, fringe religion became a
boom industry, with everything from pagan magic to Zen Buddhism
on the market. The young now complained loudly about the dead
materialism of their parents. Rock songs derided the soullessness of
living without a higher purpose, of being well respected but lacking
vision. In 1965 John Lennon chided the "Nowhere Man" who "doesn't
have a point of view / knows not where he's going to," and Mick
Jagger, in "Mother's Little Helper" (1966), lamented, "The pursuit of
happiness is just a bore."

Chemically Induced Religion

The trigger for the lurch into gnosticism, paganism and pantheism was
the hallucinogen LSD, more commonly referred to as acid, which
entered the British recreational drug market around 1964 with a reputation of being "cannabis double-plus." Within three years almost all
the most influential rock 'n' roll musicians would take it—John Lennon, Paul McCartney, George Harrison, Mick Jagger, Keith Richards, Brian Jones, Pete Townshend, Steve Winwood, Eric Burdon,

Brian Wilson, Roger McGuinn, Donovan, Cat Stevens, Jim Morrison, Eric Clapton and Jimi Hendrix among them.

LSD was the Damascus Road tablet. People started out on trips as hard-nosed materialists out for a bit of fun and emerged with their egos ripped and mauled, unsure at first whether they'd *seen* God or *were* God. Whatever they'd been through, the world appeared different. Small moments were treasured, colors burned with a new intensity, the old life appeared to have been a game. They felt suffused with feelings of benevolence, wanting to "love" everyone. "I saw God," said Beach Boy Brian Wilson when he emerged from his first trip in 1965. "I saw God and it just blew my mind."

Depending on the dosage, trips could last from five or six hours to a few days. While experiences differed in detail—Rolling Stone Brian Jones would often see demons and monsters, while McCartney felt "love and truth"—a common feeling was that the walls of the ego were collapsing so that the tripper felt merged into the rest of creation. "I am he as you are me and we are all together," as John Lennon put it in "I Am the Walrus" (1967), one of the songs that he partly composed while on a trip.

It was this temporary illusion of oneness that trippers named God. They were not confronting the biblical God of justice and love. As McCartney described it, "God is a force we are all a part of." One subject in *The Varieties of Psychedelic Experience* by R. E. L. Masters and Jean Houston (1966) recounted his feelings while on a trip. "I can dissolve," he told observers, "now that I understand what is meant by being a part of everything, what is meant by sensing the body as dissolving. I have a knowledge of my particles dissolving and becoming incorporated into a sea of particles where nothing has form or even substance. In this sea there is no individuality."

Mike Heron of the Incredible String Band, a successful Scottish folk duo that encapsulated many elements of the British hippie experience, wrote "A Very Cellular Song" (1967) while on LSD and captured this same feeling of being united with plants and animals, of being lost in an electric mass of particles.

    Black hair brown hair feather and scale
    Seed and stamen and all unnamed lives that live
    Turn your quivering nerves in my direction
    Feel the energy of my cells
    Wishes you well.

The Unmaking of a Heritage

To many young musicians such experiences were devastating. There was nothing in their background or education by which to interpret it. Literally overnight, all their values and assumptions were challenged. "It's shattering," admitted George Harrison, "because it's as though someone suddenly wipes away all you were taught or brought up to believe as a child and says, 'That's not it.' You've gone so far, your thoughts have become so lofty and there's no way of getting back."

What they had always thought of as the "real world" now seemed like a fantasy, while what they'd previously considered fantasy was real. They felt like Alices who had wandered down rabbit holes. "It just changed everything," said Jerry Garcia, leader of San Francisco's star acid-rock band the Grateful Dead. "It freed me because I suddenly realized that my little attempt at having a straight life was really a fiction."

Trippers thought that LSD showed the truth, hidden from most people, that creation is one massive heaving divinity. "We're all God," said Lennon. "I'm not *a* god or *the* God, but we're all potentially divine." Teachings that supported this idea were found not in the monotheistic religions—Islam, Judaism or Christianity—but in Hinduism, in the gnostic gospels of the first century, in occult doctrines and New Age philosophy. Here was an ear-tickling alternative to talk of having to stand before God and give account of your actions. Instead of surrendering your will to the divine will, you turned off your mind and surrendered to "the void" (as in the Beatles' "Tomorrow Never Knows").

The Beatles got into LSD more or less by accident: a dentist friend slipped a dose into Lennon's and Harrison's after-dinner coffee one night in 1965. The initial effects were, to say the least, disorienting. Lennon thought at first that he was going insane, then that he was being pursued by the devil. As the night wore on he became frantic with ideas, cracking jokes and furiously making sketches. He later admitted, "I was pretty stoned for a month or two."

From then on the two of them became serious "acid droppers"; Lennon later confessed to having been on over a thousand trips. Describing his early experiences with the drug, Harrison said, "It was like I had never tasted, smelled or heard anything before. For me it was like a flash. It just opened up something inside of me and I realized a lot of things." LSD convinced Lennon of "the existence of the human soul and of an afterlife."

The Influence of Timothy Leary

Barry Miles, the manager of the Indica Bookshop in London's Southampton Row, was under instructions to supply the Beatles with "anything interesting" being published in the newly emerging "alternative" culture. Two of the books he remembers sending were Timothy Leary's *The Psychedelic Reader* and *The Psychedelic Experience,* religious interpretations of LSD's effects. In *The Psychedelic Experience* Lennon found many of the words and ideas for *Tomorrow Never Knows,* which was included on the *Revolver* album.

Leary, at one time a Harvard professor of psychotherapy, had discovered psychedelics in 1960 at the age of forty; later he described the event as "the deepest religious experience of my life." He became a passionate advocate of the then-legal drug, preaching that if it was used widely humankind would be transformed. In the early 1970s he even predicted that in ten years' time grass would grow in New York's Times Square, an indication of a return to Eden.

In particular Leary encouraged the perception of the LSD trip as a spiritual insight. In 1963 he conducted an experiment with a group of theological students, 90 percent of whom later claimed to have had a "mystical experience." Leary persistently cited parallels with Hinduism and Tantric Buddhism, and eventually he founded the League of Spiritual Discovery, which campaigned for LSD to be recognized as a legal sacrament.

In August 1963 Leary lectured to a group of Lutheran psychologists in Philadelphia, telling them, "If you are serious about your religion, if you really want to commit yourself to the spiritual quest, you must learn how to use psychochemicals. Drugs are the religion of the twenty-first century. Pursuing the religious life today without using psychedelic drugs is like studying astronomy with the naked eye."

There was nothing new in a religion constructed around drug visions. It's possible that the "soma" mentioned in the Vedic scriptures (foundational to Hinduism) was hallucinogenic and that meditation techniques were originally developed to re-create the soma experience. Certainly the Aztec Indians of Mexico used psilocybin during their all-night festivals, believing that it enabled them to journey to the end of the world. Medieval witchcraft involved drugs such as belladonna and datura, and the mythical ride through the sky on a broomstick possibly referred to an out-of-the-body experience. In shamanistic religions the shaman (a sort of high priest who deals with the gods on behalf of a tribe) uses both drugs and music to get himself into the state where he feels able to enter the spirit world.

Leary was encouraging a return to these primitive forms, in the belief that humankind had once known the truth but had lost it beneath civilized perceptions based on dualisms of you and me, good and evil, spirit and matter, life and death. "You must retrace the ancient path yourself," he advised in 1967. "Discover your own Christhood. Stagger down from the mountain, flipped-out Moses, with your own moral code fashioned in the ecstatic despair of your own revelation."

LSD was the perfect religious experience for the consumer-boom 1960s. It could be bought, it was fun, it required no sacrifice, you made up your own commandments, and it was in color. What better marketing force could be imagined for such ideas than rock 'n' roll, the electronic art form of the generation that wanted Beethoven to roll over while Dionysus took control?

Leary certainly saw it that way, calling rock 'n' roll musicians "the philosopher-poets of the new religion." In particular he spoke of the Beatles as "four Evangelists" and "rock stars become holy men." He advised worried parents to listen to *Sergeant Pepper,* to "close your eyes and listen to the sermon from Liverpool and learn that it's the oldest message of love and peace and laughter, and trust in God and don't worry, trust in the future, and don't fight; and trust in your kids, and don't worry because it's all beautiful and right."

By 1967 Leary was a star himself, the high priest of LSD, considered by the media as much a part of the hippie phenomenon as the Beatles, beads and San Francisco. He shared the stage with the Grateful Dead, Jefferson Airplane and Quicksilver Messenger Service at the Human Be-In in January of that year. There he launched his slogan "Turn on, tune in, drop out" (turn on to LSD, tune in to the new consciousness, drop out of "straight" society). Later he befriended Lennon, who conceived "Come Together" as a campaign song for him, and Jimi Hendrix, who pressed him for interpretations of his dreams. He was immortalized in song by Lennon ("Give Peace a Chance"), the Moody Blues ("Legend of a Mind") and the Who ("The Seeker").

Music and LSD

Discovered during World War II by a Swiss biochemist working with a rye fungus, LSD had been secretly experimented with in America from the 1950s onward but didn't really hit the streets until 1961, on the East Coast. What rock 'n' roll did was to broadcast more widely the hip secret of a few. In 1962 it was estimated that only twenty-five thousand Americans had ever tried a psychedelic drug (mescaline, peyote or LSD); four years later such drugs were made illegal. Yet by 1971 it was reckoned that five million Americans had tasted of the forbidden fruit.

During 1966 and 1967 LSD transformed rock 'n' roll. It turned the Moody Blues, a rhythm and blues group from Birmingham, England, into cerebral concept-album manufacturers who felt obliged to offer spiritual advice. It saw stomping keyboard player Steve Winwood singing of elephants' eyes, bubble-gum trees and the possibility that heaven might be in our minds. Eric Burdon, a bawdy blues singer from Newcastle, became almost repentant when he thought of "all the good times I have wasted having good times," the times he spent drinking when he "should have been thinking." Burdon began wearing a black leather jacket with the message "May the baby Jesus shut your mouth and open your mind" painted on the back.

Rock musicians weren't writing gospel songs about LSD—although Jefferson Airplane came close with "White Rabbit" and its plea to "feed your head"—but the drug experience became implicit in much of what was being recorded. Distorted sounds and blurred album photographs suggested messages from the initiated. Like the first-century Gnostics, who believed that the world was divided between those who had received *gnosis* (knowledge) and those who hadn't, the "acidheads" assumed a superiority over the "straights" who had not turned on. As the writer Ken Kesey would tell his band of Merry Pranksters as they careened around the West on psychedelics, "You're either on the bus, or you're off the bus."

These were people who, like McCartney, felt they now knew "the mystery of life," but couldn't explain it because "it's impossible to put into words." The Beatles wanted to know how it felt to be one of the beautiful people ("now that you know who you are / what are you going to do?"). Jimi Hendrix asked, "Are you experienced?"

In *The Private Sea: LSD and the Search for God* (1967), William Braden explained, "The subject feels he knows, essentially, everything there is to know. He knows ultimate truth. And what's more, he knows that he knows it. Yet this sense of authority cannot be verbalized because the experience is a whole which cannot be divided." Thus Jerry Garcia could say only, "It was the truth. It's the truth like these flowers are the truth . . . or the trees. It's the truth so you know it absolutely. You don't have to wonder whether it is. It's not in the form of an idea. It's in the form of a complete reality."

Drug experiences altered the way music was made and received. "It shook all your foundations," Eric Clapton told me in 1974, referring to his first taste of LSD at the cover shoot for the 1967 Cream album *Disraeli Gears.* "After the first couple of times you realized that everything you'd been using as guidelines up until that point was actually pretty flexible if you happened to question it, which acid obviously did."

Old songwriting rules seemed irrelevant to those who'd been to the other side. They wanted to create music that would reflect the sprawling, multilayered experience of tripping, as well as something with hidden extras for those who'd be taking LSD themselves before popping on the stereo headphones. Songs broke through the three-minute barrier and went on to take up whole sides of albums, and searing guitar solos followed raga patterns.

The music of Jimi Hendrix, the Grateful Dead and Cream swirled and shimmered through the consciousness. At their shows the walls would writhe with bubbling, bursting balls of color made by projecting lights through tanks of oils. Rock 'n' roll was becoming part of the ritual, a primer for the psychedelic experience. Assaulted by sound, joss sticks and colored projections, an auditorium full of people could be made to feel like one seething organism—like part of God.

Again, this was nothing new. Almost all primitive drug cults use music. The Brazilian Tenetehara Indians chant and shake rattles while smoking cannabis and waiting for spirits to descend and heal their sick. The Navajo Indians, even today, eat peyote while singing songs. Two anthropologists who have made a special study of tribes that swallow plant hallucinogens to gain spiritual insight (M. Dobkin de Rios and F. Katz) explain that the music becomes necessary as a "set of bannisters" that can be held on to while the ego is dissolved. Leary advocated music as a "guide" to keep one "on track." Bands such as the Grateful Dead began to orchestrate their concerts to follow the graph of a typical trip, starting with gentle songs, working up to a peak and then bringing their listeners back down again.

Graham Nash, then of the Hollies, later of Crosby, Stills and Nash, explained to *Melody Maker* that so-called psychedelic music was also a simulation of a drug trip for nonusers. "Psychedelic music is trying to create an LSD session without the use of drugs," he said. "It's a question of trying to expand the consciousness to the limits. The theory is that you only use 20 per cent of your brain, but that under LSD you use 80 per cent. They aim to achieve the same thing by using combinations of sounds and lighting."

Millennial Dreams
LSD persuaded people that redemption was indeed nigh, that the kingdom of heaven was about to be established on earth. Suddenly the perplexing problem of evil appeared solvable. If only everyone could realize that we're all God, if only everyone could be filled with love, conflicts and divisions would be a thing of the past. George Harrison sang on *Sergeant Pepper* that we were only alienated from each other through a failure to see "that we're all one and life flows on / within you and without you."

So seriously was this taken at the time that suggestions were made that the water systems of major cities be spiked with the drug to forcibly induce such a realization. The Brotherhood of Eternal Love, a West Coast underground organization based loosely on Leary's League of Spiritual Discovery, manufactured LSD with the specific aim of improving the world by turning it on. One of the Brotherhood's chemists, Grateful Dead electronic adviser Tim Scully, planned to manufacture two hundred grams of the drug, which he estimated would make up to seventy million doses.

Scully also had a great interest in the complementary role of rock, in "altering consciousness and changing the culture." He said, "That became part of the general belief system, that psychedelic drugs and music were both very powerful for cultural change, and everybody I ever met in the music scene was involved in the drug scene and vice versa. Generally most of these people were aggressively interested in changing our culture."

Leary himself wrote about teenage children "mutating through acid up to a higher level of existence." He encouraged the view that through LSD humanity could make an evolutionary leap toward a near-perfect state. Open-air rock festivals, which began with the Monterey International Pop Festival in 1967, were seen as the New Age in microcosm, examples of what could happen if drugs were freely available and everyone oozed love.

They dubbed it "flower power," the power of natural growth and beauty. It was believed that acid cleaned your psyche of all the debris civilization had loaded on it, until you were able to return to the innocence of childhood. Becoming childlike was suddenly hip. Those who attended rock festivals blew bubbles, painted their bodies, frolicked in mud and tossed Frisbees. Even the notorious nudity was more an assertion of innocence than an attempt at eroticism.

The answer to everything was love. Love was all you needed. One of the effects of LSD, as witnessed by Masters and Houston, is that "this idea emerges . . . that a universal or brotherly love is possible and constitutes man's best if not only hope." This was certainly McCartney's experience. In 1967 he claimed, "The need today is for people to come to their senses and my point is that LSD can help them. We all know what we would like to see in the world today— peace. We want to be able to get on with each other. I believe the drug could heal the world. . . . I now believe the answer to everything is love."

Love became the buzzword of 1967 rock 'n' roll culture. It gave rise to a huge wave of optimism. The Beatles sang, "With our love / we could change the world," and millions of young people, for a few months, truly believed they were right. In San Francisco, "love-ins"— giant open-air festivals—were organized, and in what was to become the anthem of the summer, "San Francisco (Be Sure to Wear Some Flowers in Your Hair)," Scott McKenzie sang, "There's a whole generation / with a new explanation."

Coming Down

Ultimately a religion based solely on the LSD experience was bound to be short-lived. It suggested possibilities, but after that glimpse, where was there to go? There was no comforting revelation, no guiding light, no worship and no discipline. Now that you knew who you were (or at least thought you did), what were you going to do?

Worse than that, the drug often shortchanged people, promising them heaven but sending them to hell. Stories began to circulate of those who'd gone on trips but whose minds never returned. They became known as acid casualties. There were also those who, sincerely believing all to be one, thought no harm could come from jumping out of an upstairs window.

John Lennon was later to turn on Timothy Leary and blame LSD for undermining his confidence. The broken-down ego that was necessary to experience the oneness of the universe was an impediment once he was back in the real world, because ego assures us of our integrity and identity. "I got a message on acid that you should destroy your ego, and I did," said Lennon. "I was reading that stupid book of Leary's . . . and I destroyed myself. I destroyed my ego and I didn't believe I could do anything. I let people do what they wanted. I was nothing."

Harrison abandoned the drug for other reasons. In the summer of 1967, while *Sergeant Pepper* was riding high, he visited the Haight-Ashbury area of San Francisco, where the psychedelic culture had originated and where thousands of American teenagers had flocked that year in search of the "gentle loving" Scott McKenzie sang about. "That was the first thing that turned me off drugs," he said later. "I expected them all to be nice and clean and friendly and happy, and the first thing you see is lots of dirty people lying around on the floor."

Allen Y. Cohen, one of Leary's original followers, was similarly disenchanted. He explained,

One of the fantasies we had is demonstrably false. This is the belief that if you take enough psychedelic drugs you will become holy, spiritually sophisticated, wise, expanded consciousness, love will flow from you. It doesn't work.

The use of psychedelic chemicals did not lead to a social utopia. Our attempts failed not because of the quality of the people but because these results do not accrue from chemical-induced experiences. You can't carry over even the profound experiences you have. You can feel very loving under LSD, but can you exert that love to someone who previously you didn't like? The long-range answer is no.

Still, those who had dabbled were profoundly affected by the experience. Even though disillusionment set in, they could never erase the memory of having experienced the world as though at a submolecular level. It would make them vulnerable to a plethora of Eastern and pagan religions—spiritual systems they would have found completely uninteresting only a few years before.

My
Sweet
Lord

4

The aim of all Eastern religion, like the aim of LSD, is basically to get high.
Timothy Leary

One minute I was freaked out on acid. The next minute I was into
Meher Baba.
Pete Townshend

I wanted to have it all the time—these thoughts about the yogis
and the Himalayas and Ravi Shankar's music.
George Harrison

*I*t was with amusement that educated Indians watched as the
golden boys of Western rock 'n' roll, at the height of their earning
power and creative lives, became ascetics: meditating, refusing meat,
drugs and even marital sex, and blistering their fingers trying to master
the sitar. When one heard them speak a new form of spirito-babble,
composed of equal parts hip slang, drug talk and mysticism, it was
clear they thought they'd found an even better means of redemption
than LSD. Chemicals were now out. They didn't take you all the way.
The real high achievers, and those included the Beatles, had passed on
to Hindu teachings on meditation.

"We're all one," claimed George Harrison in 1967. "The realisation of human love reciprocated is such a gas. It's a good vibration which makes you feel good. These vibrations that you get through yoga, cosmic chants and things like that, I mean it's such a buzz. It buzzes you out of everywhere. It's nothing to do with pills. It's just in your own head, the realisation. It's such a buzz. It buzzes you right into the astral plane."

Even Paul McCartney, the "sensible" Beatle by most people's standards, was no less freaked out. "The great thing about people like Babaji and Christ, and all the governors who have transcended, is that they've got out of the reincarnation cycle," he said. "They've reached the bit where they are just there. They don't have to zoom back. So they're planning the spiritual thing for us."

The Trivialization of Spiritual Discipline

Noncommercial gurus from India were quick to disassociate themselves from the hippie tribes that began hitchhiking to Asia for enlightenment. They didn't appreciate being told by dropouts from Derby or Des Moines that the God-realisation attained after years of meditating in caves was exactly the same as what could be experienced after taking LSD at a rock 'n' roll dance. Timothy Leary's equation of Eastern transcendence with psychedelic experience was almost blasphemous to them.

Master sitarist Ravi Shankar, who'd become a college favorite after playing the Monterey Festival on a bill with Jimi Hendrix, the Who and Janis Joplin, found his American listeners taking drugs, copulating and, as he put it, "doing all sorts of things" during his performances of spiritual music. Used to being regarded as a serious classical musician, he was deeply offended.

"They took the joss sticks and the sitar," he said, "but that's very easy. You can buy them in the market along with Siddhartha, the Tibetan Book of the Dead and tantric posters. They learned the word *om,* read one or two superficial books and thought they'd got it. But it's not enough for enlightenment, just as strumming the sitar without knowing how to tune it doesn't make Indian music."

In *Karma Cola* the writer Gita Mehta, educated in Bombay and Cambridge, remembers witnessing the eastward gaze of young Westerners. "As the sitar wiped out the split-reed sax, and mantras began fouling the crystal clarity of rock 'n' roll lyrics," she wrote, "millions of wild-eyed Americans turned their backs on all that amazing equipment and pointed at us screaming, 'You guys! You've got it!' Well, talk about shabby tricks. We had been such patient wallflowers and suddenly the dance was over. Nobody wanted to shimmy. They all wanted to do the rope trick."

The Maharishi Movement

The pivotal event occurred when the Beatles encountered Maharishi Mahesh Yogi, fifty-five-year-old founder of the Spiritual Regeneration Movement. With his long hair, graying beard, white robes and beatific smile, Maharishi appeared to be everything a cosmically conscious guru should be. He spoke in riddles, talked a lot about love, and offered what he called a "mechanical path to God-realization."

The Beatles hooked up with him in August 1967, two months after the release of *Sergeant Pepper,* at a time when they were looking for ways of finding what they'd experienced on LSD without having to trip out. Just as the world had learned of their psychedelic explorations, the Beatles had altered course.

"LSD isn't a real answer," George Harrison was now telling the music press. "It doesn't give you anything. It enables you to see a lot of possibilities that you may not have noticed before, but it's not the answer. . . . It can help you to go from A to B, but when you get to B, you see C. You see that to get really high you have to do it straight. There are special ways of getting high without drugs—with yoga, meditation and all those things."

Maharishi Mahesh Yogi was understandably delighted to have bagged not only Donovan—who was to include the guru's photograph on the cover of his next album, *Gift from a Flower to a Garden*

(1968)—but also members of the Beatles, the Rolling Stones (Brian Jones and Mick Jagger were temporarily interested) and the Beach Boys (Mike Love), all in one year. "Now they're all leaping on the meditation bandwagon," announced *Disc and Music Echo* in October. Thus this rather obscure movement momentarily became as important as miniskirts and vegetarian food in the minds of style-watchers and newspaper columnists. The Maharishi was featured on the cover of *The Saturday Evening Post,* was interviewed on British television by Malcolm Muggeridge and even made a spoken-word album (side one: "Love"; side two: "The Untapped Source of Power That Lies Within").

When a British pop magazine asked him to contribute a few words to go alongside a Beatles feature, he said, "The interest of young minds in the use of drugs, even though misguided, indicates their genuine search for some form of spiritual experience. With the interest of the Beatles and the Rolling Stones in Transcendental Meditation, it has become evident that the search for higher spiritual experience among the young will not take long to reach fulfilment."

The Lure of Experience
For young white Westerners, the religion of the East was mysterious, exotic and alien enough to be fashionable. It appeared to be full of experiential high moments rather than creeds and commandments. You did things, saw things and felt things, rather than assented to doctrines and renounced the works of the devil. It seemed to have none of the dead formalism that characterized the religious observances of many of their parents.

One of the influential books of the day was *Autobiography of a Yogi* by Paramhansa Yogananda (1950), in which the founder of the Self-Realization Fellowship told his story of encounters with gurus who could, he believed, come back from the dead to deliver messages, stop breathing at will and rematerialize themselves in other places.

The Beatles were each sent a copy by Barry Miles of London's

Indica Bookshop, and when it came to choosing figures for the cover of *Sergeant Pepper* three of the gurus from the book (Sri Yukteswar, Sri Mahavatara Babaji and Sri Lahiri Mahasaya), plus Yogananda himself, were included in the lineup. "If they are planning the spiritual thing for us," mused McCartney, "what a groove that he [God] has got himself right in the middle of the Beatles' LP cover! Normal ideas of God wouldn't have him interested in Beatle music or any pop."

George Harrison, who as a child had occasionally visited a Roman Catholic church, had been left cold by formal religion. On reading Yogananda, however, he swallowed wholesale tales of gurus who could "walk on the water and materialise bodies" and of others who had levitated or had lived to be "hundreds of years old." "When you get to India," he told Barry Miles in an interview for *International Times,* "you find that this is happening all over the place, with people materialising left, right and centre."

These stories and the fact that through chanting one could get "blissed out," as he called it, appealed to his sense of value for money. Never willing to have faith in the promised unseen, he stated, "If there's a God, I want to see Him. It's pointless to believe in something without proof. . . . [Through meditation] you can actually obtain God perception. You can actually see God and hear Him, play with Him. It might sound crazy but He is actually there with you."

Music as a Means
Guitarist John McLaughlin, a prominent British blues and jazz player who converted to the teachings of Sri Chinmoy in 1972, formed the Mahavishnu Orchestra in order to explore a new form of spiritual music. Like Harrison, he'd been unmoved by his childhood experience of the Christian Church in Scotland. But after reading the work of a guru named Manamarhashi he felt that "this was the first experience I'd had of living religion. They don't view religion the way they do in the West, as dogma. In my enquiries into Indian thought, I became aware of the fact that religion and music were not separate but mixed.

I thought this was a very interesting idea."

Hinduism views music as one of the paths to God-consciousness because it releases souls trapped in the world of delusion. Music is considered a divine art, dignified by the gods Krishna, Brahma and Shiva. The Sanskrit word for musician appropriately means "he who sings the praises of God." Yogananda wrote, "Because Man himself is an expression of the Creative Word, sound has the most potent and immediate effect on him, offering a way to remembrance of his divine origin. The thrilling intensity of joy bestowed by music is caused by the vibratory awakening of one of man's occult spinal centres."

Utterly fed up with the false glamour of being a teen idol, frustrated with playing to a wall of screams, George Harrison was taken with the devotion and artistic purity of the Indian musicians he met, claiming that they produced "the greatest music ever on our level of existence." In 1966, just prior to recording *Sergeant Pepper,* he spent six weeks in Ravi Shankar's Bombay home learning the rudiments of the sitar. "Through the music you reach the spiritual," he claimed. "Music is very involved with the spiritual, as we know from the Hare Krishna mantra."

The Draw of Simplicity

Another pull, in this age of the dropout, was the simplicity of Indian life and the denial of materialism implicit in Hinduism. To young people in revolt against consumerism as a religion, who saw the Christian church as being in cahoots with the military-industrial complex, these smiling holy men, with apparently nothing more than a string of beads and a cotton robe, seemed to have discovered truly worthwhile values. "Here everybody is vibrating on a material level, which is nowhere," said Harrison of his homeland after returning from an early visit to India. "Over there, they have this great feeling of something else that's just spiritual going on."

The Beatles had experienced the best that mammon could offer. They had become millionaires at an early age. They were worshiped around the world; they'd reached the peak of their creative powers, and their place in history was assured. "Yet," said John Lennon's wife Cynthia, "human nature and the ultimate search for something new and unobtainable in their young lives drove them to experiment with anything and everything that was offered to them. The incredible speed and madness of their success story created a very large vacuum in their day-to-day existence."

Harrison's comments confirmed this observation.

Having been successful and meeting everybody we thought worth meeting, and having had more hits than anyone else and having done it bigger than everybody else was like reaching the top of a wall. Then, we looked over and there was so much more on the other side. So I felt it was part of my duty to say, okay, maybe you thought this was all you need, to be rich and famous, but actually it isn't.

Prepared by LSD

Yet the attraction of material simplicity alone wouldn't necessarily have tilted the balance in favor of Hinduism. The key factor was, without a doubt, LSD. If there had been no mass-produced LSD, there would have been no mass interest in the previously incomprehensible and culturally alien teachings of the East. The drug experience had worked as a sneak preview for yogic bliss.

Said Pete Townshend at the time, "Acid has happened, and the acceleration of spiritual thinking was obviously the purpose for it." In a similar vein, Harrison said, "Acid was the key that opened the door. From the moment I had it I wanted to have it all the time—those thoughts about yogis and the Himalayas and Ravi Shankar's music."

The collapse of the ego, the feeling that everything is part of a single consciousness, and the conviction that so-called normal life is but an illusion from which we need to escape were all acknowledged in Hindu teaching. The experiences had names. Brahman was the absolute consciousness, and *maya* was the world of illusion. It was a great consolation for many to discover that the perceptions they had been having under illegal circumstances were regarded as sacred truths in the East and had long, respected histories.

Timothy Leary had always insisted that LSD was "Western yoga." Once he claimed, "Our religious philosophy, or our philosophy about the meaning of LSD, comes closer to Hinduism than any other religion." Other popular writers such as the former Episcopal priest Alan Watts *(This Is It; The Joyous Cosmology)* and the novelist Aldous Huxley *(The Doors of Perception)* interpreted LSD and mescaline trips in Hindu and Buddhist terms, Huxley advocating what he called "biochemical mysticism."

Certainly only the shared experience of LSD would have brought John Lennon, Paul McCartney, Ringo Starr, George Harrison, Brian Jones and Mick Jagger to sit spellbound at the feet of a middle-aged religious teacher in a university hall in North Wales in the summer of 1967. Six months later the Beatles, Donovan and Beach Boy Mike Love traveled to the Maharishi's fifteen-acre ashram on the banks of the sacred River Ganges at Rishikesh, to take part in a program of lectures and intense meditation.

The rest of the world looked on in bemused wonder at just how "way out" these once flippant young men had become. Photos came back of them sitting in yoga positions, dressed in loose white cotton garments and garlanded with flowers. For one religious festival they daubed their faces with red ocher, and there was talk of Lennon and Harrison descending to underground caves for days of continuous meditation. Asked if this was yet another fad for pop stars, Maharishi retorted, "I don't care what their motive is. The moral and spiritual benefits come whether they want them or not."

The Promise of Meditation
Transcendental Meditation involves focusing the mind on a secret word (a mantra) until thoughts supposedly rise from the "gross" to the "subtle" level, where all that is experienced is awareness itself.

Schooled in the Vedanta tradition of Hinduism and a disciple of the late Brahmananda Sarasivati (also known as Guru Dev), Maharishi offered the experience of "transcendental, Absolute Being, whose nature is bliss consciousness."

This probably seemed like a complete departure from the original spirit of rock 'n' roll, but in fact Hinduism offered a coherent explanation of the human predicament. The dullness of life that rock 'n' roll screamed against was "maya," the world of illusion. Our consciousness needed to be expanded into God-consciousness so that we might rise above the "gross level of existence." Hinduism, through discipline and meditative technique, was offering a way out—heaven while on earth. It agreed with rock 'n' roll that "there's a better place for me and you" (The Animals, "We've Gotta Get Out of This Place").

Pete Townshend said in 1967, "Everything goes a lot deeper than working, living and dying. . . . If we don't reach a state of understanding of how we can escape the world situation, we'll just fade away. The only real escape is via meditation. To be able to meditate yourself to another level."

Not everyone in rock 'n' roll appeared to grasp the connection between Chuck Berry's hunger for the promised land or Eddie Cochran's summertime restlessness and this escape to another level. Instead of continuing the story and using the landmarks already set up, they tended to produce esoteric tales, recognizable to converts but baffling to everyone else. The burning passion, the admission of hunger, was lost from this sort of rock 'n' roll.

Everyone Is Brahman

Quintessence, a band based in London's Notting Hill, became the world's first Hindu rock 'n' roll band, wearing Indian robes on stage, burning incense and singing songs that were more or less religious texts put to music, such as

Everything is Brahman
Everyone is Brahman

I am Brahman

You are Brahman.

They signed with Island Records and released an album, *Dive Deep,* with a mandalic cover and tracks with titles like "Dance for the One," "Brahman" and "Sri Ram Chant."

The Moody Blues, who had graduated from LSD to TM by 1968, pioneered the lush, cerebral approach, with an accent on seriousness and instruction. Their album *In Search of the Lost Chord* was written as an expedition, starting with the crash of a sitar chord and ending with the sound of "om." On the inside cover was a yantric design (the visual equivalent of a mantra, we are told) that the listener was supposed to gaze at.

The poetry was abysmal. Blue suede shoes were left behind in favor of blue onyx seas, gamma rays, vibrations and astral planes. Instead of riding along in your automobile, you were now "speeding through the universe" or "taking a place on this trip." In one song about Timothy Leary taking you on "trips around the bay" ("Legend of a Mind"), there was confusion as to whether you were getting blissed out or ripped on acid, although Mike Pinder did confirm that "thinking is the best way to travel."

Pinder had become the most concerned in the group about religion, earning himself the nickname "Mad Monk of Cobham." In 1964, two years before experiencing LSD, he was asked by a reporter from *Disc* where rock 'n' roll would be in ten years' time. He responded, "In ten years' time we're all going to be singing hymns. Modern hymns." In a way that was what happened, but hymns don't connect with unbelievers.

Pete Townshend and Meher Baba

The one artist who did realize the redemptive heritage of rock 'n' roll was Pete Townshend, who ever since the foundation of the Who had seen the music as a violent explosion in the face of normal, civilized, suburban inertia.

"Rock 'n' roll is the single force that threatens a lot of the crap that is around at the moment in the middle class and in middle-aged politics and philosophy," he declared. "It blasts it out of sheer realism." Songs like "Anyway Anyhow Anywhere," "My Generation," "I Can't Explain" and "Substitute" filled young listeners with hope. The power of the music suggested that there was another level to which we could all rise, that our potential was much greater than we'd been led to believe. It was, years before Springsteen, a definite spit in the face of the "badlands."

Along with his peers, Townshend eventually succumbed to LSD. After the experience he came to believe that Meher Baba, a guru then still living in India, was the Avatar (manifestation of God) for this age. Baba, who claimed to be God, taught that it is ego that keeps us bound to the world of illusion, and that complete devotion to God (that is, himself) is the only way to freedom and fulfilment. Although he claimed it is possible to follow any religion and be a "Baba lover" (as his devotees are known), in truth his teachings were a heretical form of Hinduism. Certainly no orthodox Christian could accept his claims to be the Christ.

By allegiance to Baba, Townshend was able to redirect his frustrations and form new conclusions. He never disowned his earlier songs. He could see that the motivation behind "Anyway Anyhow Anywhere" ("Nothing gets in my way / Not even locked doors / Don't follow the lines / That's been laid before") was explained by Baba: "Man is constantly longing for happiness and searching desperately for some means of breaking out of the trap which life has become."

From the fresh perspective of religion, Townshend could see his mod anthems as having been a cry for salvation. He had written "Anyway Anyhow Anywhere" after listening to a Charlie Parker album, fascinated with the inner freedom suggested by the jazz of a man whose life was actually in bondage to gangsters and drug runners. "It sounded like an arrogant song, because it came through the mouthpiece of the Who," he says, "but it was a song about spiritual freedom, my earliest attempt."

In songs for the Who, Townshend had also concerned himself with false appearances. Things are never quite as they seem. A boy's mother wants him to be a girl ("I'm a Boy"), a teenager falls in love with a model on a postcard only to discover that she died long before he was born ("Pictures of Lily"), and everyone is assuming fake personalities in order to win love and respect ("Substitute," "Disguises").

Again, Meher Baba's religious teachings offered an explanation. "Even as the individual can be wrong in his convictions about his own nature, so he is often quite wrong about the nature of the world around him," Baba wrote. "In reality, it is a world of illusion that separates him from his own true birthright of freedom and happiness in oneness with the One."

Townshend's best-known line, "Hope I die before I get old," could also be invested with new meaning. Don't we all have to die in order to be reborn? "I now try to live the words in a spiritual sense," Townshend would later say. "I can't stand up and say that I wish I was dead because what I meant then was 'I hope I die before I get old and senile and out of it.' Now I see it in a spiritual sense. . . . I don't want to waste my life. I want every year to count.

"I neither want to be old before my time nor to spend the rest of eternity going through the same things again and again. I believe in reincarnation and karma. I feel that unless you face up to the fact that in the end you have to turn to God and turn to a spiritual way of living, you just spend your life eternally going through the same patterns."

From 1969 onward, the teachings of Meher Baba informed Townshend's work with the Who. The double album *Tommy,* hailed at the time as the world's first rock opera, was written as an allegory of the journey from spiritual darkness (Tommy is deaf, dumb and blind) to God-realization. "At one time [Tommy] could see only darkness and himself, a very limited view of things," said Townshend. "Then, after awakening, he was able to perceive one new thing, which was God."

Four years later *Quadrophenia* set the same allegory in the world
of the mods, confirming the continuity with Townshend's earlier anthems. He wanted to be able to discuss spiritual issues in a familiar
landscape of houses, trains and motorcycles. He wanted to prove that
the dissatisfaction that drove the mods was in essence a spiritual restlessness. His hero, Jimmy, tries to find "the real me" through the
sexual encounters he has, the company he keeps and the clothes he
wears—the traditional materialistic methods of establishing self-iden-
tity. But he really discovers himself only when he drowns in the ocean,
a symbol in Eastern mystical teaching of the all-embracing Godhead.
In "Drowned" he sings, "Oh let me flow into the ocean / Let me go
back to the sea." Explained Townshend, "It's a love song, God's love
being the ocean, and our 'selves' being the drops of water that make
it up. Meher Baba said, 'I am the ocean of love.' I want to drown in
that ocean. The 'drop' will then be an ocean itself."

Townshend opened a London Baba Centre in Victoria (later moving
it to Twickenham) and published Baba material. In 1970 he managed
to get the guru's face on the front cover of *Rolling Stone,* a space
normally reserved for the superstars of rock 'n' roll; he himself contributed an essay to the issue that he titled "In Love with Meher
Baba."

The Fortunes of Maharishi and Krishna

During their stay at the ashram in Rishikesh, the Beatles became
disillusioned with Maharishi. They claimed their teacher was himself
caught up in the gross level of existence, pumping them for financial
contributions to be paid into a Swiss bank account and making plays
for women. Maharishi had hoped the Beatles would open up their own
TM academy in London and star alongside him in promotional films
for his movement. Instead they grumbled about him in the press, and
Lennon wrote the song "Sexy Sadie," originally titled "Maharishi,"
which was a thinly disguised putdown of the man he believed had
"made a fool of everyone."

But Maharishi Mahesh Yogi was by no means the only guru who had become wise to the fertile market presented by the collapsing psychedelic culture. Swami Prabhupada, who had been commissioned in 1922 to evangelize the West, arrived in New York City in September 1965 and founded ISKCON, the International Society for Krishna Consciousness.

By 1966 he had targeted the disillusioned drug users of Greenwich Village, distributing flyers that read, "STAY HIGH FOR EVER! No more coming down. Practice Krishna Consciousness. Expand your consciousness by practicing TRANSCENDENTAL SOUND VIBRATION." Discussing drugs with new devotees, he asked, "Do you think LSD can produce ecstasy and higher consciousness? Then just imagine a room full of LSD. Krishna Consciousness is like that."

In January 1967, after Prabhupada recorded an album of Krishna mantras, ISKCON moved into the Haight-Ashbury area of San Francisco, the legendary incubator of acid culture. "The police and free clinics couldn't handle the overload of people taking LSD," commented an early Haight convert. "The police saw Prabhupada as a certain refuge."

Prabhupada saw a harvest amongst the mind-blown, but he also had a vision for rock 'n' roll as a popularizer of Krishna Consciousness. On January 27, 1967, at the Avalon Ballroom, scene of many psychedelic romps, a "Mantra-Rock Dance" was mounted. The Swami shared the stage with Bay Area acid-rock bands the Grateful Dead, Big Brother and the Holding Company, Quicksilver Messenger Service and Jefferson Airplane. All proceeds would go toward establishing a local temple.

The mix of Hinduism and hard rock was a success. Five thousand fans turned up and packed the ballroom. Prabhupada, who went on stage at ten p.m., was introduced by poet Allen Ginsberg, who announced that the Hare Krishna mantra was very important for LSD trippers because it could "stabilize their consciousness on reentry." The guru then led a mass chant that lasted for an hour. Ginsberg exulted afterward that the evening represented "the height of the Haight-Ashbury spiritual enthusiasm."

Yet Prabhupada realized that ecstatic nights in San Francisco didn't turn on the world. Already he had bigger ideas. His biographer declares that he had his eyes set on "world-wide revolution in consciousness spearheaded by Krishna Conscious Beatles." Thus ISKCON devotees began a campaign to get the Beatles' attention by sending eye-catching presentations to them at the Apple Corps headquarters in London's Savile Row. On one occasion they sent an apple pie with the Hare Krishna mantra lettered on its crust. Another time they sent in a wind-up walking apple and a recording of them chanting. When these received no response, one devotee, Syamasundara, went to the office, where he managed to catch George Harrison's attention and found him a sympathetic listener. Harrison invited Syamasundara to visit him at his home in Esher.

Within months Prabhupada had apparently replaced the Maharishi in the affections of the Beatles. He and some of his followers became house guests of Lennon at his Tittenhurst Park home near Ascot, and six Canadian devotees were invited to chant on "Give Peace a Chance." Harrison took members of the London temple into the studios to cut a single of the "Hare Krishna Mantra," which was to become a top-20 hit in 1969, and later he helped to fund their British operation. "Hare Krishna is where it's at," announced Lennon that year. "We fully believe in it."

Following the breakup of the Beatles in 1970, Harrison remained completely sold on Krishna Consciousness. In 1971 he scored a hit with "My Sweet Lord," an attempt to get radio listeners chanting the mantra that he believed to be "a method of becoming one with God." It was inspired by the surprise chart success of the gospel song "Oh Happy Day" by the Edwin Hawkins Singers. "I did the voices singing 'hallelujah' first, and then changed to 'Hare Krishna' so that people would be chanting the 'Maha mantra' before they knew what was going on."

On his solo albums *Living in the Material World* and *Dark Horse,* Harrison sang songs to Krishna and articulated the Hindu redemption promise of breaking free from the cycle of death and rebirth.

I hope to get out of this place

By the Lord Sri Krishna's Grace

My salvation from the material world.

("Living in the Material World")

On tour in America in 1974, his first since the Beatles bowed out in 1966, he led his audiences in chanting the Hare Krishna mantra, promising them, "If we can all do this for thirty seconds without any hangups, we'll blow the ceiling off this place."

No ceilings were blown off, though. For all the fascination with the Maharishi during the Summer of Love, Hindu sermons stuck in the throats of most rock 'n' roll consumers. The more religious Harrison's albums became, the less they sold. When the Beach Boys embarked on a seventeen-date U.S. tour in May 1968, with the Maharishi as an opening act, they found the fans staying away in droves, unwilling to put up with a long, unintelligible lecture before the surf music. The tour had to be aborted after a few days, causing a $500,000 loss. The group's "TM album," *Friends,* was their worst-selling ever; it was described by one of their biographers as "a boring, emotionless LP."

Disillusionment

That many of the major rock 'n' roll converts to the East subsequently abandoned their gurus suggests that not all their questions were answered. John McLaughlin, who signed up with Sri Chinmoy in 1972, left in 1978. In 1973 he had recorded *Love Devotion Surrender* with Carlos Santana, the whole inner spread being given over to a spiritual message from Chinmoy explaining that "when the finite enters into the Infinite, it becomes the Infinite all at once."

Santana, who had come to prominence through the Woodstock movie as the wiry-headed guitarist of the band that bore his name, had discovered Chinmoy through jazz guitarist Larry Coryell. "Larry showed me Sri Chinmoy," he said, "and he showed me where he was coming from, where he was channelling his music." He cut his hair short, began dressing in pure white and seemed to smile a whole lot less. Yet by 1983 Santana too had fled the fold.

The Beatles followed Maharishi for less than a year. Ringo left Rishikesh, saying it was too much like an English summer holiday camp. Lennon and McCartney quickly denounced Maharishi as a fraud. McCartney has never since shown any interest in Eastern religion. By the time Swami Prabhupada came to stay at Tittenhurst Park, Lennon was openly doubting the authority of many of these gurus. He asked Prabhupada: "How are we to tell if a spiritual master is real or not?"

Told that a true spiritual master comes from a line of succession, Lennon then asked, "But what if one of these masters who's not in the line says exactly the same as one who is? What if he says his mantra is coming from the Vedas and he seems to speak with as much authority as you?"

It was an appropriate question, because the guru was promising nothing less than eventual salvation through constantly repeating phonetic sounds. One who chanted Hare Krishna, he had said, "could be saved from falling to the lower species in the next life." When asked to trust your eternal soul to a man who once said, "Initiation means that the spiritual master accepts the student and agrees to take charge, and the student accepts the spiritual master and agrees to worship him as God," you are entitled to ask for evidence of his divinity.

Each guru was offering a slightly different technique, promising God-consciousness and disparaging all other gurus as charlatans. Meher Baba, who said, "I am the Christ. I know everything," claimed that there were only ever five Perfect Masters on earth at any one time. When, in 1971, I asked Swami Prabhupada how we should be able to tell that he was the genuine article in the then-expanding marketplace of spiritual relief, he answered, "If you want a cheap guru, there are many cheater gurus. People get cheated because they want things cheap. A genuine guru is not a businessman."

By 1970 Lennon had clearly made up his own mind. Following a short course of primal therapy under Arthur Janov in California, he resolved to face up to his own pain, failure and insecurity.

Old Hare Krishna got nothing on you

Just keep you crazy with nothing to do

Keep you occupied with pie in the sky

There ain't no guru who can see through your eyes

I found out! ("I Found Out")

Shortly after this record was released I asked Lennon why so many were searching for redemption if, as he now believed, we are isolated people in a godless universe. "They're looking for gurus," he said. "The same as I was. They're looking for some kind of Superdaddy, and I'll tell you why we look for it. We were never given enough love and touch et cetera when we were children. It's as simple as that."

For many people Eastern disciplines were far too demanding. Redemption, according to the Hindu teachers of the day, is no easy thing. You can never be quite sure how much bad karma you have to pay for or where you are on the cycle of birth to rebirth. Initiates of Krishna Consciousness vowed to chant sixteen "rounds" of the Hare Krishna mantra each day, which takes between one and a half and two hours.

Yogananda taught that Kriya Yoga quickens human evolution and that thirty seconds' practice equals "one year of natural spiritual unfoldment." He claimed, "A number of yogis achieve emancipation in six or twelve or twenty-four or forty-eight years. A yogi who dies before achieving full realization carries with him the good karma of his past Kriya effort; in his new life he is propelled towards his infinite goal." This was bad news for anyone also committed to a family, or a rock 'n' roll career.

A full-time yogi giving up eight and a half hours a day could, according to Yogananda, "in three years . . . accomplish by intelligent self-effort the same result which nature brings to pass in a million years." Yet this evolution wasn't always apparent. What are you to believe when after years of religious devotion you're still no more in control of your desires than when you first began?

After a decade as a Baba lover, Pete Townshend found himself at rock-bottom. His marriage was falling apart, he was drinking heavily, and he was addicted to heroin. Yet Baba had said, "He who loves me intensely can become God."

Once free from his addiction, Townshend closed down the Baba Centre and was clearly not so "in love" with the guru as in 1970. "I think my focus has changed," he admitted to me when I asked if his enthusiasm had waned. "I think if I went to India and was amongst other Baba lovers, his actual presence would enter in much the same way that it did. But I feel the same sensation when I go to church."

Yet it would be wrong to assume that because guruism was a short-lived fad within rock 'n' roll, it failed to have a significant effect. In truth, the combination of hallucinogenic drugs and Eastern teaching opened up a generation to other religious ideas.

So although ISKCON may have only ten thousand hardcore devotees worldwide and Sri Chinmoy claims no more than one thousand "serious followers," the impact of Hindu teaching, translated through rock 'n' roll and its attendant media, has been immeasurable. For many in the West it opened up a religious salad bar where the spiritually hungry could take their plates and design their own religious system. As John Lennon told Swami Prabhupada in 1969, "I've found that the best thing for myself is to take a little bit here and a little bit there. We have to keep sifting the sand to see who's got the best."

Sympathy for the Devil

5

There are black musicians who think we are acting as unknown agents of Lucifer and others who think we are Lucifer. Everybody's Lucifer.

Keith Richards, the Rolling Stones

I don't worship the Devil but magic does intrigue me. Magic of all kinds.

Jimmy Page, Led Zeppelin

As God has been losing his percentage, the Devil has been picking up.

John Phillips, the Mamas and the Papas

L SD made George Harrison think about the Himalayas and yogis. It propelled Pete Townshend into the arms of Meher Baba. But for the Rolling Stones it opened up a can of snakes. Their songs swirled with darkness and menace. Threats of insanity or brutality lurked at the edges. "Have You Seen Your Mother, Baby, Standing in the Shadow?" sounded like a bad trip. "Paint It Black" was plain morbid. "I look inside myself," sang Mick Jagger, "and see my heart is black."

Like no rock 'n' roll group before them, the Rolling Stones invoked the devil, titling an album *Their Satanic Majesties Request,* taking on the persona of Lucifer and frequently playing on occult associations.

For "The Rolling Stones' Rock 'n' Roll Circus" (an as yet unscreened special) Jagger ripped off his black shirt to reveal a tattoo of the devil on his chest. Later, during a David Bailey photo session, Brian Jones posed with a glass of red wine in one hand and a three-pronged fork in the other, a wicked glint evident in his heavy-lidded eyes.

If it had stopped there it would have been considered nothing more than a manufactured image, but it was known that Jagger had become fascinated with occult literature, and it was rumored that Keith Richards and his girlfriend Anita Pallenberg practiced magic rituals and witchcraft in their heavily draped bedroom, where candles continuously burned. Asked by *Rolling Stone* about the Stones' reported "Satan trip," Richards said, "It's something everybody ought to explore. There are possibilities there. . . . I'm no expert. I just try and bring it into the open a little."

The Rolling Stones had started with an image of "badness," much of it engineered by manager Andrew "Loog" Oldham, who wanted them to offer an alternative to the cooperative cheeriness of the Beatles. At this point it was hardly Satanic—just a case of a loose necktie, a weak bladder or an overdue haircut. But by 1966 there was something authentic about the dark, brooding lyrics and the hollow, wasted looks.

Fathoming Hell

Not for nothing was LSD known as "the heaven and hell drug." While some people were ushered into the Garden of Eden, others were plunged into outer darkness. Humphrey Osmond, the man who supplied Aldous Huxley with his first mescaline in the 1950s and coined the term *psychedelic,* acknowledged this in a couplet:

To fathom Hell or soar angelic

Just take a pinch of psychedelic.

Brian Jones was one of those who fathomed hell. Recalls Anita Pallenberg, "The first time Brian took acid he saw creatures coming out of the ground, the walls, the floors. He was looking in all the cupboards for people. . . . It's like he came out of it a haunted man." If Jagger's lyrics are in any way autobiographical, he too had a bad time. In "19th Nervous Breakdown" he scolds his "society girl," saying,

On our first trip I tried so hard to rearrange your mind

But after a while I realised you were disarranging mine.

It was not unusual for LSD to disarrange minds by hauling demons and monsters from the depths of the subconscious. Eric Clapton remembers hallucinating on stage in San Francisco while playing with Cream, his guitar apparently resonating with the spirit world. "Every bad lick I had, every blues lick, turned the audience into devils in red coats," he said. "Then I'd play a sweet one and they'd all turn into angels."

R. E. L. Masters and Jean Houston, during their celebrated clinical experiments with LSD during the 1960s, were startled to discover the prominence of occult and pagan images reported by the subjects. Almost half of them hallucinated demons, while a mere 7 percent saw angels. Similarly, 67 percent felt themselves transported back to the rites of ancient Greece, Rome or Egypt, whereas only 8 percent experienced Christian, Jewish or Islamic rituals.

Considering their subjects would have had nominally Christian upbringings, it caused the two researchers to question why hallucinogenics should encourage a bias toward paganism and evil. "Why, for example, do ancient and primitive rites occur in the images so often more than do contemporary ones?" they asked. "Is it because the old rites reflect and minister to deep-rooted human needs that modern rites do not or is there some other explanation? Why do angels run such a poor second to devils?"

Either the drug released monsters or suppressed fears and bad memories, or it actually tampered with consciousness in such a way that all protection from invasion by evil spiritual forces was removed. Whatever the truth, it caused some people to become intrigued with the possibility of personalized evil. Some deliberately conjured up evil in order to experience and conquer it. Jerry Garcia of the Grateful

Dead spoke about having seen things that were "intrinsically evil" while he was high on drugs; such experiences made him want to investigate further.

Breaking Out

Yet the Rolling Stones did not initially see the devil as the embodiment of evil but as an alluring glimpse of the forbidden. "It was a Baudelaire phase really," Jagger told me years later, referring to the nineteenth-century French poet who explored decadence in a search for true spiritual values. "It was an exploration of the other side of the psyche, I suppose. Letting yourself go. It's very dangerous just to let yourself drift, especially if you start using drugs to do it."

Mick Jagger, Keith Richards and Brian Jones had come from those reliably dull backgrounds that rock 'n' roll was designed to resist. Each of them knew that there must be a better life somewhere else, that there was more to life than mere decorum. Jagger and Jones came from strict homes in classically conformist English suburbs with trim lawns, bay windows and wrought-iron gates, where the unexpected was not at all welcome. Their mothers were house-proud, their fathers hardworking and disciplinarian. Cheltenham, where Jones grew up in a "semidetached," was the epitome of a town where nothing ever happened. "Brian couldn't stand Cheltenham," said one of his friends. "He simply loathed it. He couldn't stand the restrictions of Cheltenham. He couldn't stand the restrictions imposed by his family on his thinking and his general behavior."

Just as Jagger and Jones were threatened with the sterility of middle-class propriety, Richards was trapped by the ugliness of a working-class council estate (housing development). "It was soul-destroying," he later said. "A mixture of terrible apartment blocks and horrible new streets full of semidetached houses, all in a row, all new, a real concrete jungle. It was a really disgusting place. And because my father wouldn't take a gamble on anything, he wouldn't try and get us out of there."

Rock 'n' roll owes a lot to such claustrophobic surroundings, which so often provide the impulse to kick hard and loud, to cry out for something mysterious and glorious. "We were very much kicking against the mediocre aspirations of our backgrounds," admitted Jagger. "When you look back on it, it was pretty boring."

In the Stones' desire to break away from lifeless regulation, the devil suggested a glamorous impulsiveness. The devil, of course, is a ubiquitous character in the mythology of the blues music they'd fallen in love with. A persistent piece of black Southern folklore suggests that if you wait at the crossroads at midnight, the devil will appear to offer you your heart's desire in exchange for the custody of your soul. One of the Rolling Stones' favorite singers, Robert Johnson (1912-1938), was said to have done exactly that and was transformed overnight from a shy but competent guitar player into the genius composer of "Hellhound on My Trail" and "Me and the Devil Blues."

Blues men operated on the margins of their society, singing of the pain of living but never, like their gospel contemporaries, taking refuge in the Lord. Respite was always in love, sex or a convenient drug. More than most, they held on to the superstitious memories of African religion: the belief in bad omens, mojos and the curses of voodoo. Respectable church people looked down on them. They called their soulful, bumpy guitar music "the devil's music."

The Stones fancied themselves as the devil's musicians on the margins of polite British society. Anything that caused a disturbance in suburbia and rattled the values of people whose grand ambition was to buy a new lawn mower could contain the seeds of their redemption. Theirs was the devil of William Blake and Percy Bysshe Shelley. He was not the Great Deceiver of the Bible but the prototypical True Man, unhampered by tradition or moral codes. As David Dalton writes in *The Rolling Stones: The First Twenty Years,* "Satan is the rebel who promises freedom. He's always been the patron saint of blues and rock, the enemy of hypocrisy and complacency. He has nothing to live up to, and his honesty is never questioned."

The song destined to confirm their Satanic image was "Sympathy for the Devil," recorded in London during November 1968 before the cameras of Jean-Luc Godard, who was shooting *One Plus One,* and used as the opening track on *Beggars Banquet.* With its pounding African drums punctuated by screams, it was obviously designed to conjure up impressions of a sweaty jungle ritual with dancing flames and writhing bodies, and the backing track sounded like a field recording of a voodoo ceremony.

Inspired by a reading of Mikhail Bulgakov's 1938 novel *The Master and Margarita* (not published in English until 1967), "Sympathy for the Devil" was in fact an exposé of the evil one and his cunning control. Reminiscent of biblical descriptions of Satan as able to appear as "an angel of light," Jagger's portrayal shows him as "a man of wealth and taste" who inveigles his way into human affairs and claims the great catastrophes of history as examples of his work.

Yet what's remembered from the song is not the irony but the title, along with lines like "Just call me Lucifer" and

If you meet me, have some courtesy

Have some sympathy and taste

Use all your well-earned politesse

Or I'll lay your soul to waste.

Whatever the point of view of the song, this was Jagger speaking as Satan, and the Luciferian persona stuck. "I don't know how much people think of Mick as the devil or as just a good rock performer or what," confessed Keith Richards three years later. "There are black magicians who think we are acting as unknown agents of Lucifer, and others who think we are Lucifer."

Key Influences: Anger and Crowley

A significant figure in the Stones' occult education was the American filmmaker Kenneth Anger, who took up temporary residence in Chelsea during 1966. Anger, one could safely say, was drawn to the dark side of life. Raised in Hollywood, he had early on developed an appetite for the waste products of Celluloid City. While his classmates at Beverly Hills High were collecting glossy studio shots of their favorite stars, Anger was investigating local sleaze, turning up at the scenes of murders and suicides in the hope of picking up hot gossip or even a snapshot.

The eventual result of his obsession was *Hollywood Babylon,* a detailed account of the sins and downfalls of great American film stars, liberally illustrated with photographs of heads in ovens, blood on pavements and bullet holes in bodies. So libelous was it in 1960 that it had to be published in Paris to avoid prosecution. (After it was published in the United States in 1975, it became a bestseller and was followed in 1984 by *Hollywood Babylon II.*)

Anger's own films, the most famous of which remains *Scorpio Rising,* were made for the art crowd rather than for the moviegoing public. In London art-gallery owner Robert Fraser invited Anger to show his work at one of his regular home screenings. Here Anger met Mick Jagger, Brian Jones, Keith Richards, Anita Pallenberg and Marianne Faithfull, along with other interesting figures on the fringes of London's art and music scene, like interior designer Christopher Gibbs and ley-line expert John Michell. (See chapter seven, under "The New Consciousness," for a definition of *ley lines.*) They were fascinated with this visitor, who claimed his avant-garde films were informed by the magical ideas of Aleister Crowley, the self-styled "Great Beast 666" who had died in 1947. Anger said his films were "visual incantations" and "moving spells." As Michell observed, "A lot of ideas that were previously limited to occult circles had become common property through acid."

"Anger was a great tub thumper for the occult," remembers Christopher Gibbs. "I should think that single-handedly he's more responsible for the explosion of interest and for making people more aware of Crowley."

Born in 1847, Aleister Crowley had, like the Stones, rebelled against a regulated small-town background. He'd been raised in Leamington,

Warwickshire, by parents who were members of the Strict Brethren, a fundamentalist Christian sect. From an early age young Aleister identified with the enemies of God in the Bible stories that were read to him. In particular he identified with the antichrist predicted in the book of Revelation. In 1898 he joined the Hermetic Order of the Golden Dawn, a magical society.

Most of Crowley's adult life was dedicated to indulging in everything he believed God would hate: performing sex magic, taking heroin, opium, hashish, peyote and cocaine, invoking spirits, and even once offering himself to the Russian authorities to help destroy Christianity. He wrote volumes of books that he believed were dictated to him by a spirit from ancient Egypt called Aiwass. "To worship me take wine and strange drugs," the spirit conveniently told him. "Lust, enjoy all things of sense and rapture. Fear not that any God shall deny thee for this."

In the middle of the 1960s, to a rock 'n' roll culture wanting to smash taboos in order to raise a new, liberated society, Crowley became a cult figure. Anger considered him "one of the unique geniuses of the twentieth century. A Promethean Man." *International Times* voted him "the unsung hero of the hippies." Even the Beatles tipped their hats to the magician, making him one of the faces in the crowd on the cover of *Sergeant Pepper*.

In retrospect it would seem that for the Stones, Crowley was a passing fancy, a convenient justification for their self-indulgent lifestyle. Anger has certainly come to believe so, calling them "spoiled, self-deluded brats" who remain "totally ignorant" of Crowley's "magickal" system. "Mick Jagger thinks everything is a gimmick," he says. "If it's to do with magick, there's a gimmick behind it. You press two buttons and discover the secret that makes you top dog. He wants to know how he can use things. It's not for his spiritual enlightenment."

Today Jagger is equally damning of Anger: "I thought he was really ridiculous," he says, "although he's talented in many ways. I thought he definitely had talents as a filmmaker, but his whole religious experience was a load of crap."

David Bowie

Also temporarily drawn into a fascination with Crowley was David Bowie, who'd made reference both to Crowley and to the Golden Dawn in "Quicksand," on his album *The Man Who Sold the World.* It has always been difficult to assess how serious Bowie is about anything because of his jackdawlike tendency to pick up on whatever happens to be sparkling most brightly. However, by his own admission the period around the filming of *The Man Who Fell to Earth* was one of decadence and self-destruction. Excessive cocaine usage had emaciated him and filled him with paranoia. He made wild comments to the press about the need for the cleansing effect of a right-wing dictatorship in the West, and he claimed that rock 'n' roll was "the Devil's Music."

Friends who visited Bowie in Los Angeles reported that he was living in a room with the curtains permanently drawn, a bowl of cocaine prominently displayed on the coffee table. Scattered around the floor were books of occultism and mysticism. On the walls he'd scrawled magic pentagrams as protection against the curses he believed had been uttered against him.

So convinced did he become that black magicians were planning to destroy him that he hired a white witch to perform an exorcism involving the burning of blue and white candles and the sprinkling of salt. Later (1983) he was to talk vaguely of "dark obsessions" characterizing the period, a time when the "Lower Elements" were allowed into his life and music.

Jimmy Page

More obviously serious and devoted was guitarist Jimmy Page. Although members of Led Zeppelin never posed in magicians' robes or introduced diabolic imagery into their songs (the lyrics were written by Robert Plant, who was more interested in Celtic mysticism), many fans and critics found their music more oppressive and connotative of evil than the Rolling Stones'. Rumors of the ritual slaughter of lambs, a privately recorded album of death chants, and a pact with the devil made by three members of the group all aided the impression.

Page was a leading collector of Crowleyiana, gathering together not only his manuscripts and first editions but also his paintings, robes, hats, canes and tarot pack. In 1970 he bought Boleskine House, the mansion on the shores of Loch Ness that Crowley had acquired in 1900 specifically to allow him to perform a magic ritual that required water, mountains and a building facing a certain direction. Crowley wrote how he summoned up so many demons in the house that they ran amok, causing one of his workmen to go mad, a housekeeper to leave because of the "eeriness" and a visiting clairvoyant to turn to prostitution.

When Page bought the house, he hired Satanist Charles Pace to paint it with murals that would restore it to its "original condition." When he stayed there with friends, he said, "it crystallizes things in a very short time." Five years later he financed an occult bookstore for his astrologer in Holland Street, Kensington, naming it the Equinox after a magazine that Crowley edited and using it to publish out-of-print works by the magician. (It closed in 1979, after the lease ran out.)

From the sparse pieces of information Page has let slip in interviews, it appears that he first encountered Crowley's work as an eleven-year-old, when he read *Magic in Theory and Practice,* Not surprisingly, however, he says he didn't understand much of what he had read until years later. Like Anger, he considers the magician "a misunderstood genius" whose message was "liberation of the person." He told one magazine, "You can't ignore evil if you study the supernatural as I do. I have many books on the subject and I've also attended a number of seances. I want to go on studying it. . . . Magic is very important if people can go through it."

Like most magicians, Crowley insisted he wasn't a black magician, but even his fellow occultists regarded him as a black sorcerer. The argument is semantic, for what he taught and practiced, although not intended to harm others, was evil by most civilized standards. Richard Cavendish, in his 1967 book *The Black Arts,* succinctly describes the driving force behind black magic as "hunger for power." Its ultimate aim, he says, was best stated by the serpent in the Garden of Eden.

> Black Magic is rooted in the darkest levels of the mind, and that is a large part of its attraction, but it is much more than a product of the love of evil or a liking for mysterious mumbo-jumbo. It is a titanic attempt to exalt the stature of man, to put man in the place which religious thought reserves for God. In spite of its crudities and squalors this gives it a certain magnificence.

Central to Crowley's philosophy was the need to find the "true will," the pure human instinct unhindered by morality. "There is no law," he wrote, "beyond do what thou wilt." (Page had "Do What Thou Wilt" inscribed in the plastic surrounding the label of *Led Zeppelin III.*) Drugs, alcohol and sex rituals were a means to this end. The mind had to be continually deranged to rid it of all inherited values. "Bind nothing!" he instructed. "Let there be no difference made among you between one thing and any other thing, for thereby cometh hurt."

The individual was therefore installed in God's position, beholden to no one, self-realized through obedience to his or her own almighty will. This is certainly the message that Page collected from Crowley's works. "What I can relate to is Crowley's system of self-liberation in which repression is the greatest work of sin," he said. "When you've discovered your true will you should just forge ahead like a steam train. If you put all your energies into it there's no doubt you'll succeed because that's your true will. It may take a little while to work out what that is, but when you discover it, it's all there."

The redemption message of the serpent is that, like God, we can be transported beyond the duality of good and evil. Yet this redemption comes not through the defeat of evil, as in Christ's death and resurrection, but by the acceptance of evil. Christ says we can be relieved of our guilt through faith. The devil says we can be relieved by giving in, by anesthetizing our consciences through repetitious sin.

Jim Morrison

The Doors' Jim Morrison, son of a rear admiral in the U.S. Navy, became convinced that he was inhabited by the spirit of a Pueblo Indian he had seen dying by the roadside when he was a boy of four. He believed that indulgence in evil could lead to spiritual purification. He saw himself as a shaman figure negotiating with dark powers on behalf of his rock 'n' roll tribe, and the songs he wrote suggest a journey through darkness toward some new purity. He sang of taking "the highway to the end of the night," of "riding the snake," of breaking through "to the other side."

In his life Morrison was appropriately excessive, downing copious amounts of drugs and alcohol, brutalizing women and behaving erratically and abusively. In 1970 he married the priestess of a witches' coven in a Wicca ceremony that involved calling up the presence of the goddess, stepping over a broomstick and mingling their blood in a chalice of consecrated wine.

Describing the Doors' music, Morrison said,

It's a search, an opening of one door after another. As yet there's no consistent philosophy or politics. Sensuousness and evil is an attractive image to us now, but think of it as a snakeskin that will be shed sometime. Right now I'm more interested in the dark side of life, the evil thing, the dark side of the moon, the night-time. But in our music it seems to me that we're seeking, striving, trying to break through to some clearer, freer realm.

It's like a purification ritual in the alchemical sense. First you have to have the period of disorder, chaos, returning to a primeval disaster region. Out of that you purify the elements and find the new seed of life, which transforms all life and all matter and the personality, until finally, hopefully, you emerge and marry all those dualisms and opposites. Then you're not talking about evil and good any more but something unified and pure.

It was fine talk, appealing to anyone who'd ever despaired of taming their wilder appetites. A reversal of Christian morality, it called restraint a sin and saw the dissolute life as a means of redemption. It promoted as truth William Blake's "Proverbs of Hell": "The road of excess leads to the palace of wisdom," and "He who desires but acts not, breeds pestilence." Yet in practice, as with Eve in the Garden of Eden, it led to moral disintegration, despair and, in Morrison's own case, premature death.

Descent into Darkness

Those who promoted this point of view illustrated by their lives that while abandonment to dark impulses promises liberation and purity, it ultimately enslaves and corrupts. Set free from conscience and external moral restraint, the human mind descends to the depths rather than ascends to the heights. As in experimentation with LSD, angels run a poor second to demons when the imagination is unchained.

Those who dabbled in evil became distinguished by their dark moods, sudden violence, sexual abuse, flaunted decadence and almost permanent intoxication of one sort or another. Led Zeppelin biographer Stephen Davis says the group regarded Los Angeles as their "Sodom and Gomorrah, an improbable sub-tropical fantasyland which offered them its most nubile daughters and every conceivable vice on a platter." Jimmy Page was known for carrying a collection of whips in his luggage and for delighting in humiliating the groupies who slept with him. "Crowley didn't have a very high opinion of women," he told one interviewer, "and I don't think he was wrong."

Heroin eventually got a grip on many of them—Keith Richards, Anita Pallenberg and Jimmy Page all became addicts who had to spend years in search of an effective cure. Graham Bond, an influential British rhythm and blues singer who genuinely thought he was Crowley's illegitimate son and who recorded albums of rituals with his band Holy Magick, was also addicted to heroin. Crowley himself finished his life as a sick, wasted heroin addict given to black rages and doubts about the value of his life's work. His last words as he passed into a coma on December 1, 1947, were "I am perplexed . . ."

As the acid culture fragmented, the forces of darkness seem to have closed in. Peddlers on Sunset Strip were no longer handing out flowers but voodoo candles and Satanic crosses. American universities were offering courses in magic and occultism. Commented Cal McCrystal in *The Sunday Times* of London in August 1970, "The witchcraft craze sweeping America is fairly recent. Last year students had been preoccupied with flowers and free love, Transcendental Meditation, Timothy Leary and Senator McCarthy. This year the fashion is witchcraft and hippie communes."

Heritage of Horror

One of the lasting legacies of this period, characterized in Britain by the emergence of Black Sabbath (who wanted to do a rock 'n' roll version of the horror movie genre) and Black Widow (who performed rituals on stage and became associated with Alex Sanders, "King of the Witches"), has been the adoption of demonic imagery by heavy metal groups. This ranged from the frivolous (Ozzy Osbourne as a werewolf) through the dangerous (AC/DC requesting to be sent on a "highway to hell") to the apparent seriousness of black metal and death metal bands such as Venom, Slayer, Cloven Hoof, Celtic Frost, Immortal, Emperor, Darkthrone, Deicide and Morbid Angel.

Much of this is not done with the seriousness of the artists from the 1960s discussed above, but simply to fulfill audience expectations. "It's just a show-biz thing," said Ozzy Osbourne, once of Black Sabbath. "It's not that we're Satanists. I wouldn't know how to conjure a rabbit out of a hat, never mind a devil."

John Tardy, vocalist with the death metal band Obituary, says that "horror metal" would be a better description of what his band does. "There is a group of people who like horror movies and horror books. That's really what we're doing. It's not meant to be any more serious than a Steven Spielberg movie."

Tommy Lee of Motley Crue *(Shout at the Devil)* says much the same: "The kids want something that's either gonna scare them or make their ears bleed or is gonna make them happy. If you cover all three angles—man, you've got it locked up! They like it loud, they like it scary and they like it crazy, because they've seen everything else before."

Even those who claim to practice the black arts are not reliable informants, because black metal thrives on adverse publicity. Cloven Hoof, for example, sent out a press release saying that the group name meant "followers at the feet of the Devil" and that the title track of their debut album was drawn from a witchcraft document. Venom (sample song titles—"Welcome to Hell," "In League with Satan," "Heaven's on Fire") claimed to sing about "the dark forces of hell." Holland's King Diamond let it be known that he had a Satanist altar at home, and he mounted his microphone on a stand made of human leg bones.

Glen Benton of Florida-based death metal band Deicide, which sings about the joys of killing Jesus in songs like "Crucifixation" and "Deicide," branded an inverted cross into his forehead, named his son Daemon ("master of the supernatural") and claimed to have been involved in animal sacrifices. "Don't call yourself death metal if you're not Satanic," said the group's bass player, Eric Hoffman. "Death metal is Satanic. We relay our music all into Satanism. We take it 100 percent."

In Norway black metal followers are believed to have been responsible for a series of arson attacks on churches, and in May 1994 Varg Vikernes of Burzum was sentenced to twenty-one years' imprisonment for church burning and murdering Oystein Aarseth of the band Mayhem. Mayhem and Burzum were leading Norwegian black metal bands, and the murder was believed to have been the outcome of a feud over supremacy. In court Vikernes said, "Through church burning and black metal music we will reawaken the Norwegians' feelings of belonging to Odin." In an earlier interview with the British magazine *Ultrakill!* Vikernes had explained that he worshiped the Viking god of war and death. "Burzum exists exclusively for Odin," he said. "Odin is the one-eyed enemy of the Christian God."

Whether as serious as Vikernes or as flippant as Ozzy Osbourne, the effect of such forays into the occult is to trivialize something that has spiritual consequences and to make it appear a mere daring exploit on the level of getting drunk or driving too fast. In one well-publicized murder case in the United States during 1984, a seventeen-year-old was tortured and then had his eyes gouged out by boys who were drunk, high on "angel dust" and convinced they were Satanists after hours of listening to heavy metal. When one of them, Richard Kasso, was led off to jail, he was wearing an AC/DC sweatshirt. Two days later he hung himself in his cell.

"Probably 95 percent of the teenagers who check out death metal are doing it for the thrill, and because it's something that's floating around in the adolescent environment," says Cynthia Kisser of Chicago's Cult Awareness Network. "But there is going to be a small percentage that is going to tap into it and could be introduced to other people who are engaged in activities that glorify the Satanist philosophy. That's where a small pool of vulnerable adolescents could get pulled into a more sophisticated, and perhaps adult-run, underground organization."

Bitter Fruit

Back in 1970, when Black Sabbath was playing its first dance gigs, cult members prowling the streets of Los Angeles and San Francisco dressed in purple cloaks called themselves Process, or the Church of the Final Judgment. They preached a coming Armageddon from which only a few would be saved, and a reconciliation between Jehovah, Lucifer and Satan through Jesus Christ. "Through love, Christ and Satan have destroyed their enmity," read their brochures. "Christ said love your enemies. Christ's enemy was Satan. Love Christ and Satan."

The cult formed a rock band, the Black Swan, that worked the clubs of Los Angeles while audiences were proselytized by other members. Anxious to cut an album, they contacted Mama Cass and John Phillips of the Mamas and the Papas, but no recording ever materialized. Phillips later admitted, "There's a lot of black magic going on. As God has been losing his percentage, the devil has been picking up. Things have become very demonic."

One of the cult's contacts was a failed musician called Charles Manson, who had already absorbed what he could of Hinduism, Buddhism, Scientology and LSD and was working with Beach Boy Brian Wilson on a demonstration record. Manson, who was to use the ego-destroying techniques of Eastern religion and hallucinogenic drugs to gain control over followers whom he would then send out to murder, took mindless spirituality to its frighteningly logical conclusion. "If God is One," he reasoned, "what is bad?"

Much earlier, Robert Johnson, who had supposedly received his gift from the devil, recorded twenty-nine songs and was then murdered under mysterious circumstances in 1938. The word went out that the "black arts" did it, and a look at his songs suggested that he knew it was inevitable. Somewhere around the corner was that "hellhound," coming to escort him away. Bluesologist Samuel Charters noted that six of Johnson's recorded songs make reference to the devil or voodoo. "It seemed to force its presence on some of his greatest music," he concluded.

The same was true of the rock 'n' roll people who danced too closely with the devil: there was a price to pay. Blessed with brilliance and earthly glory for a brief moment, they were then discarded to become empty shells bereft of creativity. Brian Jones, unable to get the music out of his head and into his fingers, finally ended up dead in his own swimming pool. Jim Morrison went to Paris to try and halt his own deterioration, but instead he died in his bathtub. Graham Bond was crushed by the wheels of a London subway train. Led Zeppelin was brought to a halt by the sudden death of John Bonham; Jimmy Page has remained a virtual recluse ever since.

There would seem to be an abundance of evidence that those who mess with the devil get messed by the devil. In the words of the prophet Isaiah, "Woe to those who call evil good and good evil, who put darkness for light and light for darkness" (Isaiah 5:20 NIV).

The Dream Is Over

6

The dream is over. . . . We've got to get down to so-called reality.
John Lennon

I do feel sad that the spiritual thing does not seem to have gone anywhere.
Mick Jagger

I believe the only thing left in life is to fall in love totally or become spiritual.
Cat Stevens

I n 1969 everyone involved in what was becoming known as "rock culture" believed it looked as though redemption was indeed drawing nigh. The mutant beings that Timothy Leary promised would result from widespread LSD consumption had arrived. The Golden Age prophesied by the gurus was about to dawn. The lost secrets of earlier ages were being uncovered. The Garden of Eden was about to be regained.

There was a call to return to values, many of which could have been endorsed by the early Christian church. People were not to be judged by their outward appearance but by the content of their hearts. Greed, gossip, violence, prejudice and hypocrisy were to be exposed as hideous sins. Natural beauty was to be celebrated. Brotherhood and sisterhood were to be enjoyed. Communal living was to be encouraged. Above all, there was to be love.

For a while young people the world over appeared united in their appreciation of these simple values and in their avowed rejection of materialism. The most significant conduit for these ideas was rock 'n' roll. Without rock 'n' roll the news about LSD would have taken a long time to travel from New York and San Francisco to Tokyo, Peking, Moscow, London and Paris. How many would have heard of an Indian guru or an English magician without an introduction by the Beatles or the Rolling Stones?

It wasn't the music alone that spread the word, but the attendant culture of newspapers, magazines, books, events, happenings, festivals and posters. Interviews with musicians regarded as spokesmen were awaited with anticipation. What will Lennon have to say about the revolution? What is Jagger's stand on Marxism? Does Dylan think psychedelics are necessary to spiritual growth?

The Woodstock Spirit

The event that now stands as a consummation of all this religious yearning was the Woodstock Music and Art Fair, mounted in upstate New York during August 1969. Much of the festival was an orgy of self-congratulation, with newspaper and radio reports of the chaos caused by the sudden influx of people being gleefully quoted from the stage. The owner of the land on which the festival was held announced, "If these are the kids who are going to inherit the world, I don't fear for it." The organizers modestly promoted the "Aquarian Exposition" as "Three Days of Peace and Music."

Over that three-day period half a million young people gathered on rough farmland in the Catskill Mountains to listen to some of the era's best rock 'n' roll acts—including Jimi Hendrix, the Who, the Band, the Grateful Dead, Santana and Joe Cocker. Social order was maintained without the assistance of outside security forces or riot police. The fences broke down early on, so that it became a free festival. The sanitation gave out, there was hardly enough food, it rained—but there was no stampede, no violence and no abuse.

There were hundreds of "freak outs" from badly produced LSD, there was one birth and one death (from a heroin overdose), but none of the problems expected from such massive crowds and inadequate facilities. The young people's remarkable behavior inspired amazement and delight. "We're all feeding from each other," said one overwhelmed stage announcer. "We must be in heaven, man!"

John Sebastian, whose Lovin' Spoonful had been among the pioneer folk-rock bands, had arrived not expecting to play. Slightly stoned and wearing a tie-dyed jean jacket, he was the embodiment of the wide-eyed, groovy, Lennonesque hippie who believed that the kingdom had come but who had been rendered partially inarticulate by the glory of it all. When he was finally coaxed on stage, he gazed out over the solid mass of humanity and marveled, "Far out! Far around! Far down! Far up! You're truly amazing. You're a whole city. And it's so groovy to come here and see all you people living in tents. A flop-house is all you need if you've got love, I tell you."

The myth of Woodstock was the same myth that Scott McKenzie's "San Francisco" had promoted two years before: "There's a whole generation / With a new explanation." It was suggested that this was a generation "come of age," able to coexist without the frictions of greed and enmity and free of the interfering hand of the law. These were people who needed only to obey the dictates of their own pure hearts.

The subsequent Warner Brothers film, which was to become most people's experience of Woodstock, was edited in such a way that it appeared to endorse the idea of a return to primal innocence. Fans wallowed in mud like newly discovered tribespeople, as if to show that cleanliness was no longer next to godliness. Newly acquainted couples wandered off naked into the long grass to copulate without shame. Good vibrations and happy smiles abounded. Calling for a return to the Garden of Eden, Joni Mitchell wrote "Woodstock," a song that suggested the festival was evidence of an evolutionary surge forward.

But Woodstock lasted for only a weekend. For many attenders it was nothing more than a chance to see acts like Jefferson Airplane, Janis Joplin and Crosby, Stills & Nash for free. It was naive to speculate on great changes in human nature simply because a well-behaved audience had imbibed free rock 'n' roll. Change the circumstances, change the crowd, change the setting, and you could equally well have ended up with a disaster.

The "peace and music" line was upheld because people desperately wanted to believe a change had come. In the decade of Vietnam, assassinations and urban riots, they wanted to prove themselves capable of a new way of living. Drugs, meditation and the good thoughts inspired by music made them feel as though they had all the love that was needed to bring the world back from the brink. Woodstock was a microcosm of the coming order.

End of the Dream

Yet Woodstock fever was short-lived. Within four months came the first of several blows to the notion that a human remedy for sin had been discovered. On a California racetrack, the Rolling Stones were to give a free concert. To illustrate the point that the new generation didn't need the law, it was suggested that instead of security guards, Hell's Angels, the original "noble savages" of postwar American subculture, would serve. It was a symbolic gesture, using society's outlaws to uphold law. These guards wouldn't be paid in cash, but in beer.

But everything that had gone right at Woodstock went wrong at Altamont. Before the day arrived, local astrologers were warning of an ominous conjunction of the planets. On the day itself, bad LSD was producing surges of violence through the crowd. When the Rolling Stones began to play "Sympathy for the Devil," some Hell's Angels knifed a black teenager to death in view of the stage. Mick Jagger turned to his band, saying, "Something very funny happens when we start that number."

In the ensuing commotion Jagger pathetically tried to restore order.

His whole message had been based on individual morality—"I'm free to do what I want any old time" ("I'm Free")—and now he was having to play headmaster. "I mean, like people, who's fighting and what for? Hey, people! I mean, who's fighting and what for? Why are we fighting? Why are we fighting? We don't want to fight. Come on. Who wants to fight? I mean, like every other scene has been cool . . ." Confronted with the unacceptable face of evil, His Satanic Majesty was powerless, appealing fruitlessly to reason in the heat of violence, calling not for righteousness but for coolness. It was a terrifying evening, and a sobering vision for those who saw *Gimme Shelter,* the documentary record of the event. On Jagger's next tour of the United States, observers later noted, he wore a large crucifix around his neck.

Although only another rock festival, Altamont is now regarded as the beginning of the end of the utopian dreams of the 1960s. The idea was dawning that maybe the new generation was no different from the old generation; it just had longer hair, a more varied sexual life and a different range of preferred drugs. "There's nothing in the streets / Looks any different to me," wrote Pete Townshend on the Who single "Won't Get Fooled Again"; "Meet the new boss / Same as the old boss." "Nothing happened except that we all dressed up," commented John Lennon. "The same bastards are in control, the same people are running everything, it's exactly the same. They hyped the kids and the generation."

Other events crowded in to confirm the idea. The deaths, within two years, of Brian Jones, Janis Joplin, Jim Morrison and Jimi Hendrix intensified the general mood of depression, not just because these musicians had been removed as figureheads but also because in each case an uninhibited lifestyle had been responsible for the death.

The breakup of the Beatles amid considerable acrimony not only removed the one group that appeared to unify rock culture but also raised a poignant question: if even the legendary composers of "All You Need Is Love" can't see eye to eye, can *anyone* get along?

The Manson Logic

Equally significant were the series of murders carried out in Los Angeles during 1969 by the Charles Manson "family." Manson had
picked up on the dream of a new dispensation, was a regular user of
LSD, had dabbled in religion, wrote songs, played guitar, lived in a
commune and idolized the Beatles. Yet Manson had strange dreams.
He saw John, Paul, George and Ringo as the four horsemen of the
Apocalypse and took his LSD vision of everything as God to terrifying
logical conclusions.

Manson argued that as we are all God, it's no crime for one part
of God to stick a blade into another part of God. The only moral
consideration is whether you feel love as you do it. Love is all you
need. He reasoned, "If God is one, what can be evil?" Having instructed his followers to destroy their egos, usually with drugs, he then had
them murder for him as they awaited the final holocaust out of which
only he and his chosen few would emerge to start the world anew.

Where most people paddled, Manson dived in deep. Where most
traveled light, he accumulated baggage, until his head was filled with
all the fragmented, half-digested philosophies of hippiedom. What was
particularly chilling about Manson, though, was the logic. Having
dispensed with the idea of an objective God "out there," he jettisoned
the morals associated with such a God. He raised the specter of a
world of annihilated egos where the strongest ruled and nothing really
mattered anyway, because all was part of the anonymous One.

"Charles Manson believed in the ancient Hindu assertion that, from
the absolute point of view, good and evil, order and disorder, are
reconciled in the One," noted R. C. Zaehner, an Oxford professor of
Eastern religion. "Believing, he acted on his beliefs, and many a 'rich
pig' was to meet a gruesome and untimely end because Charlie, so far
from being mad, seems to have had a lucidly logical mind. He took
the ambiguities and ambivalences of Indian religion as transmitted to
him seriously, but drew conclusions that were the exact opposite of
conclusions conventionally drawn."

Diminished Expectations

Thus the 1960s closed with an air of apprehension. No one wanted to let go of all the small victories of the decade, but then it was hard to believe in an imminent change in the human condition. Writer David Downing captured the mood in an essay on Crosby, Stills, Nash & Young when he commented that "no new premises have been laid down, no other path has been publicly accepted."

He continued, "The rejection of one set of social and personal values did not in itself create a new set. That is a long process. In the meantime you . . . create a little harmony for the world of jagged edges little changed by your understanding of it. Crosby, Stills, Nash & Young do that, and only that. No amount of talent can pull a rabbit out of no hat."

The spokesmen of rock 'n' roll beat a retreat into rural domesticity, clutching to the most traditional forms of security. On his first post-Beatles album, John Lennon announced, "The dream is over," and in "God" he systematically denied the "myths" of religion, politics and rock 'n' roll. Having traveled the long and winding road of the 1960s, he could trust only "Yoko and me / That's reality."

In a celebrated *Rolling Stone* interview in 1970 Lennon set the tone for the new decade. "I no longer believe in myth, and the Beatles is another myth," he said. "I don't believe in it; the dream is over. And I'm not just talking about the Beatles. I'm talking about the generation thing. The dream is over. It's over and we've got to get down to so-called reality."

Getting down to "reality" characterized the new mood of resignation. Paul McCartney retreated to his Scottish farm and forsook the "poetry" that had become associated with Beatles songs.

Bob Dylan, now looking more like a Jewish businessman than a rock 'n' roll star, also went into the country and started writing songs that had a considerably narrower focus than anything he'd done before. The celebrated prophet-poet was now content to sing about holding each other tight "the whole night through" and to rhyme "night" with "shining bright." On the albums *Nashville Skyline* (1969) and *New Morning* (1970) he would set up problems only to have them neatly resolved in the arms of his baby.

The Eagles and Jackson Browne

New songwriters coming of age in the 1970s had arrived with hopes of being part of a movement, only to find that the concerns had changed. Instead of looking outward or upward, they folded in on themselves, examining their own anxieties in the face of cultural inertia.

This mood of spiritual desolation was perhaps best captured by the Eagles and Jackson Browne, musicians reared on sixties optimism who didn't get into the recording studio until the party was all over. The renewed search for meaning in a world stripped of illusion was to become their subject matter.

As Don Henley of the Eagles observed,

The first half of the seventies has been a big escape. We'd come to the end of the sixties when there were people in the streets and everybody took acid and thought it was going to change the world. People were in shock that it really didn't change anything. I'm not saying people should let go of all their dreams and myths, but the seventies seem to have a big value gap.

Hotel California is about trying to look at things in a different way, to go from here and try to develop a new set of values and a new thrill that is more meaningful and more valid than one just built on sand. Some of the first thrills had no base, no real root in anything.

The songs of the Eagles, with their sweet vocals and country roll, dealt rather self-pityingly with the pilgrimage of laid-back Californians as they gorged themselves on the good things of life while hoping for the peace of mind discovered by mystics and ascetics. Even as they protested the wear and tear they suffered in the fast lane, they seemed to like telling you about the excesses they'd been through to discover the fruitlessness of it all.

Just as the writer of Ecclesiastes had complained, "Vanity of vanities, all is vanity" (KJV), and then proceeded to chase the fleeting pleasures of life to try and prove the assumption wrong, so the Eagles took to the road, drove fast cars, chased women, accepted adulation and downed tequila before writing such remorseful songs as "Take It to the Limit" and "After the Thrill Is Gone."

They really warmed to the theme of hollow hedonism on the concept album *Desperado* (1973). The desperado of the song is a restless man who tries to slake his thirst with earthly pleasures. His problem is that the more he gets, the thirstier he becomes. Whatever fine things are laid before him, he's always yearning for what he doesn't have.

Years later I asked founding member Bernie Leadon (by now a Christian) what he felt when he looked back on these songs.

I still think they were all very perceptive of the human condition. But ultimately they offered no answer. There have been a lot of fine blessings laid on our tables, but in the end we do want the things we can't get. Are we ever going to be satisfied? The ultimate answer must be no.

In "Hotel California" they ended up saying we're stuck, we can't get out. It's like we've got all the fast cars and credit cards, but we're trapped. We're victims of our own appetites. We're on a treadmill where we just try to satisfy our physical desires or our emotional needs and so we need more sex, more money and more food. Then we need more exciting sex and better-tasting food. I've heard people say, "Give me more of everything and then I'll be satisfied." But ultimately you're not.

Jackson Browne was never as self-pitying, but the sense of searching for a lost dream permeates much of his work. Tucked away in his songs are references to the quest for truth and the need to be lifted to a higher level of existence.

It was on *The Pretender* that the subject really came into focus for him. Recognizing that a life devoid of purpose eventually immobilizes, Browne made the Pretender a sixties idealist going through a crisis of faith, needing something to believe in yet aware that his earlier dreams have receded. He decides to go for gold, to leap back into the mainstream of life, the epitome of everything he once railed against. Having started out as a bold young optimist, he finally surrenders.

Exotic Conversions

Not everyone returned to life as normal. There were those who had lost their bearings after the formless experience of drugs and yoga and who looked for more authoritarian forms of religion where your thoughts were sorted out for you ahead of time. Tired of highs, unsure of what was right and wrong, they wanted to subscribe to strict rules and put themselves under a daily discipline.

On an American tour with Fleetwood Mac in 1971, guitarist Jeremy Spencer went missing overnight. Four days later he turned up as a member of the Children of God, a heretical "Christian" cult that later used prostitutes to lure male converts and brainwashing techniques to retain those it already held. When the group's manager finally tracked him down, he found that Spencer had cut his hair, didn't want to rejoin Fleetwood Mac and was from then on to be known as Jonathan.

"He'd been brainwashed, and it nearly killed me to see him," said a roadie who had also gone along to the Children of God commune. "He just mumbled 'Jesus loves you.' He was with about five hundred of these people and they're just like vegetables." Spencer was later allowed by the cult to record albums under his own name, with lyrics that followed the party line.

Only the year before, founding member Peter Green had suddenly quit Fleetwood Mac after a London concert, apparently unable to reconcile his growing social concerns with his status and lifestyle as a superstar. There has always been speculation about the role of LSD in this sudden "conversion," but Green took to giving his royalties away to charity and studying Christianity and Judaism. He has never returned to the limelight.

The most remarkable conversion came when Cat Stevens, a Catholic by birth, became a Muslim, abandoned his recording career, sold his gold discs and took up life as a religious educator under the name Yusef Islam. He had been a typical product of his spiritually hungry generation, taking LSD, checking into Buddhism and meditation, playing around with numerology and astrology. Then, in 1975, as one of the superstars of the business, he was to be found saying, "I believe the only thing left in life is to fall in love totally or become spiritual," and "The only person I believe in now is God."

Four years later he was handed a copy of the Qur'an, and he converted shortly afterward. "Up until that point," he says, "I felt that all religions had some facet of the truth, but not the complete and comprehensive truth. When I read the Qur'an I realized that religion was not something you could concoct. It is either true religion, which means that it is God's religion, or it is not God's religion. Islam means 'surrender,' and it's God's religion."

Stevens began to adopt the white robes of Middle Eastern Muslims, prayed faithfully five times a day and set up the Islamic Circle, an educational trust based in an old warehouse in north London. He stopped listening to rock 'n' roll, auctioned off his guitars because there was "some doubt about the lawfulness of playing stringed instruments," and regarded his past life as a rock star with detachment.

I used to believe in astrology. I used to believe in I Ching. I used to believe in everything. But it deluded me into thinking I was getting somewhere. When you finally find the right way of living, you can't make it up yourself. If you want the freedom to go on making mistakes, it's up to you. If you find something that's guaranteed, that's going to take you where you want to go, you no longer have to exhaust yourself looking. Your final destination on this earth is the grave. So what's the point?

Into
the
Mystic

7

I think music is spiritual. Singing, playing an instrument is spiritual.
It's coming from a spiritual world.
Van Morrison

Music has always been religious. Music is a passion and a vehicle
for the understanding of why we are here. It's a remembering
of the past and of ritual.
Jon Anderson, Yes

I always like to take people on trips. That's why music is magic.
Jimi Hendrix

S piritual issues were at the top of the agenda in sixties rock 'n'
roll. The major artists of the decade—the Beatles, the Rolling
Stones, Bob Dylan, the Beach Boys, the Who, Marvin Gaye, the Doors,
the Grateful Dead, Jimi Hendrix—had all publicly wrestled with the
religious questions of where we came from, why we are here and where
we are going. Through the Beatles, ancient religious texts were to spill
through modern hi-fi systems. Through the Who, the teachings of a
Hindu mystic became the stuff of rock opera. Through Dylan, theological concepts such as collective guilt ("Who Killed Davy Moore?") and
the just war ("With God on Our Side") were debated in song.

These artists saw their work in religious terms. They may have been using all the machinery of show business, but there was a dimension believed to have a continuity with the earliest religious rituals. Brian Jones felt an affinity with the trance musicians of the Moroccan Rif mountains. Jim Morrison saw himself as an electric update of the Siberian shaman and the Doors' music as performing a purification ceremony.

The seventies represented a change: these issues were no longer of such importance. For the new stars like Elton John and Rod Stewart, the emphasis was on glamour and good times. In Britain the battle for the Beatles' newly vacated top spot was fought out between groups like Slade, the Bay City Rollers, David Cassidy and the Osmonds. It was a period of light relief after a very intense decade. The less hardy of the Woodstock generation had probably already stopped buying albums in favor of paying off mortgages, and their younger brothers and sisters wanted something new.

The New Consciousness
Yet the question did live on in some minds. The death of the sixties dream may have sent some into despair and others into unbridled hedonism, but there were still idealists who saw the new decade as a time for reassessment. American Jerry Rubin, a well-known student activist in the 1960s and a member of the notorious Chicago Seven, correctly concluded in the early 1970s that a new way of living hadn't emerged because even those with the sharpest vision of what it should be like were guilty of the sins they condemned in others.

The way forward, he conjectured, was to concentrate on personal growth so that in the eighties the spiritual and the political could come together in a new maturity. "Revolution is only as high as the people that make it," he said. "I had expected the revolution apocalyptically, but have since discovered that revolution is an evolutionary process. . . . People out of touch with bodies-and souls cannot make positive change."

Rubin was an early convert to what is now known as the New Consciousness or New Age movement. Between 1971 and 1975 he enrolled in a host of courses in human potential, including Gestalt therapy, est, biomechanics, Tai Chi, hypnotism, meditation, Silva Mind Control and yoga. "As the consciousness movement expands, its natural evolution will be towards changing society," he said. "We have the opportunity to transform the planet."

The New Consciousness movement had obvious appeal to those who had walked the popularly prescribed spiritual pathway through the sixties. It accepted the notion of an indefinable power behind the universe and taught that through the correct technique this power could be tapped. The New Consciousness was the consciousness that could harness the power. The New Age was the world restored to harmony by a spreading knowledge of the hidden forces that control events. To anyone who had dabbled in magic, meditated or tripped on LSD, this made sense.

Jon Anderson, singer and songwriter with Yes, was one such musician. He had taken LSD in imitation of his hero Paul McCartney ("it introduced me to the other world"), had attempted "astral travel" (an out-of-body experience) and later embarked on the teachings of Paramahansa Yogananda. His gleanings from Hinduism were mixed with beliefs about UFOs as bearers of arcane knowledge and the coming New Age in lyrics for sprawling concept albums with pompous music and titles like *Tales from Topographic Oceans* and *Going for the One.*

Derided often in the music press for cosmic pretentiousness, Anderson remained unmoved in his conviction about the New Age. "Everybody is a part of it," he insisted. "When the Beatles sang 'All You Need Is Love,' a seed was planted in everybody who heard and enjoyed it. This little seed is growing every day. I know it's going to happen. It's the next stage of our consciousness. . . . Things will change and things will be for the better. It takes just a little bit of faith."

The New Age movement saw itself as a return to ancient times when, it was fondly imagined, human beings lived in harmony with their environment and one another. They were able to live this way because they recognized and respectfully used the powers around them. Over the centuries the secrets had been lost, leaving only standing stones, pyramids, hieroglyphics and myths as evidence of the Golden Age.

The New Consciousness was to push for a rediscovery of ancient arts. It concerned itself with the "ley-line" system, channels of energy believed to run across the world, on whose junctions our ancestors built their most sacred buildings in order to trap the power. It tried to plumb the mysteries of old religious monuments. "We appear today to have lost touch with some source of inspiration known in former times," wrote John Michell in his classic study of geomancy, *A View over Atlantis.*

Jimi Hendrix and New Consciousness Music

More important for musicians was the theory that sound contains healing qualities. In ancient times, it was said, people knew certain musical formulas that could bring ecstasy, physical healing and universal harmony. Musicians in these times didn't need to sing about solutions—they could create them. They could be doctors, surgeons, priests, therapists and politicians, all through their instruments.

The idea that music could bring about states of altered consciousness needed no extra evidence for rock 'n' roll musicians. They were all familiar with the trancelike states that some of their most ardent fans could get themselves into. Yet could this effect be extended to introduce states of peace, moments of insight or flashes of transcendence? Could rock 'n' roll bring healing and harmony if the right notes were found?

Before his death Jimi Hendrix had become an avid student of occult literature, taking guidance from astrologers and heavily underlining copies of books with titles such as *Secret Places of the Lion, Spacemen in the Ancient East* and *Secrets of the Andes.* In combination with the drugs he was using, this information led him to bizarre conclusions. He told friends he'd been born in outer space and had been sent to earth on a divine mission. His task, he said, was to lead humanity back to a harmonious relationship with the cosmic powers. He also believed he was visited by spirit guides and could travel on the astral plane.

Hendrix spent his brief post-Woodstock period trying to develop a music that would help him achieve this. He imagined a music that would have an impact on the mind similar to that of psychedelic drugs; it would be a sound that would actually alter consciousness and "open people's eyes to cosmic powers." He called it "raw spiritual music" or "electric church music." He openly wondered about the possibility of transmitting guitar sounds over great distances to affect everyone in their path, and he studied theories of sound-color healing.

Hendrix's experimentation peaked at his famous Rainbow Bridge concert, mounted in an open-air amphitheater on the Hawaiian island of Maui. Seeing the event as redemptive, he utilized occult knowledge to bring his audience back into union with the unnamed powers. The seating was arranged according to the astrological signs of ticket holders. Hendrix himself wore the shirt of an Indian medicine man, meditated beforehand in a sacred Hopi tent and consulted a sooth-sayer.

Before Hendrix took to the stage, an announcement was made that the purpose of the concert was to build a bridge between the hearts of those listening and "the spiritual centers of the planetary being." All the audience had to do was listen and "let Jimi let us across that bridge." By way of preparation, everyone was encouraged to chant the sacred *om* sound. After the concert, residents of the island called the local radio station to report noises emitting from rocks and sightings of unidentified flying objects.

The Grateful Dead

The Grateful Dead were similarly intrigued with the possibility of putting their music at the service of unknown powers. "I can envisage a new world in which society has a way for there to be music whose function it is to get you high," said Jerry Garcia in 1972. "That's the sort of thing we're hammering at. . . . To get really high is to forget yourself and to forget yourself is to see everything else. To see everything else is to be an understanding molecule in evolution, a conscious tool of the universe."

Beginning the previous year, the group had entered what they would later refer to as their "gnostic period," devouring all the information they could find on ancient mysteries. They raided occult bookstores in London and Paris and brought back folio editions to California. They even managed to get a reader's ticket to London's Warburg Institute, where the most complete collection of magical books in the English language is housed along with many of Aleister Crowley's manuscripts.

The Grateful Dead had grown particularly interested in the idea of power and its ultimate source. Playing to large audiences, especially while on LSD, they experienced what they thought were waves of spiritual power that they could use and feed back through the music. Drummer Mickey Hart would even personalize this power by speaking of it as "the wolf," which would appear at a certain point during the excitement of a performance. "That's what it feels like to me," he said. "I look around, I see the music getting to larger proportions than was intended, or even expected."

Their reading introduced them to the idea that certain points of the globe contain concentrations of this universal energy. They began to contemplate what might happen if they were to stage Grateful Dead concerts close to these recognized power centers. Would they gain access to something no rock 'n' roll band had yet experienced if they were to perform in these energy traps?

In 1978 the Grateful Dead put their theory to the test. In one of the most ambitious stagings for a modern rock 'n' roll band, they played concerts at the pyramids of Giza. While no one knows exactly how or why these monuments were built in Egypt, it seems certain that they had great religious significance and that the proportions correspond to astrological plans.

Guitarist Phil Lesh said,

I was one of the first people in the group who was on the trip of playing at places of power; power, that is, that has been preserved from the ancient world. The pyramids are the obvious number one choice, because no matter what anyone thinks they might be, there is definitely some kind of mojo about the pyramids. The power there is the same kind of power we get from an audience, only there's more of it, because it's older and because of what was built into it.

Yet the Grateful Dead's pyramid concerts failed to produce the hoped-for alchemy. "At least it was interesting to do it," commented Jerry Garcia afterward. "The fact that the Pyramid didn't open up and flying saucers pour out didn't make it less of an experience." Added Bob Weir, "We tried to use the King's Chamber as an echo chamber but, for one reason or another, it didn't work. So, I'm not entirely sure that what we do bears any direct relevance to what is happening at those places."

Pyramidmania

To seekers of New Consciousness, the pyramids represented one of the keys to lost knowledge. John Michell's opinion is representative when he says of the Great Pyramid, "It was constructed for a magical and sacred purpose, as a vehicle for transcending the material state, for travel in space, through time and into further dimensions."

Some came to believe, however, that not only could the pyramids of Giza act as energy conduits, but the geometric proportions themselves held the secret. Lyall Watson, in his 1973 book *Supernature,* claimed that a blunt razor blade placed beneath a cardboard replica of a pyramid would regain its sharpness. Likewise, the body of an animal would resist decay.

Musicians affected by New Age thinking were quick to grasp the implications. Hawkwind's Nik Turner had a stage set constructed that closely followed the proportions of the Great Pyramid ("I play healing music and I think the pyramid helps to harmonize what I'm doing"), and in 1976 he recorded flute music in the King's Chamber for use on an album *(Xitintoday),* which was a setting of the Egyptian Book of the Dead.

The original stage for the Glastonbury Festival (Glastonbury is recognized as one of Britain's mystical power centers) was covered by a pyramid one-tenth the size of Cheops. Todd Rundgren, who after an intense period with LSD found himself "seeing things differently" and writing Egyptian fantasies, toured in the 1970s with a pyramid, making a spectacular dive from the apex during his performance.

Even soul-funk outfit Earth, Wind and Fire incorporated Egyptology under the guidance of Maurice White, a onetime Southern Baptist who had dipped into Buddhism and concluded that all religions are one. "The group is very heavily into Egyptology," he said in 1977, going on to explain that he believed the group was being used by the Creator. "We felt that there were many secrets from that era that had never been totally worked out. Our total concept is to create an illusory effect in our public's mind. We're trying to reacquaint them with the Egyptian's civilization so that they can search and find out new things about themselves."

Van Morrison

Van Morrison had always been enthusiastically accepted by the hippies (1968's *Astral Weeks,* universally recognized as one of the greatest albums of the rock 'n' roll years, was essential baggage on the hippie trail), although he himself consistently avoided hallucinogenic drugs ("I'd always had experiences without drugs. Anything like that would impair it"), and was far too much of a maverick to adopt any trendy lifestyle. What drew hippies to his work and made them sense they'd discovered a kindred spirit was Morrison's acceptance of the mystical experience and his songs' underlying hope for a new beginning.

From *Astral Weeks* on, Morrison's work has been marked by the evolving theme of personal transformation through an experience that he has variously described in his work as a "sense of wonder," a "beautiful vision," "mystical ecstasy" and "my rapture." His songs, while often set in the visible world, always contain a strong sense of an equally real world beyond. He may start off walking down Cypress Avenue like any other Belfast citizen, but he's soon "caught up" or in a "trance." Watching the girls walk by "in their summer fashions," he suddenly finds "the angel of imagination / Opened up my gaze." His voice, too, glides beautifully from the whisky-edge sound of blues to heavenly gospel.

The song "Astral Weeks" was the ball of wool he's been unraveling ever since. It's an almost perfect song of redemption, moving from the dreamlike landscape of Leadbelly, steel rims, back roads and red shoes to the yearning to be set free from a world in which he feels an alien— "nothin' but a stranger in this world." His real home is "on high . . . in another land so far away." He longs to be "way up in the heaven / In another time / In another place."

The longing in Morrison's work over the years has been to tear down the veil that separates this world from the deeper, unseen mystery. As a child he had unprovoked mystical experiences, sudden senses of wonder, which he later wrote about in songs such as "She Gives Me Religion," "Cypress Avenue" and "Madame George." At the time he had no one to confide in and no point of reference by which to understand these experiences. Later he came across the poetry of William Blake and John Donne, writers who he realized had had similar awakenings.

"I can never remember talking about it with anyone when I was a child," he says. "It was something I kept to myself because I didn't feel there was even the possibility of talking to anyone about this. I also didn't really feel the need."

A classic outsider who genuinely hates the dross of show business and the shallowness of contemporary popular culture, Morrison seems to need to know why he feels so out of place in this world and what it is that beckons him from the other side. His quest has led him to study Buddhism, Christianity and Hinduism and to enroll in Scientology courses. "All I was interested in," he says, "was somewhere to put my experiences. To find out what they were."

Morrison feels he is guided to do his work. "It's like I'm receiving some sort of inner direction," he explains. "There's something inside of me that directs me to do this, and I don't know why myself. It directs me to do my work and my study, to study religion and to study various aspects of this in relation to experiences."

Out of this investigation came a parallel search for a music that might facilitate this sense of rapture. In 1982 Morrison was saying that now it was much more important to

> explore real things, like on the level of healing. Music as a healing force. . . . I've just done some research and there's things I've been finding out, ancient teachings about different keys and things, and what they do. Apparently in the old days if someone was sick they'd get a harp and play a C chord to heal the affliction, or whatever. And these teachings are still floating around in various religious sects. They've been lost, but you can still dig them out.

Five years later Morrison copresented a weekend conference at Loughborough University under the title "The Secret Heart of Music: An Exploration into the Power of Music to Change Consciousness." The biographical note in the prospectus, presumably written with his approval, revealed what he now saw as his musical goals. It read, in part,

> His own work is now increasingly intended as a means for inducing contemplation and for healing and uplifting the soul. On albums like *Beautiful Vision, Inarticulate Speech of the Heart* and *No Guru, No Method, No Teacher,* he has acknowledged the influence of people such as William Blake, Alice Bailey and Krishnamurti. His struggle to reconcile the mythic, almost otherworldly vision of the Celts and his own search for spiritual satisfaction with the

apparent hedonism of blues and soul music has produced many inspired and visionary performances.

Encouraged by books such as David Tame's *The Secret Power of Music* and Cyril Scott's *Music: Its Secret Influence Throughout the Ages,* Morrison continues to research the possibility of a music that will bring about higher states of awareness. Asked what effect he wants his music to have, he says, "Ideally, to induce states of meditation and ecstasy as well as to make people think." He says he himself had such experiences as a child of three while listening to his father's records of Mahalia Jackson.

To categorize Morrison as New Age would be to belittle his talent. He is clearly an artist endowed with a great spiritual sensitivity, a fact that both excites and troubles him. There's privilege involved in being able to discern a world beyond the material, but it implies a responsibility in determining what one should be doing in relation to that higher world. "If you say that we all have a basic purpose for being here then that's why I'm here," he says. "I've tried running away from it. I've tried ignoring it. I've tried suppressing it. I've tried everything there is to get away from this because at times it seems it's a hell of a big responsibility."

Morrison's *Avalon Sunset,* released in 1989, contained what appeared to be specific Christian indications. The first single from the album, "Whenever God Shines His Light," was recorded with Cliff Richard, the best-known Christian convert in British pop, and featured lines such as "He heals the sick and heals the lame / Says you can do it too in Jesus' name." Another track, "When Will I Ever Learn to Live in God," revealed Morrison in a rare penitent state of mind. He even included two traditional hymns, "Just a Closer Walk with Thee" and "Be Thou My Vision," on his 1991 double album *Hymns to the Silence.* But for Morrison this was a reflection on the religious tapestry of his childhood rather than an announcement of a recent conversion. "I'm into it all, orthodox or otherwise," he told *New Musical Express* when pressed for a statement of his beliefs. "I don't accept or reject any of it. . . . I'm just groping in the dark for a bit more light."

When asked for this book how he would now describe himself, he said that he felt "Christian mystic" was the best label. As he had earlier admitted to being unable to accept that Jesus Christ was God, he was asked why he regarded his mysticism as specifically Christian. "Because I'm not a Buddhist or a Hindu," he answered. "I was born in a Christian environment in a Christian country, and I was born after the Christ event. So that makes me a Christian."

Morrison's preoccupations remain focused on the universal power that reveals itself in nature and through what writer Colin Wilson calls "peak experiences." He recognizes now that as far back as the late 1960s he was attempting a music that could perhaps stimulate such peaks, what he calls "meditation music," but was frustrated because it had to be marketed as pop.

"At that point they didn't know what to do with it," Morrison says. "It didn't fit in with Woodstock or rock 'n' roll. It didn't fit in with anything. I just pulled back because there was an avenue which was closed. Since then there has been the New Age thing which has created an avenue where people know, well, this isn't rock 'n' roll."

"A New Kind of Man" ("You're part of the plan / For a new kind of man to come through") appeared to indicate that Morrison too had taken out a subscription to the New Age movement. In fact, he's not certain of a coming new dispensation, and the song was titled after a book on William Blake.

It stressed the point that Blake was very New Age and that maybe this could be developed now. I think it's a possibility, but I think it would be very difficult because at the present time you have future shock and it's very difficult to have that and your New Age at the same time.

I read New Age magazines, but you have to analyze this sort of stuff because it could end up the same as the rock 'n' roll business. . . . You could have your New Age superstars who have their *Sex and Drugs and New Age!* You have to ask whether it's safe. You have to probe it.

New Age Music

New Age albums, mainly instrumental, are marketed through esoteric bookshops and health food stores as well as through traditional record outlets. Although much of it may be easy listening for yuppies or for anyone else grown tired of the loud thump of rock 'n' roll, it began as music designed to produce states of meditation and involved musicians acquainted with the power of trance music.

A glance through any catalog of New Age music confirms the point made by Carl A. Raschke, a professor of religious studies at the University of Denver: "the New Age movement is essentially the maturing of the hippie movements of the sixties." The imagery is almost exclusively occult or Hindu, and advertising copy promises that, for example, *The Trance Tapes* by Ojas can act "as a catalyst for altering states of consciousness" and David Naegele's *Journeys out of the Body* is "ideal for promoting enhanced awareness."

One of the stars of the genre, a flautist who goes under the name Larkin, has typically arrived as a New Ager after experiencing LSD and becoming a student of Hatha Yoga and Korean Buddhism. "Music is now my meditation," he says. "It's the place where I really melt into the Oneness. . . . I feel a lot of us are instruments for healing the planet, for tuning people back into nature."

The New Age movement has become a powerful force, attracting those disillusioned with materialism and holding on to the generation that passed through experiences with drugs, mysticism and magic. Although not commanding as much attention as the spiritual antics of the 1960s, it will have long-term effects that are likely to be more profound.

Elvis Presley (pictured here with the Jordanaires in 1956) claimed that his first love was "spiritual music" and frequently used gospel singers to back him.

Most soul singers came out of the church. Al Green went back to it, becoming a pastor in 1974 and combining his distinctive soul style with a gospel message.

Thomas Dorsey (inset) is credited with being "the father of gospel music," having introduced the rhythms of jazz and blues into American churches during the 1920s.

Rishikesh, India, March 1968: Donovan, George Harrison, Mike Love (Beach Boys) and John Lennon sing for guru Maharishi Mahesh Yogi. Suddenly religion was acceptable within rock 'n' roll.

The Rolling Stones were captivated by the occult theories of filmmaker Kenneth Anger (lying down). Marianne Faithfull, Keith Richards, Anita Pallenberg and Mick Jagger are pictured in 1968 at Woolhope Church, Herefordshire, while searching for ley lines.

Bono's Luciferian creation MacPhisto debuted on the 1993 Zoo TV tour by U2. MacPhisto liked religion, he said, because it stopped people getting to know God.

Although Bob Dylan started making overtly Christian statements following his 1979 album *Slow Train Coming,* he had always expressed spiritual concerns in his writings.

MICK GARLAND 1990

Van Morrison, pictured playing at St. Mary's Church, Stogumber, Somerset, had mystical experiences as a child which he has spent much of his life investigating. His songs reflect this search.

For Rastafarian Bob Marley, Haile Selassie was God, Ethiopia was heaven and the drug ganja facilitated prayer. "When you smoke," he said, "you meditate."

The influence of drug prophet Terence McKenna (left) can be heard in the work of the Shamen, founded by Colin Angus (right). They shared a belief that spiritual transformation can be brought about by psychedelics and music.

Public Enemy, featuring Chuck D. (left) and Flavor Flav (right), fused the biting social realism of rap with an appeal to the tenets of the Nation of Islam.

Madonna explains her juxtaposition of sleaze and Catholicism as an attempt to purge herself of guilt feelings.

Rivers of Babylon

8

If God hadn't given me a song to sing, I wouldn't have a song to sing.
Bob Marley

Musicians do the work of God.
Toots Hibbert

I will know my work is over because I will feel myself satisfied,
and I will feel like I am tired. And God will see and tell me. It is
redemption now, yunno. No one can stop it.
Bob Marley

*F*or Rastafarians like Bob Marley, the New Age was to be a
political kingdom. They weren't waiting for the world to evolve
to a higher stage of consciousness; they were waiting to be set free
from the ugly poverty that was an inheritance of slavery. They were
literally "strangers in a strange land," being descended from West
African slaves who were transported across the ocean to work the
sugar plantations.

These people had grown understandably alienated from a Christian
gospel (presented to them by well-to-do white missionaries) that assumed they'd bear all their burdens with a smile since they knew there
was equality in heaven. If the white people could enjoy a bit of heaven

now, why couldn't they? Or was heaven itself possibly a white trick to keep them content and obedient?

Rastafarianism developed out of such thinking. "We're sick and tired of your bullshit game / Die and go to heaven in Jesus' name," as Marley sang in "Get Up, Stand Up." It grew into a religious cult with adherents wherever there were Jamaican communities. It drew on favorite passages from the Bible, added doctrines of black supremacy and interpreted the mixture through a psychedelic consciousness. Taken literally, it was nonsense. Taken as a source of pride, identity and hope, it was very powerful.

Roots of Rastafarianism

The roots of the Rastafarian movement go back to 1914, when Marcus Garvey, a Jamaican labor organizer born in 1887, founded the Universal Negro Improvement and Conservation Association. Garvey promoted the idea of Ethiopia as the cradle of civilization, the black person as the superior being. During the same period a "Negro Bible" was compiled, purporting to prove that God and his prophets were all black. This book was not published in America until 1924.

Garvey's teachings and the Black Bible influenced Leonard Howell, an acknowledged founder of Rastafarianism, who developed a theory of black supremacy and the eventual return of all exiled blacks to their homeland. Yet it wasn't until Bob Marley bound these doctrines to the hypnotic beat of reggae that the world at large became aware of this Caribbean cult religion.

Marley's Message

"Exodus," one of Marley's best-known songs, recorded in 1977, clearly spelled out the Rastafarian hope of redemption:

Open your eyes and look within
Are you satisfied with the life you're livin'?
We know where we're goin'!
We know where we're from

We're leaving Babylon

We're goin' to our Father's land.

Regarded by Rastas as a prophet, healer and priest, Marley toured the world, sold over $250 million worth of records and was eventually elevated to the pantheon of rock greats. He was admired by Eric Clapton, Bob Dylan, Keith Richards and Johnny Rotten alike. When Marley died in 1981, he was given a state funeral, his body lying in an open coffin in Jamaica's National Arena while thousands of mourners filed past.

Outlaw Fundamentalism

At a time when white rock 'n' roll was getting fat and comfortable, reggae came along with dirt on its shoes and fire in its belly. Like the blues, it was the black person's response to poverty, hopelessness and exploitation. Like the earliest rock 'n' roll, it drew sustenance from the church and provided a Pentecostal type of experience for its audience.

Hard-core white rock 'n' roll fans loved it. This was outlaw music, created in the purest of conditions for independent record labels. The musicians' swirling spirals of hair and religious use of drugs added a bit of hippie nonconformity that appealed to veterans of the 1960s. Rastafarian teachings, which would have been derided if they had originated among poor white people, were respected. To have called Rastafarians cranky fundamentalists would have marked the accuser as a patronizing middle-class bigot.

Essential to the appeal of Rasta-inspired reggae, both to Jamaican followers and to white onlookers, was the redemption story. Whereas in rock 'n' roll the sense of being in the wrong place and searching for the true home was shadowy, in reggae it was made clear. The badlands were real shantytowns where the gang warfare raged. Heaven wasn't some vague place off down the tracks; it could be pointed out on any world map.

Rastas saw themselves as modern-day children of Israel, in captivity in a foreign land and looking for a savior to lead them to their promised land. Those parts of the Old Testament that told of the Israelites' being held in Egypt before their forty-year-trek through the wilderness under Moses, culminating in their reaching the "land of milk and honey" and the later captivity by the Babylonians, resonated with Rastas' own experience.

Young Jamaicans brought up in teetering shacks of corrugated iron and packing-case wood, in a society plagued by corrupt government officials and exploitative Western business interests, felt they didn't have to look any further for Babylon. It was all around them.

They took comfort from the Israelites' plight, although their appreciation of the Bible was highly selective. As one local historian noted, "To the Rastafarians, the Bible is a holy book, but not all of its contents are acceptable." Best of all they loved the Psalms with their poetry of blues interspersed with great exaltation, and the book of Revelation with its graphic description of the eventual destruction of Babylon. They drew strength from these accounts, and reggae artists regularly quoted from the Psalms.

"Rivers of Babylon," a hit for Boney M (and one of Britain's best-selling singles ever), but originally recorded by the Melodians, was an adaptation of Psalm 137, where the dejected Israelites are portrayed in captivity and are taunted by their captors to sing songs of their homeland, Zion. They answer, "How shall we sing the Lord's song in a strange land?"

Marley himself was a regular reader of the Psalms, carrying around a battered Bible, quoting his favorite passages and encouraging others to read it. When he lay in state, a Bible was placed on his chest, open at Psalm 23: "The LORD is my shepherd; I shall not want. He maketh me to lie down in green pastures: he leadeth me beside the still waters. He restoreth my soul" (vv. 1-2 KJV).

Messianic Hope

In the Psalms, Rastas found notice of their coming savior. Two verses (Psalm 68:4; 89:8) make mention of JAH, a contraction of Jehovah.

In 1924 Marcus Garvey (some historians claim it could have been one of his associates) prophesied that such a savior would soon come. "Look to Africa, for the crowning of a black King," he instructed his followers. "He shall be the Redeemer." Haile Selassie's coronation six years later in Addis Ababa, in which he took the titles King of Kings and Conquering Lion of Judah, was seen as prophecy fulfilled. "Princes shall come out of Egypt," Psalm 68:31 (KJV) promised; "Ethiopia shall soon stretch out her hands unto God."

Selassie himself, though a great advocate of the Bible who apparently believed he was descended from King Solomon, was bemused by the accolade. He kept silent on the subject when he made a state visit to Jamaica in 1966 and was met by a crowd of 100,000 at the airport. Yet his silence only fanned the flames of belief. As Marley said when asked why Selassie hadn't owned up to his divinity, "How God gonna come tell you he's God? God don't own no one no obligations."

Selassie was born Tafari Makonnen, the great-grandson of King Saheka Selassie of Shoa, and inherited the title Ras, the equivalent of an English duke. Thus he was Ras Tafari, and believers in his divinity became known as Rastafari, Rastafarians or simply Rastas.

Selassie's position in the cult is undeniably Christlike. He's seen as being both God and man—JAH Ras Tafari. He is dead (he died in August 1975), yet he lives. He has gone away, yet he will return for the faithful few. His image decorated record sleeves, T-shirts and posters. Bob Marley's first words on hitting the stage would be a Rastafarian blessing: "Greetings in the name of Selassie. JAH Ras Tafari. Ever living, ever faithful, ever true." Behind him would be a huge painted scrim bearing the face of the late emperor.

The earliest Rastafarians believed that Selassie would arrange for steamships to take them from Jamaica to Ethiopia and that they would be resettled in a glorious land where they would prosper and be accepted. Some even believed that their homecoming would be the start of an African revival, that Africa would triumph in the world, becoming equal, if not superior, to the superpowers.

Winston Rodney, who records as Burning Spear, is a shaman figure like Marley. His songs "Marcus Garvey" and "Slavery Days" ("do you remember the days of slavery?") have become Rasta reggae classics. Singing since 1969, he remains a convinced Rasta, attending bimonthly meetings of the Twelve Tribes of Judah (one of the two main Rasta sects) and believing passionately in the continuing presence of Selassie ("JAH no dead").

Despite the apparent logistical impossibility and political undesirability of relocating Jamaican cult followers in northeast Africa, the faith of Burning Spear and many others remains undimmed. Ethiopia is Zion. Babylon is to be judged and condemned, just as outlined in the book of Revelation, and God's elect will live peacefully in his kingdom.

Asked if Ethiopia retains its attraction as a heavenly destination despite crippling famine, war and political corruption, Burning Spear says none of this matters.

Don't mind in what area is violence or famine or whatever it is. Africa must be free. Africa is for Africans—those abroad, those at home. The foundation of the whole world is Africa. The first civilized person is from Africa, and civilization is from Africa. So I don't mind what's going on right now. I don't know how it might look. That's immaterial. Africa must be free.

Redemptive Rhythms
Yet before reaching Zion, the Rasta thinks he has techniques that can elevate him into the divine presence. He has music and he has ganja.

The music has always been important. Before the 1960s advent of reggae, which had evolved out of the softer bluebeat and ska styles, there were Ras Tafari orchestras that played Sunday-night meetings on rattles, tambourines, saxophones and a rhumba box. Behind ska and bluebeat is an ancestry of church music (Toots Hibbert of Toots and the Maytals, for example, started by recording gospel songs), rhythm and blues songs picked up from radio stations broadcasting out of New Orleans, some rock 'n' roll and Kumina drumming. In Jamaican religious cults—whether voodoo or Baptist revivalism—drumming and chanting were central. The idea of using hypnotic rhythms to bring about altered states of consciousness in a religious setting was commonplace in Jamaica; it was a variation of the frenzy that Elvis Presley, Little Richard, Jerry Lee Lewis and Ray Charles had experienced as young churchgoing Americans.

Norman Grant, vocalist and drummer for the Twinkle Brothers, a Jamaican-based reggae band, recalls his own Baptist childhood. "You clapped and stamped your feet and you really got into it," he says. "People even got into the Spirit. They would fall down in a trance and start to roll on the ground."

Reggae, with its shuddering bass line driving up from the concrete floors and the slap of the drums that can make it sound as though the side of an ocean liner is being used as a wobbly board, is a physical experience; you can literally vibrate with the sound. Describing a Burning Spear performance, Stephen Davis wrote in *Reggae Bloodlines,* "Every song is arranged to first embrace the listener with tension and apprehension, and then to release him via hypnotic repetition."

"The music take people closer to everything which is good," says Burning Spear of his own work. "It take them in every clean and proper direction. It's the right music. It's uplifting music. It's music of convenience for every nation and color. It speak about truth and right."

Spiritual Herb

Ganja, a hemp originally grown in India by mystics for use in meditation, became a Rasta sacrament. It is viewed with mystical reverence, not just as a means of temporarily escaping from the Babylonian existence but as a means of purifying the heart, of entering the presence of JAH and bringing about harmony between people.

"When you smoke you meditate," Bob Marley told a journalist. "JAH made it for a purpose. (The beauty of herb is, you know . . .

herb is a plant, right, but the Devil know that if people smoke this herb they will communicate together.)" Marley was a very heavy smoker, often sitting up late at night with his Bible and his ganja. "Herb reveal yourself to you," he would say. "All the wickedness you do, the herb reveal it all to yourself."

As with almost all Rasta beliefs, the practice of smoking ganja is seen to be authorized by a clutch of disconnected Scriptures, in this case from Genesis ("Behold, I have given you every herb bearing seed," 1:29 KJV) to Revelation ("And the leaves of the tree [of life] were for the healing of the nations," 22:2 KJV). Rasta activists have fought, unsuccessfully so far, to have the drug legalized on the basis that for them it's a religious sacrament equal to the bread and wine of the Christian church.

Says Norman Grant, "Herb help you meditate on the Father even more. It pull you closer to him. When you're burning the hash it takes all the evil things out of you. Herb is spiritual really. By smoking it you take everything else out of your mind and then you just dealing with the Father. It's good! It's wonderful really, to deal with the Father himself."

Bob Marley

Bob Marley, though, was something more than a Rastafarian believing in exile and eventual redemption: he was an African medicine man with an electric guitar. Born in 1945 to a woman made pregnant by a white military man, he grew up surrounded by the lingering paganism of his Ashanti tribal ancestors. Ghosts and omens, demons and spirits, dreams and visions, prophecies and possession were the stuff of ordinary life.

His mother, Cedelia, belonged to a church where Pentecostalism was allowed to accommodate some of these Africanisms. Alongside straight Bible preaching there was drumming, chanting and dancing—means of producing pocomania, "the little madness." Marley's grandfather, in whose house he was raised, was a myalaman—a white witch—who used magic to block the activities of evil spirits. It was thought that Marley might inherit his powers, but he chose music instead.

What Marley did was to fuse Rastafarianism with the visionary aspects of African religion. West Indian historian Leonard Barrett, in his book *The Sun and the Drum,* describes the African medicine man in a way that fits Marley. The medicine man, says Barrett, is a healer and a diviner. He knows about sorcery but uses his powers to counter it: he heals with herbs and rituals.

For Marley the herb was ganja and the ritual was reggae. The herb, he would say again and again, is the healer of nations. "Politicians are devils who corrupt," he once said. "They don't smoke herb because when you smoke you think alike and they don't want that." The year before his death he was still preaching on the same theme. "The Devil know that if people smoke this herb they will communicate together."

His music too was medicine. "One good thing about music," he sang in "Trenchtown Rock," "when it hits, you feel no pain." It united people and took them out of the mundanity of their ordinary lives. He saw his concerts as consciousness-raising events; in 1980 he explained to a journalist, "We are a consciousness, raising consciousness."

Barrett's medicine man is also a diviner, a foreteller of the future. Accounts of Marley growing up portray him as having psychic ability, being able as a child to read palms and discern past events in a person's life. He would experience omens at the time of imminent deaths. At the age of thirty-two he predicted that his own death would come at thirty-six after a powerful three-year ministry, much like that of Jesus Christ.

His near-murder by gunmen who attacked his home in Kingston came to him in a dream that he'd already written up as the song "Ambush in the Night." "Every song we sing come true," he said afterward. "It all happen in real life. Some songs are too early, some happen immediately, but all of them happen."

Beyond these personal calamities, Marley claimed he could see the end of Babylon. He saw himself as a prophet warning of impending destruction. Rastafarianism, like Pentecostalism, teaches that the end is nigh. Marley had been affected by reading *The Late Great Planet Earth,* a popular interpretation of Bible prophecies relating to Armageddon, written by an American evangelical Christian, Hal Lindsey. The same book was to influence Bob Dylan shortly after his "born-again" experience in 1979. "It's the last days without a doubt," Marley said. "It's the last quarter before the year 2000 and righteousness, the positive way of thinking, must win. Good over evil. We're confident of victory."

The medicine man is able to see that which the rest of the tribe are ignorant of, says Barrett. Marley was reported to have a permanently distant look, his head cocked as if he was tuned in to some mystical frequency. "JAH appear to me in a vision," he confidently announced to one sympathetic music journalist. "Every time he look just a bit older than me. Him don't look ninety years old or anything. If I'm thirty, then he look about thirty-five. Man, it's so sweet. It's me brother, me father, me mother, me creator, everything . . ."

The Splintering of Reggae

With the death of Marley, Rasta lost its figurehead. Major reggae artists like Dennis Brown, Burning Spear and Gregory Isaacs still prospered, but there was no one as inspirational and international as the composer of "Exodus," "Jamming" and "No Woman, No Cry." Younger reggae artists no longer automatically became Rastas, and young West Indians increasingly turned to rap and soul. In 1987 Peter Tosh, a founding member of the Wailers, was shot dead.

Ragga music, spearheaded by Shabba Ranks, began to eclipse reggae. It was secular, sexual and often given to boasts about violence. But then some ragga stars like Buju Banton and Capleton started to turn back to Rasta, singing praises to Selassie to a ragga beat and opening up the prospect of a renewed interest in Rasta among an audience looking for an alternative to the culture of guns and sex.

Fatal Flaws

The weakness of Rastafarianism, if it can be called a weakness, is that this belief system offers a patently false hope. Haile Selassie is not going to return and lead the descendants of the Shanti to the wonderful land of Ethiopia while the Western world stands in ruins. Drugs, though they undoubtedly can bring moments of peace and illusions of human harmony, do nothing in the long term except erode motivation and distort useful perception.

At the end of it all, the dedicated Rasta is as far as ever from his longed-for redemption. Reggae has a commitment and passion that make it one of the truly inspiring types of electric music, but no one can be saved by commitment alone. The story of the journey from Babylon to Zion has a certain beauty that corresponds to a genuine realization that we are all exiled and were created for a better place, but beauty does not equal truth, and truth counts in matters as vital as this.

West Indian poet Linton Kwesi Johnson, who records his poems with reggae musicians, believes Rastafarianism is a mythical way of making sense of political reality, but dangerous in that it blinds its followers to the real picture.

It has a great deal which is positive in so far as it brought back to the Jamaican masses a sense of dignity. It gave them a sense of pride in their African heritage which British colonialism had done a great deal to destroy. So it culturally enriched the lives of the masses and the language of the people. But all this talk of going back to Africa . . . it's a pipe-dream.

There are Rastas who beat their drums and chant their chants and get high, and for a moment they can find themselves in Ethiopia at the foot of Selassie or sitting on the Golden Throne. But after the weed wear off, and after the music finish playing, then it's back to the harsh and ugly reality of life. One of the things about Rastafarianism is that it has prevented the masses from seeing who their real enemies are.

No Future

9

They try to ruin you from the start. They take away your soul. They destroy you. You have no future. Nothing.
Johnny Rotten, the Sex Pistols

Punk was at its most spiritual in the Sex Pistols.
Malcolm McLaren, manager of the Sex Pistols

I don't believe that Lucifer was evil. I believe he was a rebel.
Eve's desires weren't material, she had a desire for wisdom.
Adam was like a mindless acid head.
Patti Smith

*T*he commercial rise of reggae (Bob Marley had his first British hit single in September 1975) coincided with the emergence of punk (the Sex Pistols made their first appearance in November 1975). In many respects the two couldn't have been more different (punks scorned long hair, drugs and any form of mysticism), yet there was a great affinity at a roots level.

Punks and Rastas both felt pushed to the margins of society; they felt out of place. They felt as if they were capable of greater things than society would ever let them attempt, and they wanted to shout at a world that trampled on their dignity. Both groups went out of their way to exacerbate the feeling of separation—the Rastas with their fearful-looking dreadlocks, the punks with matted hair, chains, spikes and provocative T-shirts. They wanted to look as trashy and alienated as they felt inside.

Marley acknowledged the shared grievances, recording "Punky Reggae Party" and saying, "Listen, punk love reggae and some of them say things that Babylon no like. . . . Them resist society and say, 'Me a punk 'cos I don't want you to shove me where I don't like it.' "

The difference, though, came in their response. Whereas Rastas had constructed a religion of hope, punks wallowed in hopelessness and mediocrity. Rastas spoke of universal brotherhood, but the Sex Pistols sang,

I'm in love with myself
My pretty little self
And nobody else.

Bob Marley longed for Zion; Johnny Rotten claimed there was "no future for you / no future for me."

Yet it would be wrong to assume that punks were simply nihilists. They experienced the same sense of isolation that galvanized the rock 'n' roll greats before them, but instead of searching for transcendence they raged, and hoped that the noise of the rage would make a difference.

The Sterility of Mid-1970s Rock

Punk was born of necessity. Rock 'n' roll, at its creative best when expressing rebellion against sterile living, had itself become sterile. Adventurous spirits such as Bob Dylan and Van Morrison understandably didn't connect with sixteen-year-olds living in urban tenements and wondering whether they'd ever be employed. The pilgrimages of these now mature men made sense only if you'd followed them from the beginning.

Glamour stars such as Rod Stewart, Elton John and Queen were an irrelevance for those who expected rock 'n' roll to articulate their dreams and frustrations. The music that had started as do-it-yourself entertainment had drifted out of the reach of most teenagers. In order to succeed you needed expensive equipment and instrumental proficiency. The pit between the stage and the audience had grown ever wider.

In January 1976 *New Musical Express* writer Mick Farren was complaining that rock stars had become little more than management investments, increasingly detached from the outside world. A photo of partying superstars such as Eric Clapton and Keith Moon was contrasted with a bombed-out Belfast hotel and the question asked: "What does the rich lifestyle of the rock 'n' roll aristocracy have to do with these vital contemporary issues?" Six months later, with things apparently not much improved, Farren launched another attack on what he called the "tired ideas left over from the sixties" that were littering the charts.

Did we really come through the fantasy, fear and psychic mess of the last decade to make rock 'n' roll safe for the Queen, Princess Margaret and Liz Taylor? If rock becomes safe, it's all over. It's vibrant, vital music that from its very roots has always been a burst of colour and excitement against a backdrop of dullness, hardship or frustration.

From the blues onwards, the essential core of the music has been the rough side of humanity. It's a core of rebellion, sexuality, assertion and even violence. All the things that have always been unacceptable to a ruling establishment. Once that vigorous, horny-handed core is extracted from rock 'n' roll, you're left with little more than muzak.

Farren ended his piece by calling for a new generation's music to push aside the old, even though he recognized the difficulty in the current economic climate. "It may be a question of taking rock back to street level and starting all over again. . . . Putting the Beatles back together isn't going to be the salvation of rock 'n' roll. Four kids playing to their own contemporaries in a dirty cellar night club might."

The Sex Pistols

As Farren wrote, four kids of the type he envisaged were doing exactly that. They were Steve Jones, Glen Matlock, Paul Cook and Johnny Rotten. Their manager, clothes-shop owner and former art student Malcolm McLaren, had called them the Sex Pistols. His manipulation of the group has since been widely exposed, but for a brief time they burned bright, threatening the security of superstars, rousing record companies out of their complacency and inspiring thousands of young people to pick up guitars in the spirit of "if they can do it, we can do it too."

The Sex Pistols' music, like early Elvis Presley, came from the gut. To see them play was to feel that you were in the engine room of youth culture. This wasn't just a show; it was an event, a piece of history. It reflected the real frustrations of powerless people.

Johnny Rotten portrayed himself as morally depraved and philo-sophically redundant. He was an anarchist and an antichrist. He had no feelings, no future and no hope. He was lazy, selfish and vacant. His almost crippled posture on stage and the petulance with which he both spoke and sang seemed to confirm that, as he said, "I mean it maaan." In "God Save the Queen" he pictured his generation as a discarded beauty ("the flowers in the dustbin") and queried whether morality could exist in the face of extinction. If everything is to end in oblivion, what is the source of justice? "When there's no future / how can there be sin?"

In interviews Rotten promoted himself as a jaded youth, fed up with sex, cynical of love and happy to amuse himself by stubbing out lighted cigarettes on the back of his hand. In turn the journalists, excited by the discovery of such an urban primitive, exaggerated the conditions of his background—the "unyielding concrete environ-ment," as Caroline Coon described it in *Melody Maker*.

"We really want to do something for our own sakes as much as anyone else's," said Rotten. "We want to be people with a mind of our own. We are doing our bit to punch the rest of 1976 away. Our songs

are ideas. Spend one night in London and you'll become disgusted
with the old ways. You're bound to get ideas from that. And soon this
country will be just one city. What'll happen then?"

Cosmic Boredom

Other punk bands, in both Britain and America, fostered similar pos-
tures of ennui. The Clash were bored with London, bored with America,
bored with Elvis, the Beatles and the Stones. They were anxious for
action, any action, that would authenticate their lives. More political
than the Sex Pistols, they blamed oppressive systems of control, whether
government or record company, for inducing widespread catatonia.

In New York, Richard Hell, who originated the symbolic shredded
T-shirt that was to become the premier punk fashion artifact, sang of
the "Blank Generation." The Ramones perfected an attitude of dumb-
ness in songs of studied boredom, insanity and violence, all delivered
in the language of a high-school dropout.

Ten years before they would have become hippies or political activists, but as far as they were concerned that had been a failed experiment; it was something their older brothers and sisters had tried.
Johnny Rotten himself was sneering toward hippies. "They were so
complacent," he said. "They let the drug culture flop around them.
They were so dosed out of their heads the whole time. Yeah man.
Peace and love! Don't let anything affect you!"

Ironically, the older generation who assisted punk's birth were children of the 1960s. Journalists like Mick Farren and Caroline Coon
had been active in the London "underground," Farren as a vocalist
with the Social Deviants, Coon as the founder of Release, an agency
set up to aid those arrested on drug charges. Clash manager Bernie
Rhodes had shared a flat with Graham Bond (of Holy Magick) and
sold shirts in Granny Takes a Trip, one of Chelsea's hottest boutiques
in 1967.

Malcolm McLaren had been to art school, had attended sit-ins, had
participated in the Paris riots of 1968 and was acquainted with Ger-

man political activist Daniel Cohn-Bendit. His real love was early rock 'n' roll, and he'd lost interest when Elvis went into the army.

McLaren was able to see that the natural frustration of the kids who dropped by his King's Road clothing shop could be channeled into a rock 'n' roll spectacle that could have a social impact. It was he who encouraged the anarchic spirit that came to characterize the Sex Pistols. He'd been inspired by a little-known political art movement called Situationism, where public events were set up in which "the individual would be made aware of the repressive structure of urban life."

Once asked whether the Sex Pistols hadn't been totally destructive, he agreed: "For me the very destructive nature of the idea was ultimately its most creative point. To me that was what it was all about." He believed that out of the resulting chaos would come a "tremendous lease of life."

Punk's long-term effect was not what McLaren imagined, and society at large was not shaken out of its apathy. The dreaded high-rises and urban wastelands still exist, and twenty years after "Anarchy in the UK" unemployment remains a problem. Punks themselves, now evolved into leather-jacketed young people with brightly colored Mohawk haircuts, are an acceptable sideshow, turning up on London postcards alongside Beefeaters and policemen.

The greatest effect of the Sex Pistols lay in the musicians it inspired, many of whom were to go on to enjoy longer recording lives than Rotten and company. With just one album the Pistols had restored many people's faith in the possibility that rock 'n' roll might regain its old vitality. They proved that great rock 'n' roll had more to do with passion than with proficiency. Once again, as in the days of hillbilly trios or London skifflers, anyone could do it. The release of *Never Mind the Bollocks* was to rank with the release of "Heartbreak Hotel" and the Beatles' first appearance on *The Ed Sullivan Show* as one of the crucial moments in the history of rock 'n' roll.

Yet the punk of the Clash, the Sex Pistols and hundreds of other now-forgotten groups was inevitably short-lived. It was impossible to attempt to be that destructive without, in the end, destroying yourself. McLaren boasted that he'd created a spectacle with the group that people were willing to pay for, but "with the spectacle there is a tremendous sense of poison that ultimately wrings the neck of society."

With the Sex Pistols, the poison flowed back into their own system. Sid Vicious, who had replaced Glen Matlock on bass guitar, was brought in for his aggressive image rather than his musical ability, which was nonexistent. He didn't disappoint, ending up covered in blood during one of the band's last American concerts and dying of a heroin overdose while awaiting trial on a murder charge. Eighteen months after the release of their first single, the Sex Pistols disintegrated in an atmosphere of violence and recrimination.

Patti Smith

Patti Smith, an anorexic-looking writer and poet from New Jersey, had been inspired by the unlikely combination of Little Richard and Arthur Rimbaud. Where the Clash insisted, "No more Elvis, Beatles and Rolling Stones in 1977," Smith was proud to admit drawing sustenance from Jim Morrison, Jimi Hendrix, Bob Dylan and Keith Richards. Unique among punks, she saw herself in a shamanistic role, negotiating with God during her performances. "We're able to nourish the future and give inspiration," she said of her group. "We're able to put our hands to the young kids who also salute the older guard. I always think of us as guardians of history."

Of those Smith admired, she was closest to Jim Morrison, believing that real spiritual freedom comes through a synthesis of moral opposites. Having grown up with an atheist father and a fervently religious mother, she found that she'd inherited both tendencies. Part of her was drawn to absolute evil, part to purity. "My father taught me not to be a pawn in God's game," she once said. "He used to blaspheme and swear against God, putting him down. I got that side of me from him. The religious part is from my mother, who was a complete religious fanatic."

The poet Rimbaud interested her because he too had suffered this tension. Born into a Catholic family, he was deeply religious as a boy and even considered becoming a missionary. Later he developed an artistic vision that saw obedience to any outside authority as a spiritual impediment. He tried to resolve this conflict by submitting to blasphemy and obscenity, debauchery and drugs, magic and Satanism, hoping to neutralize sin by letting it have its way. "He imagined he could cut down the tree of good and evil," wrote his biographer Enid Starkie, "to atrophy its roots and thus wipe out the conflict."

Smith, too, tried to befriend her dark side. "I've done everything I can to taste who I am," she claimed. "I don't feel cheated out of anything." She read the Bible and fell in love with Cain, Eve and Lucifer, whom she saw as bold and instinctive characters. She particularly admired Eve and her search for wisdom. A *New York Times* writer observed, "She sees evil as an inextricable part of human nature, herself as the bearer of the poison fruit of human knowledge."

Smith could not accept the teaching of original sin, that all are born separated from God because of a flawed moral character. "Jesus died for somebody's sins / but not mine," she boldly asserted in "Gloria." On her *Easter* album (1978) she repeated the words of Psalm 23 ("The LORD is my shepherd, I shall not want . . .") and then added her own: "Goddam, goddam, goddam." Later she commented, "I've been called a blasphemer a thousand times, but I said that [in 'Gloria'] because I refuse to accept that I came into this world as a sinner."

Nevertheless, she was always aware of the religious function of rock 'n' roll. She claimed that rock 'n' roll was about "trying to touch the tongue of God" and felt shamanistic about her work on stage. "When I pull out my mike and fall on my knees in a state of grace I can inspire people," she said. "I always opt for communication with God, and in that pursuit you can enter some very dangerous territory. I also have to realize that total communication with God is physical death." Dave Marsh, writing in *Rolling Stone,* was to call her "the most profoundly religious popular American performer since Jim Morrison."

Doors Revival

At the turn of the 1980s, Morrison, who had by then been dead for almost a decade, was coming alive again as an influence within rock 'n' roll. With his good looks, punk attitude and spiritual objectives, he was a suitable bridge with the 1960s. Morrison at least had never worn flowers in his hair or kissed the feet of the Maharishi. He could never stand accused of being a drippy hippie. A biography by Jerry Hopkins and Danny Sugarman, *No One Here Gets Out Alive,* made the *New York Times* nonfiction bestseller list in 1980, a rare occurrence for a rock 'n' roll book.

Oliver Stone's film *The Doors* (1991) did even more for Morrison's name. Stone consciously promoted him as a shamanistic figure from whom great spiritual lessons could be learned, rather than as a drunken loser who threw away his career and killed himself through a lack of self-control.

The Doors' music was to prove arguably even more influential than it had been in the 1960s, shaping the sounds of a host of postpunk bands such as the Stranglers, Joy Division, Echo and the Bunnymen, Simple Minds and the Lords of the New Church. As punk became little more than a rag bag of empty attitudes and designer clothes, musicians in the early 1980s seemed to turn back to the wellsprings of the 1960s for inspiration. Musical and spiritual exploration was suddenly back in fashion.

New
Gold
Dream

10

We're just a group writing songs and yet we have all this holy stuff written about us. The thing is, I half believe it.
Ian McCulloch, Echo and the Bunnymen

I believe inspiration comes through me and that I channel it.
Jim Kerr, Simple Minds

You have to come to terms with the gods and demons who populate your unconsciousness and your dreams.
Sting

*E*cho and the Bunnymen were typical of a new kind of band emerging in the 1980s. They'd been inspired to pick up instruments by exposure to punk; they used spiritual images in their songs (sample titles—"Gods Will Be Gods," "Heaven Up Here," "Higher Hell," "My White Devil") and were regarded by fans with what one newspaper called "religious reverence."

It was all a lot grander and more intense than punk. They didn't snarl at cameras or pull faces; they wore dark clothing and posed in graveyards or in front of church buildings. They talked about having "communion" with their audience; they were conscious of a spiritual dimension and eager to acknowledge it in their music.

Yet Echo and the Bunnymen were not believers in any religious teaching. They simply acknowledged the evocative power of the language and symbols of religion, and a generation that had grown up ignorant of its spiritual heritage responded to this mystery.

"I use the word *heaven* a lot in my songs because it sounds good," admitted Ian McCulloch, singer for Echo and the Bunnymen. "I think I write spiritually rather than religiously, a personal spiritual view. *Heaven* is a word that seems to sum up some great thing that we can't ever imagine. It's not an orthodox use of the word."

When Echo and the Bunnymen toured Britain in 1983, this religious aura was heightened by their use of a back projection of stained-glass windows and recordings of organ music played just prior to their entrance on stage. "You do experience things that you don't usually at a rock concert," admitted McCulloch. "We found there was an attitude towards us that was something more than 'music.' . . . There seemed to be a religious type of following. Some people do actually love us. Our albums are like their versions of the Bible."

Simple Minds (singer and lyricist Jim Kerr was raised a Roman Catholic in Scotland) worked in similar territory. They used Crusader crosses, sacred hearts, an open Bible and the flame of Pentecost on their album covers. Although Kerr had no fixed religious commitment, he utilized the emotive capital of words like *miracle, faith, heaven* and *angel* in his songs.

The titles of the group's songs suggested much more than they actually delivered—"Promised You a Miracle," "Somebody Up There Likes You," "East at Easter," "Shake Off the Ghosts." One of their most popular songs was mysteriously entitled "Sanctify Yourself" ("Sanctify / sanctify yourself / set yourself free").

Because of this religious veneer, Simple Minds' albums breathed a sense of hope that punk never had, and some of the glory of the great theological words lit them up. Kerr seemed always to be reaching toward a source of new life, of new light, desperately wanting to pass on a promise of a better life to come, a "sparkle in the rain," a "new gold dream," although never suggesting any *reason* we should all be so optimistic.

Sting

In a secularized culture where mystery had been displaced by intrigue, grandeur by glamour, it was not surprising that the trappings of religion, invested with centuries of faith, should command an unusual sense of awe. In the vanguard of the new positive postpunk movement it was also not surprising to find a collection of lapsed Roman Catholics who, while not subscribing to the ethics and power structure of the church, nevertheless found themselves using the church's symbols as a way of discussing the battle between good and evil.

These were people deeply respectful of religious ritual, moved by the language and typology of the Bible, but skeptical of church teachings. Sting, raised in a Catholic family in Newcastle and educated by Jesuits, said that being brought up "rooted in magic and religion" left him feeling set apart from the hedonistic rock 'n' roll world.

In his songs he grappled with angels and demons. In his private life he studied ferociously, trying to make sense of fears and guilt. He admitted,

I'm not a devout Catholic. I don't go to Mass, but I'm not sure that I've broken away from it. All that was inculcated into my brain as a small child—that there is a heaven and a hell, mortal sins and venial sins—is inside my psyche and will never come out. I think human psychology is such that we invent gods and demons anyway, and the Catholic ones are tried and tested archetypes. The ones we invent for ourselves are much more dangerous in a way.

Catholicism is useful to me as a creative artist in that there is a whole creative reservoir—the man on the cross with blood pouring out of him, the crown of thorns, all that imagery. The incredible imagery of hellfire which James Joyce explored so brilliantly. It's so rich and, for an artist, it's essential. You need something like that to scare the living daylights out of you in order to write. You write as a defense.

Brian Eno and David Byrne

Brian Eno—"I was brought up as a Catholic but I don't suppose I am now really"—was another for whom rock 'n' roll closed the gap that the church had once filled. "It was the only thing I had which was a spiritual experience," he told me. "I wasn't religious at that time. That part of my life was occupied by music." During the 1970s, when less rock 'n' roll was being produced that could fulfill a spiritual function, he began to look elsewhere.

He was searching for an ecstatic music, something that reminded people that they were spiritual beings, not ciphers. He found it in what might be called religious performance. Eno began visiting Brooklyn's First Baptist Tabernacle of Christ, finding the gospel singing "extremely moving," sufficient to leave him elated for days afterward. He also began to listen to gospel albums, amassing quite a collection in his New York apartment. "As a music, gospel has the power to move me in a way that rock music ceased to do a long time ago," he said.

At the same time Eno was tuning in to local radio stations and becoming fascinated with religious orators whom he felt demonstrated "a kind of lust for the life of the spirit." These people burned with a conviction that changed the very quality of their voices, turning them into musical instruments. They were earthly voices crying out to heaven. With David Byrne, whom he had produced when he was in Talking Heads, he set about recontextualizing these sounds, turning them into a soundtrack.

The result was their joint album *My Life in the Bush of Ghosts* (1981), where the voices of radio evangelists, exorcists, gospel singers and Algerian Muslims chanting the Qur'an were taped from broadcasts and meshed in with guitars, bass, drums and synthesizers to create an uncanny collage of excited voices reaching out with yearning and the familiar beat of rock 'n' roll.

Explaining the thinking behind the project, Eno said,

Both David and I were interested in what you might call "ecstatic spirituality," and for me that was because I had become disenchanted with the ordinary concerns of rock music which are normally to do with one's relationship with other people, to do with a society of teenagers. I'd become interested in musical forms which were either to do with your relationship with the world of nature or with the spiritual world. In other words, an exploration of the dilemma between a physical life and a spiritual life.

Both Byrne and Eno were highly regarded for their ability to stay in the forefront of creative rock, continually anticipating trends. Talking Heads had been the most original American band to grasp the opportunities offered by punk, taking contemporary art-school ideas into the club scene opened up by people like the Ramones and Richard Hell, and Eno had impeccable avant-garde credentials going back to his days as keyboard player with Roxy Music. *My Life in the Bush of Ghosts* became a significant pointer toward new currents flowing in rock 'n' roll.

In 1983, when I interviewed Eno, he had not yet met U2 (he was later to produce or coproduce several albums, including *The Unforgettable Fire* and *The Joshua Tree*), but already his thinking on spirituality was rolling in a direction compatible with U2's approach. "I get thoroughly fed up of hearing about people's mystical drug experiences," he told me.

I don't see the experiences doing anything. I know people who've been having sublime experiences on drugs for years and they're still the same people. It doesn't seem to have affected their behavior in any way.

I think the measure of a spiritual discipline is that it doesn't just remain spiritual. It alters the way you are as a person and the way you move through the world. The experience I want from music at the moment is seeing my own significance diminished in my eyes. The experiences I consider spiritual, that make a difference to how

I feel about the world, are always to do with stepping away from myself in some way. Stepping away from me as being such a big important thing.

In 1988 Byrne directed a documentary film, *The House of Life,* which studied the lives of people from the Bahia region of Brazil who follow the African-rooted religion Candomble. He was particularly interested in the drumming and chanting rituals in which followers believe they are taken over by whichever god the ceremony is dedicated to. "It's a big part of where our popular music comes from," he later said of this form of trance music. "Rock 'n' roll comes from those traditions, and I believe that the power and influence it has had has come because it carries a small part of that energy with it. It may be a very small part, but I think it's that which makes rock 'n' roll different from Perry Como or Frank Sinatra."

Bruce Springsteen

Bruce Springsteen, born to Americans with Irish and Italian roots, received his junior education from Catholic nuns and later became an altar boy. Almost more than any other rock 'n' roller, he understands the redemptive theme. He sees music as being essentially about holding out or getting out. It is a resistance movement against an unnamable force that threatens to crush the human spirit.

Springsteen isn't religious, but he seems to have acquired a good basic knowledge of theology, enough to be able to refer to sin, redemption and atonement in his songs. He never talks much about this interest, having come the closest when he suggested that *Born to Run* was a "religious album" and that he did sometimes read the Bible. "I tried to read it for a while," he admitted to an interviewer. "It was great. It was fascinating. I got into it quite a ways. There are some great stories."

The human problem, as Springsteen defines it in his work, is a basic lack of fulfillment. Surrounded by death, pain and fear, we human beings have to break our backs even to survive. Yet all the time we know, deep in our hearts, that we were created for greater things.

Everybody's got a hunger

A hunger they can't resist

There's so much that you want

You deserve much more than this. ("Prove It All Night")

This tension between, as it were, humankind's heavenly calling and its earthly imprisonment has been the theme of Springsteen's best work. In a typical small-town situation he sees two different sorts of people. There are those who resign themselves to mediocrity and those who burn with a passion to transcend their circumstances. There are those who "just give up living," and there are those who go "racin' in the street." There are those whose blood never burns in their veins, and those who are compelled to walk into the darkness on the edge of town, where the mysteries exist.

Springsteen presents himself as being on the side of the hungry, the ones who know they are strangers in a strange land. You either grab hold of a dream that can save you, he says, or you're stuffed full of manufactured dreams. But how must we be saved? It's one thing to know that you're in the wrong place, but how do you get out? How is a person able to be spiritually fulfilled, to find the promised land?

Here Springsteen necessarily fudges the issue. Having articulated a religious question, he doesn't have a religious answer. Springsteen, I believe, realizes that a religious answer is needed and compensates by dressing essentially existential advice in glorious heavenly language. When he's really urging those trapped in mediocrity to "go for it," to quit procrastinating and grab hold of their dreams, he sings,

I believe in the hope that can save me

I believe in the faith

And I pray that someday it may raise me

Above these badlands. ("Badlands")

Yet this kind of faith, hope and prayer is no more than positive thinking.

Throughout *Born to Run* and *Darkness on the Edge of Town,*

Springsteen portrays his heroes, those who have acknowledged their bondage and are doing something about it, as leaping into cars or onto the backs of motorcycles, authenticating themselves by an existential act. The car, from Chuck Berry onward, has been a prime symbol of pride and freedom. Driving along a freeway with no particular place to go supplies a feeling of release and escape. As Hazel Motes says in Flannery O'Connor's novel *Wise Blood,* "Anybody with a good car needs no justification."

Springsteen invests the activity of driving with religious significance. You don't just ride your car, you "have faith in your machine" ("Night"); you don't drive down streets but "through mansions of glory" ("Born to Run"), because "Heaven's waiting on down the tracks" ("Thunder Road"). To his girl in "Thunder Road" he unmistakably offers the car ride as means of salvation. He urges her not to pray for "a savior to rise from these streets," saying,

> Well I'm no hero
> That's understood
> All the redemption I can offer, girl
> Is beneath this dirty hood
> With a chance to make it good somehow
> Hey what else can we do now?

I suspect that even Springsteen himself is disappointed at such inadequate solutions. With his music he tries to elevate people, to remind them of their dignity, but at the end of the day, when you strip away the ornate decoration and turn down the volume, he has no more to tell us than "think positive," "believe in yourself" and "why not go for a ride?"

Two songs on *Nebraska* (1982) appeared, in a veiled way, to deal with the dilemma he's faced with, which is how we can be reconciled to God—if indeed God is the one to whom we need to be reconciled. What is it that separates us from our Maker? When writing "Mansion on the Hill" and "My Father's House," was Springsteen aware of Christ's statement about heaven, "In my Father's house are many mansions" (John 14:2 KJV)? It would seem so, for both songs are about an experience of ultimate exclusion. They both also appear to contain a twist on the parable of the prodigal son, who returns home from a dissolute life in the city to be reconciled with his father, who not only welcomes him but mounts a huge celebratory party.

In "Mansion on the Hill" Springsteen finds himself on the outside of this wonderful house, looking longingly in to where

The lights would shine

There'd be music playin'

People laughin' all the time.

In "My Father's House" it's even worse. He dreams he's running from the devil, who is "snappin' at my heels," on his way to a reunion with his father. Falling into his father's arms, he promises never again to let anything come between them. Yet when he wakes and runs to the house for real, he finds that his father is no longer the occupant. No one knows where he went; there can be no reconciliation. The song ends,

My father's house shines hard and bright

It stands like a beacon calling me in the night

Calling and calling so cold and alone

Shining 'cross this dark highway where our sins lie unatoned.

This theme of being exiled from God's forgiveness cropped up again and again on the simultaneously released albums *Lucky Town* and *Human Touch* (1992). In "Human Touch" Springsteen appeared resigned to the conclusion that in the absence of forgiveness, the best we're left with is human love and consolation: "Ain't no mercy on the streets of this town / Ain't no bread from heavenly skies." In "My Beautiful Reward" he even returned to the image of the mansion on the hill where he goes in search of his reward: "From a house on a hill a sacred light shines / I walk through these rooms but none of them are mine."

For Springsteen, witnessing the birth of his first child was the closest he could get to feeling God's presence in his life. In "Living Proof" he describes the little boy in his wife's arms as "a little piece of the Lord's undying light," an answer to a prayer he could barely articulate:

In a world so hard and dirty
So fouled and confused
Searching for a little bit of God's mercy
I found living proof.

Springsteen can take a huge amount of credit for pioneering a new mood of positivism in rock 'n' roll. Clean-living, opposed to the use of drugs, committed to his music, loving his country, concerned over social issues and without a trace of cynicism toward his audience, he's been a force for good. He genuinely seeks to enlarge people's experience; he believes that the best rock 'n' roll has an inspirational effect, encouraging the brokenhearted and restoring their faith in human potential. "Rock 'n' roll is never about giving up," he says. "To me it's a totally positive force. Not optimistic all the time, but positive. It was never, never about giving up."

Bob Geldof

The same new positive mood enabled Band Aid and Live Aid to happen. Here, shunning orthodox approaches to famine relief, the entire rock 'n' roll community united to raise money for Ethiopia. It was a remarkable act in a business more often characterized by self-indulgence and self-promotion. For a short period rock 'n' roll worked alongside Christian missionary organizations supplying money, clothes, trucks and medicine for a country on the brink of extinction.

The man whose vision it had been, Bob Geldof, had a big heart and an equally big mouth. He could spend time with Mother Teresa—indeed, at times he was even compared with that great worker among Calcutta's sick and dying—yet was second to none when it came to stringing obscenities together. Nicknamed Saint Bob for his charity work, he seemed determined to prove that this saint still enjoyed his sin.

As a Boomtown Rat (his group formed in Dublin) he'd never made a lasting impact, although the group had several records; but as a motivator of people, a tireless worker and a passionate debater, he found his niche. He became the first rock 'n' roll star to meet heads of state and get them to listen. His questions were blunt to the point of rudeness, but the public loved him because he was asking what they'd ask and had no diplomatic relations to jeopardize.

Geldof, too, was raised a Roman Catholic. He now strenuously denied Catholic beliefs, but it was possible to see in him some of the same motivation that sends Jesuits out into remote villages to live alongside the poor. Was it entirely a coincidence that the man who for a new generation became almost as much of a saint as Martin Luther King Jr. was educated by priests?

"I think I've always been fairly religious," says Sting, who appeared on the Band Aid record and played at Live Aid.

I suppose like most Catholic boys who went to grammar school, we were conditioned to believe that the best of us would become priests. I suppose we all seriously thought about what was called a "vocation," being "called" to the priesthood.

I, in fact, came to believe I should give up all else to do music. In a cautious and roundabout way it was my vocation. I think if you look at someone like Bob Geldof, he's now fired by his almost messianic spirit of doing good, which I'm sure was instilled in him by the Christian Brothers.

Geldof's bestselling biography *Is That It?* ended with a poignant description of the aftermath of Live Aid, the greatest assembly of rock musicians ever, watched by more people than any other event in history—an event that succeeded in raising a massive amount of money for Ethiopia.

In London, Geldof got ready to jump into a taxi as Wembley Stadium was being cleared of litter. In Philadelphia, promoter Bill Graham stepped on the stage to watch the crowds leaving and a kid shouted up to him, "Hey you, Bill Graham. Is that it?" When he heard this story, Geldof was struck with all the other implications of such a question. Was his own mission in life over? Had he been chosen just for this year? Was that really it? "It's something," he wrote, "that I keep asking myself."

Knockin' on Heaven's Door

11

I think art can lead you to God. I think that's the purpose of everything.
If it's not doing that, what's it doing? It's leading you the other way.
It's certainly not leading you nowhere.

Bob Dylan

Christianity has survived Christians for two thousand years now,
which from my point of view is evidence that maybe something
is going on there.

T-Bone Burnett

I thought when we were doing *Hallowed Ground* that maybe, in a few
years' time, people would be saying, "Remember that band Violent Femmes?
They really blew it when they started to do that gospel stuff."

Gordon Gano, Violent Femmes

*W*hat must seem quite remarkable to anyone who has followed
this story so far is that up until the 1980s there was no effective Christian contribution to rock 'n' roll. No one with the stature of
John Lennon, Mick Jagger, Van Morrison or Pete Townshend was
offering the gospel story of redemption to the ongoing debate. There
were numerous rock 'n' roll musicians who had converted to Christianity, but either this happened long after their voices really counted

(Barry McGuire, Noel Paul Stookey of Peter, Paul and Mary, Bernie
Leadon of the Eagles, Roger McGuinn of the Byrds), or they saw a
clear division between their "secular" music and their "gospel" music
(Cliff Richard, Johnny Cash, Little Richard, Philip Bailey of Earth,
Wind and Fire). Some decided to concentrate exclusively on evangelistic work, leaving the rock 'n' roll business behind and becoming
celebrities on the church circuit.

The "Christian Case" Against Rock 'n' Roll

Why was it that at a time when issues that are central to the Christian
message—our estranged state, the need for personal renewal, the
search for love, the desire to return to the Garden of Eden—were being
aired in one of popular culture's most potent media, Christians were
notable only by their absence?

The answer goes back to the case of Jerry Lee Lewis. He was one
of many early rock 'n' rollers who were persuaded to see rock 'n' roll
as "the devil's music" and believed the only way to make a contribution was to jeopardize one's own salvation. When he said, "Can you
imagine Jesus singing 'Great Balls of Fire'?" he was voicing the conviction of many Christian ministers who believed that rock 'n' roll and
the gospel were incompatible. Redemption as unfolded in the Bible is
not to be tainted with the rhythms of Africa.

The argument still goes on. In the United States, Bob Larson has
made a career out of writing books against rock 'n' roll *(Rock 'n' Roll:
The Devil's Diversion; The Day Music Died; Rock and the Church),*
while in Britain one evangelical preacher, John Blanchard, has stirred
up a controversy over whether Christians should even use rock 'n' roll
as an "evangelistic tool." These men tend to extract the worst behavior
of well-known performers and use it to generalize about rock 'n' roll
as a whole, rather like detailing the sexual preferences of a fallen TV
evangelist to discredit evangelicalism. Often their information is completely wrong (the claim that Black Sabbath held black masses "on
stage," for example, or that part of *Goats Head Soup* by the Rolling

Stones was recorded at a voodoo ritual). They quote musicians talking palpable rubbish if it supports their argument.

So you have John Oates (of Hall and Oates) claiming that "rock 'n' roll is 99 per cent sex" and Frank Zappa saying that "rock 'n' roll is sex." John Blanchard lumps together Olivia Newton-John, Prince, Jethro Tull and Pink Floyd as examples of sexual depravity. His book *Pop Goes the Gospel* is riddled with inaccuracies, misspellings and opinions attributed to highly dubious sources.

True, some rock 'n' roll stars have chosen appallingly selfish and destructive lifestyles. But the question for Christians is whether this is essential to the music. Do you have to break the Ten Commandments to be a good rock 'n' roll performer? Christians have too often been conned by the arrogant talk of young stars and their publicists, who realize that what offends parents quite often pleases kids.

A second objection to rock 'n' roll has been its rhythm. The earliest critics didn't like it because they said it aroused savage passions and animal behavior, it was "jungle music," not fit to be listened to by civilized teenagers. In the mid-1950s there was horror at the idea that white children were coming under the influence not only of music with roots in Africa but of *black men* such as Chuck Berry and Little Richard.

Since then the arguments have become a little more superficially sophisticated, with the addition of "scientific evidence." Still, the criticisms betray fears that rock 'n' roll's "hypnotic" rhythms either open people up to subliminal communication (the idea being that rock 'n' roll singers are subverting their audience by planting messages) or cause them to become sexually aroused.

Bob Larson, in *The Day Music Died,* is quite specific about this second point. He suggests that low bass tones slow down the pulsation of cerebrospinal fluid, ultimately causing hormones to be released to the sex glands. "Because of the hormone secretion I have described," he writes, "the sex glands have an over-stimulation without a normal release. Not only is that the prelude to the release that will occur in the parked car after the dance, it is a direct cause of the bodily obscenities that occur on the dancefloor."

Other writers are convinced that certain rhythms put audiences into trance states in which they become open to demonic interference. Considerable interest has developed in the subject of "backward masking," the idea that subliminal backward messages are included on albums, messages that are picked up and stored by the subconscious mind.

Arguments such as these, which tend not to discriminate between a fourteen-year-old sitting in the front row of a Guns 'n' Roses concert snorting cocaine and a thirty-five-year-old listening to Van Morrison on a Sony Walkman, have little supportive evidence from ordinary concertgoers. The most significant factor governing crowd behavior tends not to be volume or the repetition of sound but the expectations brought to the event.

Forty years ago the now innocuous-sounding, "jumped-up" country and western swing of Bill Haley, transmitted through small speakers and with no accompanying light show, sent people into spasms. Today it would attract polite applause from the middle-aged and indifference from teenagers. What has changed is not the music but the social context. In 1955 children born during the war years and raised in austerity saw rock 'n' roll as a symbolic release from the power of their parents' generation. It wasn't the rhythms that caused the disturbing behavior as much as what those rhythms signified.

Jesus Rock

Yet arguments such as those of Larson and Blanchard kept Christians out of rock 'n' roll. When believers did take up the electric guitar (acoustic guitars were much more acceptable), it was to produce something called Jesus Rock, which failed to understand the tradition it was hoping to enter. Almost none of the musicians playing Jesus Rock, which developed at the end of the 1960s, had bothered to learn the language of rock 'n' roll. They weren't astute enough to take and subvert what was already there, but came in heavy-handedly hoping to "use" rock 'n' roll to "convey a Christian message."

Making the music secondary to the message created impotent rock 'n' roll. Nothing was allowed to grow out of the subconscious; there was no mystery; and every song had to be in some way about Jesus. It was as if these people didn't really want to make a contribution to the history of the music but to use it as a Trojan horse out of which they could leap while brandishing Bibles.

Jesus Rock had no effect on mainstream rock 'n' roll; it was produced by church-based musicians for church audiences. The Jesus Rock industry had its own "contemporary Christian" record labels, its own news magazines and its own concert circuit. In the aftermath of Woodstock, there were even Jesus festivals. But the average reader of *Rolling Stone* in America or *New Musical Express* in Britain would remain blissfully oblivious to the likes of Randy Matthews, Chuck Girard, Love Song, Sheep and the Resurrection Band.

Breaking a Taboo
The earliest examples of Jesus Rock had been stimulated by an awareness that the secular industry was now house-training Jesus. There had been two smash rock musicals, *Godspell* and *Jesus Christ Superstar,* which, not composed by believers, were reaching the same people who turned out for *Hair.* Norman Greenbaum had made the top ten with "Spirit in the Sky," which could have been sung to almost any deity but did mention having a "friend in Jesus." James Taylor, in "Fire and Rain," a song partly about the agonies of heroin addiction, begged Jesus to "look down" on him.

At the time these were significant moves in rock 'n' roll, because before then the name of Jesus Christ had been an absolute no-no in music intended for mainstream commercial success. When Paul Simon wrote the line "Jesus loves you more than you will know" in "Mrs. Robinson" (1968), his soundtrack song for the movie *The Graduate,* he was conscious that he was breaking a taboo, just as two years earlier the Beach Boys had broken the God taboo by releasing "God Only Knows" as a single.

"Nobody had said Jesus before," Simon later noted. "People thought it was a word you couldn't say in pop music. They wouldn't play it on the radio. . . . Now it's a word that's readily acceptable in popular music, but when we released 'Mrs. Robinson,' Columbia Records was keeping its fingers crossed."

Larry Norman

One of the few artists associated with Jesus Rock who did understand the redemptive theme was Larry Norman, a Californian musician who had started out in a San Francisco band called People. He had a real love for rock 'n' roll and was a great admirer of the Beatles, Rolling Stones and Bob Dylan. Although he played on the Christian circuit, he rarely played it as expected. Norman was considered moody and unpredictable, he didn't have the regulation born-again smile when he played, and he would shock interviewers by telling them that he wouldn't answer any "religious" questions—a tactic actually designed to get them talking about his songs, out of which would naturally flow discussion of religion.

He could write unashamed propaganda like "Why Don't You Look into Jesus?" and "Why Should the Devil Have All the Good Music?" (songs that predated Dylan's gospel songs by a good six years, but that employed the same approach) and then devote three albums to unfolding the story of redemption from the Fall *(So Long Ago the Garden)* through this life *(Only Visiting This Planet)* to paradise *(In Another Land)*. On these albums he was often as oblique about his faith in Christ as Pete Townshend was about his Baba beliefs on *Tommy*. He tried to work through the emotional truths of the Fall and redemption, rather than the doctrinal truths only. The songs of loss and brokenness on *So Long Ago the Garden* led his Christian constituency to believe rumors that he'd deserted the faith and was now living in a nudist colony on a Greek island. The fact that on the album cover he was portrayed as the naked Adam with the Lion of Christ emerging from his heart didn't help matters.

"There aren't enough clues in the songs," he said in his defense. "It's stuff that isn't understood immediately by Christians as being religious product. It doesn't fit into the categories that have been established over the past twenty years. This music makes more sense to a nonreligious disc jockey than it often does to a long-term Christian."

Bob Dylan

A small Bible study in Norman's Hollywood home grew into a church, the Vineyard Fellowship. One day in 1978 Bob Dylan came to this church in the company of a young black Christian woman by the name of Mary Alice Artes. She had recently rededicated her life to God and had asked two of the church's ministers, Larry Myers and Paul Esmond, to meet Dylan, who was at that time her boyfriend.

The outcome of that meeting was to shock and astound the rock 'n' roll community. Dylan began to accept, in his own words, "that Jesus was real and I wanted that. . . . One thing led to another . . . until I had this feeling, this vision and feeling. I truly had a born-again experience, if you want to call it that. It's an overused term, but it's something that people can relate to."

Once asked what *born again* meant, Dylan replied, "Born once is born with the spirit from below, which is when you're born. It's the spirit you're born with. Born again is born with the Spirit from above, which is a little bit different."

Following this experience he spent five days a week for three and a half months at the church's School of Discipleship, studying the life of Christ, principles of discipleship, spiritual growth and the Sermon on the Mount. The results of his brisk education showed up on *Slow Train Coming,* where every track was a gospel song, almost all of them clearly based on specific New Testament passages.

It was not the album that Bob Dylan fans had been waiting for. It was too definite and too accusatory. They preferred albums like *John Wesley Hardin* (1968), "the first biblical rock album," as Dylan had called it, where any number of interpretations could be placed on the songs. Hadn't Dylan himself once praised ambiguity by saying (in 1966), "Anybody can be specific and obvious. That's always been the easy way. . . . It's not that it's so difficult to be unspecific and less obvious. It's just that there's nothing, absolutely nothing, to be specific and obvious about"?

He'd been attracted to Zen Buddhism, which teaches that the truth lies beyond any attempt to categorize it. In songs like "Ballad of a Thin Man" and "Love Minus Zero" he had played Zen-like exercises. He admired the ideal woman who could speak "like silence," the one who "knows too much to argue or to judge," and he mocked the rational man "with his pencil in his hand" who would bother with such questions as "For what reason?"

Much of Dylan's appeal lay in such mystery. To writer Stephen Pickering he was a Jewish mystic in the Hasidic tradition. Allen Ginsberg, a Hindu later to become a Buddhist, when asked in 1965 whether Dylan had "sold out" by going electric, stated that he had only "sold out to God." Irwin Silber declared in *Sing Out* that *Highway 61 Revisited* showed Dylan's "essentially existentialist philosophy," while Steven Goldberg, writing in *Saturday Review,* said that "the mystical experience in which all separations fuse into the infinite unity . . . pervades all that Dylan has written since 1964."

Slow Train Coming couldn't be anything but Christian. There was no other interpretation, although some tried to convince themselves that Dylan was merely extending his longtime love of the Bible or that he was speaking of the need for rebirth in a general sense. Gone was the tantalizing poetry that allowed individual interpretation, and in its place was a series of commercials for the gospel of Jesus Christ.

This record and its follow-up, *Saved,* sounded impetuous. It was as if Dylan wanted to deliver the complete truth about the need to repent ("Change My Way of Thinking") and be saved in language that couldn't possibly be misunderstood because the return of Jesus Christ was so imminent.

Saved was an inferior record (with possibly two redeeming songs), packed with Christian clichés that would make even many young evangelicals wince. It was as though Dylan had simply set his Bible notes to a beat. At least in "I Believe in You" and "Precious Angel" you got a glimpse of how the artist felt; on songs like "Saved" and "Solid Rock" you felt as if he was simply dispensing information.

Rock critic Greil Marcus put it well when reviewing *Slow Train Coming* for *New West* magazine: "Throughout his career, Dylan has taken Biblical allegory as a second language; themes of spiritual exile and homecoming, and of personal and national salvation, have been central to his work. . . . What is new is Dylan's use of religious imagery, not to discover and shape a vision of what's at stake in the world, but to sell a pre-packed doctrine he's received from someone else."

Dylan's reason for doing it was understandable. He'd been converted, he had something to say, and he had an audience. He was overwhelmed by the new truths before they'd had time to sink from his head to his heart and work their way out into his life and actions. In concert, however, his audiences became restless. The clichés, true as they were, were recognized only as pieces of religious propaganda. They didn't engage listeners' imaginations in the way Dylan's earlier work had done.

The music critic for the *San Francisco Tribune* expressed the view of many fans when, after Dylan's first postconversion concerts at the Warfield Theatre (November 1979), he commented, "After half an hour the lyrics became repetitious. They didn't move me as his songs once did, maybe because in the past Dylan wrote about problems and situations, provided questions and let the listener figure it out. Now the answer in every song is the same one."

Dylan more or less admitted later that he'd tried to do it all in one shot. "I've made my statement and I don't think I could make it any

better than in some of those songs," he said. "Once I've said what I
need to say in a song, that's it. I didn't want to repeat myself." Asked
in 1983 whether he regretted anything from the *Slow Train Coming*
period, he answered, "I don't particularly regret telling people how to
get their souls saved. . . . Whoever was supposed to pick it up, picked
it up."

Critics were also irritated because for the first time Dylan was saying that judgment might well fall on them if they didn't repent. Before
he'd always pointed the accusatory finger at others, and they'd been
able to sit back and nod in pleased agreement. The redemption story
was fine for most people if it only mentioned the glory of the saved;
but Dylan now tackled the destiny of those who ignore or reject Jesus
Christ.

It was all perfectly orthodox Christianity, but of course "perfectly
orthodox Christianity," with its warning of impending hell for those
who neglect the offer of redemption, is always an offense to human
pride. There's no really polite way of stating the truth that if we die
exiled from God we spend eternity in that same condition. Too much
artistry would blunt the point. It's not a truth for public admiration.

Charles Shaar Murray, reviewing *Slow Train Coming* for *New Musical Express,* was typical in wanting to hear only of a God whose love
was stripped of holiness and justice, the old Uncle in the Sky who lets
you do anything as long as you don't make too much noise. "What
Dylan is preaching talks not of liberation but of punishment, and in
sour and elitist terms," he wrote. "If we aren't talking about a God of
love, then FORGET IT."

The shortcomings of *Slow Train Coming* and *Saved* began to be
ironed out by the time of *Shot of Love.* Here, while holding to the
same gospel message, Dylan was able to start looking at the world
with eyes opened by faith. He could include a song appreciating comic
Lenny Bruce's battle against hypocrisy in the 1950s and 1960s, even
though Bruce said many things offensive to Christians.

"Every Grain of Sand," the album's closing number, was a classic.

Here, at last, Dylan viewed his transformation without the compulsion to spell it out in words that any Sunday-school child would understand. He was now able to deal with his own sinfulness rather than exclusively pointing out the shortcomings of others.

> I gaze into the doorway of temptation's angry flame
> And every time I pass that way I always hear my name
> Then onward in my journey I come to understand
> That every hair is numbered like every grain of sand.

At that time (1981) Dylan explained what he was now trying to do.

> I just have to hope that in some way this music that I've always played is a healing kind of music. If it isn't I don't want to do it because there's enough so-called music out there which is sick music, made by sick people and played to sick people to further a whole world of sickness. If I can't do something that is telling people that whatever that sickness is—and we're all sick—you can be healed and set straight, I'd just as soon be on a boat or hiking through the woods.

Slow Train Coming, Saved and *Shot of Love* are now regarded as Dylan's "born-again trilogy," which raises the question whether he has maintained his belief in Christ as Savior. In the absence of an answer from the songwriter himself, it's fruitless to speculate. All that can be said is that later albums such as *Oh Mercy* and *Under the Red Sky* continued to acknowledge the existence of an all-knowing God, and that songs such as "Gotta Serve Somebody," "I Believe in You" and "In the Garden" still featured prominently in his stage set.

Dylan did clearly retreat from the hot gospeling song introductions of 1981, in which he warned of the end of the world, and he avoided being labeled "born-again" by interviewers. "Whatever label is put on you, the purpose is to limit your accessibility to people," he told *USA Today* in 1989. In the same interview he denied that the trilogy was "religious," saying that the songs were "based on my experience in daily matters, what you run up against and how you respond to things."

At first glance this seemed to be nonsense. How could he argue that songs about Jesus and the need to be saved, which sometimes quoted directly from the Bible, were not "religious"? Actually, however, Dylan appears to have been making the profound point that Jesus didn't come to start a religion but to enable people to know and glorify God in their everyday life. Dylan was writing observations not of religion but of his "experience in daily matters." It just so happened that Jesus had become a part of those matters. "Make something religious and people don't have to deal with it," he had observed in 1985. "They can say it's irrelevant."

For those looking for intimations of Dylan's coming conversion to Christianity, there were more than enough in *Renaldo and Clara,* his four-hour film based loosely on the 1976 Rolling Thunder Tour of America. In the graveyard where Jack Kerouac lies buried, Dylan and Allen Ginsberg are shown strolling, stopping at each of the stations of the cross. Ginsberg asks a young boy what God looks like. Does he play a guitar? Back on the bus, the musicians start singing gospel songs. Out the window a fundamentalist preacher stands on top of a van before a rival pulls him off.

After the tour several of the musicians, in unconnected circumstances, became Christians. Roger McGuinn had what he termed "a traumatic spiritual experience. The Holy Spirit brought me to a realization of my need for God and of the provision of Jesus." Arlo Guthrie, son of Dylan's original inspiration Woody Guthrie, became a Franciscan monk. David Mansfield, Steven Soles and T-Bone Burnett formed the Alpha Band, offering their first album "to the triune God."

T-Bone Burnett

"I have no idea what happened on that tour," says Burnett, who went on to produce Elvis Costello, Los Lobos and Counting Crows, among others, "but it is interesting that so many people either became Christians or went back to church by the time it ended." Burnett himself would eventually achieve the unique position of being a songwriting Christian who garnered great critical respect, with *Rolling Stone* reviewer Ken Tucker calling him in 1982 "the best singer-songwriter in the country right now." In the same review Tucker said, "With his folk roots and his insistence upon knowing right and wrong in all the important moments of his life, Burnett is making music that is the implicit opposite of nearly everything that weasels its way into the Top Ten these days. Yet there is no reason why he shouldn't be a star."

Burnett's approach to integrating his faith with his music was markedly different from Bob Dylan's in *Slow Train Coming* and *Saved*. He didn't see himself as an evangelist but as an artist given the responsibility primarily to write well-crafted songs drawn from his observations of human behavior. He drew inspiration not from Jesus Rock or even gospel music but from Catholic novelist Flannery O'Connor, Anglican poet T. S. Eliot and Catholic writer G. K. Chesterton.

He remembered that C. S. Lewis, the great Oxford don and Christian apologist, had once said, "I believe in God like I believe in the sun. Not just because I can see Him, but because by Him I can see everything else." Interviewed by the *L.A. Weekly* in 1980, Burnett commented, "If Jesus is the Light of the World, there are two kinds of songs you can write. You can write songs about the light, or you can write songs about what you can see from the light. That's what I try to do. I'm still looking."

His songs like "Madison Avenue," "House of Mirrors" and "Hefner and Disney" dealt with the power of illusion in the contemporary world. In order to face spiritual truth, people must first be stripped of their illusions. "Our battle is to bring down every deceptive fantasy and every imposing defense that men erect against the true knowledge of God," as Paul wrote in his second letter to the Corinthians (2 Corinthians 10:5 Phillips).

But Burnett was also aware of his own power of self-delusion.

I find it hard sometimes to say the way that I feel

I do the very things I hate to do

I act like a child and I'm afraid of what is real
And so I try to cover up the truth.
I stumble like a drunk along this crazy path I walk
I have a hundred thousand questions too
I'll go to any length to prove nothing is my fault
Then later on I will deny the proof. ("Shut It Tight")

In "Criminals" (1992) he admitted his own guilt:

He's capable of anything
Of any vicious act
This criminal is dangerous
The criminal under my own hat.

Some Christians believed he was forsaking his duty by raising more questions than answers, by talking about the "power of love" rather than naming God. Yet it was this questioning attitude plus the admission of his own struggle that has drawn hardened critics into his work. Wrote one: "Burnett's songs don't hammer home the name 'Jesus,' they just talk about the things that concern this man who happens to feel that humanity is in deep trouble of its own making."

For Burnett a bad piece of songwriting was never redeemed by a spiritually accurate lyric. As he explained to *Rolling Stone* in 1982, "A bricklayer's job is to build a good wall that will stand against the rain and wind. Writing JESUS on it isn't going to help it withstand the storms."

Bruce Cockburn

Other Christian musicians with a similar approach began to emerge during the 1980s—Maria McKee with Lone Justice, Mike Peters with the Alarm, Gordon Gano with Violent Femmes, Peter Garrett with Midnight Oil, Ricky Ross with Deacon Blue. In Britain the open-air Greenbelt Festival could attract twenty-five thousand people each year to lectures on social and spiritual issues alongside main-stage concerts with Christian performers such as Deniece Williams, the Clarke Sisters and Maria Muldaur. In 1981 U2 played an unannounced set, and six years later Bono returned as an onlooker, disguising himself as a crowd-control attendant.

Greenbelt particularly encouraged musicians who were able to integrate their spiritual convictions in their social observations. Such a one is Canadian songwriter Bruce Cockburn, who is known as much for his biting political commentary as for his Christian imagery. In the 1970s, with albums like *Circles in the Stream* and *Joy Will Find a Way,* he was regarded as a happy mystic; but in the 1980s, with *Stealing Fire* and *Big Circumstances,* he displayed an increasing concern with human rights and environmental issues.

This wasn't simply a change of tack; it was an application of his personal beliefs. Cockburn cared about the poor because God cared for the poor. He cared for the forests because God planted them. "My faith determines how I see things," he said. "So the way I write songs will be affected very much. But I don't see the music as a means of selling that faith. It doesn't feel right to me. Songs are an expression of things I feel and see, things that touch me. Therefore, my faith comes into it indirectly, determining my reaction to what I see and experience."

Johnny Cash

Prior to his 1994 album *American Recordings* Johnny Cash was regarded as a singer and songwriter who saved gospel music for special occasions (in 1973 he recorded a double album, *Gospel Road,* on the life of Christ) and made his living from singing about hard living and bad times. Now for the first time he brilliantly intertwined the two. Songs of betrayal, loneliness and wild living were neatly contrasted with songs of forgiveness and hope. All of them fully deserved their place on the album. The sinful resignation of Nick Lowe's "The Beast in Me" was made to lead to the penitence of Kris Kristofferson's "Why Me, Lord," and the thwarted aspirations of Leonard Cohen's "Bird on a Wire" were resolved in Tom Waits's "Down There by the Train." The cornerstone of the album was one of Cash's own songs, "Redemp-

tion," which unashamedly used biblical language to claim that true
spiritual freedom had its source in the crucifixion of Christ:

And the blood gave life to the branches of the tree
And the blood was the price that set the captives free
And the numbers that came through the fire and the flood
Clung to the tree and were redeemed by the blood.

Because of his legendary status Cash could be specific about the source
of forgiveness without losing the attention of the audience. He had
spent the best part of four decades trying to find salvation through
wild excess. Now, at the age of sixty-two, he could afford to preach
a little. "The theme of the album is sin and redemption," he declared
at the 1994 Glastonbury Festival. "Thank God for redemption. I
wouldn't be here without it."

Mysterious Ways

12

Once I thought that rock 'n' roll didn't have a place for spiritual concerns. But I've since discovered that a lot of the artists who have inspired me—Bob Dylan, Van Morrison, Patti Smith, Al Green and Marvin Gaye—were in a similar position. . . . That's why I'm more at ease.

Bono, U2

I think that art can be a light at the end of the tunnel, not just a mirror held up to society.

The Edge, U2

I'm still interested in the things of the spirit and God and the mind-boggling idea that he might be interested in us.

Bono, U2

*T*here were twitterings in the British music press when it was discovered that the Irish band U2, who had come riding in on the immediate postpunk wave with a reputation for aggression and passion, had three members who were Christians. There was nothing vague or wishy-washy about their Christianity, either. In fact, their shared faith was a key to understanding their music.

In his first newspaper interview (*Hot Press,* March 1979) Bono said that U2 was dealing with "spiritual questions, ones that few groups ever touch." For a *New Musical Express* "Consumer File" (June 1981) he placed the Bible at the top of his list of favorite books.

Rock journalists were puzzled. They loved the music but regarded Christianity as antithetical to the spirit of rock 'n' roll. They could tolerate most expressions of religion (although they privately derided mumbo-jumbo mysticism), but Christianity seemed to represent everything that rock 'n' roll had come to deliver them from. Black musicians were the only artists who could legitimately express Christian faith; gospel music, because it was a roots music and displayed physical passion, was actually admired.

The orthodox position of rock 'n' roll criticism was exemplified by Barry Miles in *New Musical Express* when reviewing After the Fire, a CBS band well-known at the time for its Christian commitment. "To me, rock 'n' roll is the music of rebellion and sexual liberation," he wrote. "It's music which cuts through hypocrisy and guilt, music which attacks patriarchy and authoritarianism, and as such constitutes a direct attack on what I think of as traditional Christian values."

The Bible and Rock 'n' Roll

Bono (Paul Hewson), the Edge (Dave Evans), Larry Mullen and Adam Clayton met as teenagers at Mount Temple, a progressive secondary school in Dublin. During their time there, largely through the efforts of a particularly good religious-education teacher, three of the boys (Edge, Bono and Mullen) became interested in Christianity— interested enough to visit a charismatic house-group known as Shalom, and later to announce themselves as believing Christians.

In a country saturated with "religion," where the young often blame the official church for not moving with the times, it was unusual in the mid-1970s for three youngsters to be turned on by both the Sex Pistols and the Holy Bible. Their peers would have advised them to be wary of groups of charismatic Christians, and charismatic Christians would have warned them off punk rock. Rock journalists would have told them not to contemplate fusing the anger of Johnny Rotten with the compassion of Jesus Christ. But U2 ignored all these pressures.

Christian faith clarified U2's vision. They viewed the Bible not as an archaic, outmoded rule book but as an exciting and socially relevant document. Bono saw David's psalms as early versions of the blues. The Edge quoted passages of Jeremiah and Isaiah at band meetings. The Jesus who emerged from the pages of the New Testament was more of a street person than a pillar of society, and they could relate to both his compassion and his anger.

"Jesus Christ has been given the image of a weakling, a sort of 'Sunday' image, a 'religious' image," complained Bono in the days just before the band began to become well known. "This is not the case. Christ came to 'bring a sword,' not flowers." The Christ they'd come to believe in not only washed the feet of his followers but also overturned the tables of his enemies. What was missing, in their opinion, was a well-rounded portrayal. Why was "Christian music" inevitably a label for anemic, unchallenging sounds?

For young people in the British Isles, prior to the Bob Dylan of *Slow Train Coming* there was only one notable precedent for a Christian in pop or rock, and that was Cliff Richard, who had announced his conversion in 1966 during a Billy Graham rally in London. Richard, who had virtually abandoned rock 'n' roll in the late 1950s for a broader, safer style of pop, was not a songwriter, didn't see his music as a means of self-exploration and was by nature a comfortable, "nice" person. (An earlier rock 'n' roll convert, Terry Dene, England's "answer to Elvis" in 1957, had given it all up to become a traveling evangelist.)

Although he was never frightened of expressing unpopular opinions and suffered ceaseless personal ridicule for his faith, Cliff Richard was never combative in performance. Whatever anger and frustrations he felt, they were not fuel for his music. There was nothing restless or urgent in the Cliff Richard experience. There were no abrasive edges.

His musical career was neatly divided between the gospel songs he performed for charity and the inoffensively pleasant pop he produced for money. He did not provide a useful role model for the likes of U2.

U2 began to dream of a rock 'n' roll that would blend the indignation of punk with the loving idealism of the hippie era. They were as inspired by John Lennon and Jimi Hendrix (whose music they'd heard from big brothers) as they were by Patti Smith and the Sex Pistols. In 1981 Bono said,

> The Sex Pistols' first single, "Anarchy in the UK," shocked the whole world. It changed a lot of things in music. What the music meant to us was a return to what I thought rock 'n' roll was supposed to be, which was aggressive, loud and glorious.
>
> I'd like to think that U2 is aggressive, loud and emotional. I think that's good. I think that the people who I see parallels with are people like John the Baptist or Jeremiah. They were very loud, quite aggressive, yet gloryful. And I believe they had an answer and a hope. In that sense I think we have a love and an emotion without the flowers in our hair, and we have an aggression without the safety pins in our noses.

Shiny Moments

This blend of loving hippyism and punkish belligerence characterized the first important stage in U2's career, which lasted from *Boy* to *Rattle and Hum,* bringing them fans with roots in both subcultures. They would wave the white flag and the aerosol spray can with equal dexterity, winning the respect of Joan Baez and Bob Dylan as well as Lou Reed and Iggy Pop.

They had perceived that beneath the froth of rock 'n' roll's "teenage rebellion" and knee-jerk antiauthoritarianism there was a desire for what Bono would later call "the shiny moments"—for personal transcendence and social renewal. Rock 'n' roll railed against the mediocrity that shackles the human spirit, and this gave it an exhilarating kick of energy; but too often the kick itself had to make do as the solution. Rock 'n' roll was the only answer.

Bono had felt the same frustrations but had been able to satisfy them spiritually. Speaking in March 1982, he said,

> I felt that I just couldn't put up with that cycle of things where you just grow up, get a job, get married and die. Maybe this is where Christ comes in, as far as my life is concerned. Because I can't believe we just appeared here out of gas. I can't believe that, and maybe that's where my spiritual nature comes from, that fight. From wanting to break out of that type of conventionalism.

The traditional conversion of a rock star comes when he or she is at the end of a rope, usually when the gods of fame, sex and money have been tried and found wanting. What was different about U2 was that it had come from an adolescent search for meaning, the same search that provides rock 'n' roll with its most enduring moments. This was why the group found it relatively easy to incorporate their beliefs in their music.

They began with a conviction that they should not tailor their material for secular expectations, despite the occasional advice to cool the fervor. In 1983 Bono admitted,

> A few people pressed the panic button, but I was determined. John Lennon—there was a man who, however unfashionable, however uncontemporary his beliefs were, because they were his beliefs, he exposed himself. He was saying, well this is it, what do you want— no music or the truth? Because if I lie, the music will choke on itself. That's the choice. And I was going through that on *October*—what is the choice, write about Johnny and Mary or what?

A Poetry of Repentance

October, U2's second album, released in 1981, established the group's early approach toward matters of faith. This was not to be gospel music, but music that consistently acknowledged the spiritual dimension. It would have been easy to trot out theologically correct quotes and lyrics, but the members were aware that the impact of U2 was not in word alone and needed to last for a whole career. Personal behavior, business ethics, social concern, packaging and performance all had to communicate the same message.

The opening track, "Gloria," was a song of submission that reflected the group's interest in Watchman Nee, a Chinese preacher whose three-volume work *The Spiritual Man* (1927) stressed the need for the individual "self" to die in order for Christ to live. With a lyric composed in the vocal booth, Bono had drawn on his memory of Gregorian chant to produce what in effect was a spontaneous prayer, pleading with God to show him how to use his life:

Oh Lord, if I have anything

Anything at all

I give it to you.

At the time the three Christians in the band were undergoing a crisis of conscience, wondering how to reconcile the demands of Jesus with the demands of potential rock 'n' roll stardom. Remembers Bono:

Watchman Nee's idea was "Unless a seed shall die and be crushed in the earth it cannot bear fruit," whereas rock 'n' roll had the idea: "Look at me!" "Outta my way," "Look out for number one!" "I can't get no satisfaction!" Watchman Nee's attitude to that would be "So what? What's so important about you anyway?"

They resolved the issue through believing that a life in rock 'n' roll, far from being a compromise, was exactly where God wanted them to be. "We let the Lord guide our music," the Edge told a gathering of Christian musicians in 1981. "We let him guide how we dress, the lyrics—everything. All our decisions go through the Lord. . . . Our most useful position will be at the top of our field. If we can get ourselves into a position of usefulness to the Lord, I think that's where he wants us."

Their approach during this period was to avoid detailed discussions of their faith in the press for fear of being misquoted; instead they relied on implications in the songs. "What I have to say is so important that I'd only trust a song or personal conversation," Bono said. "I wouldn't trust print. I think people would get a misinterpretation." Mention of the need for personal change was the closest they got to preaching, and often this was directed to themselves. In "Sunday Bloody Sunday" on their 1983 album *War,* they discussed Ireland's problems in terms of the "trenches dug within our hearts." In "Like a Song" they said, "A new heart is what I need."

"Rebellion has to start within you," explained Bono in one interview. Speaking in March 1982 on a U.S. tour promoting *October,* he added, "There are too many people pointing the finger, saying that what you need to do is this. All the great writers that I respond to, be they in the Bible or otherwise, are people who said 'we,' as in '*we* need to get down on our knees. *We* need to turn about. *We* are going wrong.' "

Most often—in songs like "Fire," "With a Shout" and "Stranger in a Strange Land"—they maintained a spiritual feel but avoided specific advice. "New Year's Day," reportedly written about the Solidarity movement in Poland, contained what appeared to be references to the Second Coming of Christ—"the chosen few" and the "blood-red sky" drawn from passages in Matthew and Revelation. "Sunday Bloody Sunday" was quite specific in calling the resurrection "the victory Jesus won / on a Sunday bloody Sunday."

U2's most undeniably Christian song, "I Still Haven't Found What I'm Looking For," contained the seeds of their future preoccupation with uncertainty. With its biblically derived images of broken bonds and loosed chains, it went about as far as it is possible to go in a rock 'n' roll song to detail the extent of Christian salvation. Yet by admitting that he hadn't immediately been swept into the Celestial City, Bono avoided triumphalism. "People expect you, as a believer, to have all the answers, when really all you have is a whole new set of questions," he explained. "I think that if 'I Still Haven't Found What I'm Looking For' is successful, it's because it's not affirmative in the ordinary way of a gospel song. It's restless, yet there's a pure joy in it somewhere."

A New Irreverence

During the early 1990s the fervent evangelical vision that U2 had shared a decade before was less obvious, leading some to believe that they'd given up, that those who had warned them about the downward pull of rock 'n' roll had been right. U2 often seemed frivolous in interviews, used obscenities with more relish than even the Rolling Stones at the height of their decadence, appeared drunk in front of reporters and issued free "Zooropa" condoms at their concerts. This was in contrast to the Bono of 1981, who had said, "Compromise makes you useless. If you compromise, you're just like any other band."

At times when interviewed Bono appeared to be creating his own theology without respect for the previous two thousand years of Christian history. He suggested, for instance, that being led by the Holy Spirit is a form of anarchy, that catechisms are not useful guides to the spiritual life and that organized religion is "the enemy of God." In the Zooropa concerts he dressed as the devil and said that the pope and the archbishop of Canterbury (the evangelical George Carey) were "doing his work." To a journalist from *Mother Jones* who asked whether he liked being intoxicated, he replied, "It's better to be drunk of the Spirit—however, a bottle of Jack Daniel's is sometimes handier."

All of this fostered the impression that the group members had become embarrassed about their Christian connections and were now keen to show that they could be as unspiritual as anyone else in the rock 'n' roll business. After being told by *Mother Jones* that U2 had a 'chaste image', they began talking and singing a lot more about sex, featuring a full frontal nude photo of bassist Adam Clayton on their next album cover and dressing in drag for a photo shoot. During an interview with *The Face* in April 1992, Bono stripped naked in a London restaurant, earning himself a cover story titled "Saint Bono Unfrocked."

Christians who had been overjoyed that a band powered by Christian conviction was competing in the higher echelons of rock were naturally dismayed. They felt let down and hurt; they felt that having gained the ears of millions, U2 was squandering its opportunity. "U2 are not just a rock band for many Christians but the embodiment of an ideal," wrote Dave Roberts in the British magazine *Alpha.*

> They were the band that proved that you could take radical Christianity into the heart of contemporary culture and perhaps begin to transform it, creating a culture that began to rediscover faith. U2 in our eyes were sowing seeds that others would reap. For those who had ears to hear, there were messages of faith in their early lyrics which drew heavily from the biblical imagery of Isaiah and the Psalms. For some, however, our idealism is beginning to wane as we see the band being seduced by the world they set out to prophetically transform.

And it wasn't only Christians who expressed disappointment. After seeing the band on tour in America during 1992, *Melody Maker* observed, "They've given up on sermons and diatribes, allowing the kids to find the 'truth' by following their hearts (and Bono's lyrics) down the path to wisdom and enlightenment." A year later a review of the album *Zooropa* in the same paper commented, "The erstwhile Dublin urchin that stared God in the face and bawled, 'If you walk away / I will follow' is found muttering 'I have no compass / And I have no map . . . And I have no religion,' rendered virtually inaudible by Brian Eno's desolate, inhumane keyboards. The man that once had so many answers now sounds simply confused."

Reinventing U2

According to group members, none of this was the result of spiritual confusion, but simply a different approach to the problems that had bothered them around the time of *October.* They now felt that rather than trying precariously to negotiate their way through the thorny moral problems of being Christian believers in the often fleshly world of rock 'n' roll, they had to embrace the contradictions. "In the eye of the contradiction, that's the place to be," said Bono, paraphrasing American writer/actor Sam Shepard.

They had also decided to reinvent U2 because they thought *The Joshua Tree* image of four serious young men in an arid desert with the weight of the world on their shoulders was a limiting one and revealed only one aspect of their concerns. In 1992, shortly after the release of the bleak-sounding album *Achtung Baby,* Bono said,

> No matter how much we strip away the mythology, the spirit of U2 remains constant. Hopefully what's happened is that our audience don't expect so much from us as people, but they still expect an awful lot from the music. That suits me fine. I never wanted to be seen as a righteous person. I've found that there is a great freedom when you have your feet in two so-called mutually exclusive worlds—the world of irony and the world of soul, the world of flesh and the world of the spirit, the world of surface and the world of depth. That's where most people live. That's where U2 live.

The intention with *Achtung Baby* was to take an unflinching look at the dark side of human relationships, an area U2 had previously ignored as they unswervingly promoted light and hope. "You've got to start with your own hypocrisy before you start pointing it out in others," Bono explained. "The same person who is capable of high ideas is also capable of base acts."

For those who cared to look deeply enough there was the same spiritual backbone as there had been in the earlier work, but this time it was like reading a dark passage from the book of Job or a particularly distraught psalm rather than an uplifting promise from the Gospels. In "Until the End of the World" Judas was overheard addressing the resurrected Jesus, "The Fly" appeared to be about the fall of Lucifer from heaven, and "Acrobat" touched on Bono's feelings of alienation from the established church.

"Mysterious Ways," on one level a love song, was a reference to the workings of the Holy Spirit in the words of the eighteenth-century British poet William Cowper, who wrote, "God moves in a mysterious way / His wonders to perform." Bono sang, "If you want to kiss the sky / Better learn how to kneel," suggesting that if you want a truly transcendent life you shouldn't bother swallowing chemicals à la Jimi Hendrix (" 'Scuse me while I kiss the sky"—"Purple Haze"); instead you should start talking to God. This was pretty potent stuff.

A lot of the confusion over *Achtung Baby* was to do with the context. The high-soaring sound of *The Joshua Tree* had been replaced by something hard and industrial, the almost Quaker-style clothes had given way to glam, and there was an air of carnival about the new stage show, which featured banks of flashing TV screens, costume changes, dancing girls and flashed aphorisms such as "Everything you know is false." As Bono had warned, "I found in amongst the trash to be a great place to develop my loftier ideas, and a great disguise as well."

Zooropa, released in 1993, continued the exploration of doubt and darkness but focused more on the media's role in inoculating us against truth. The title song was packed with advertising clichés; "Babyface" was about someone whose life is controlled by video imagery, and "Numb" dealt with sensory overload. When playing the tapes to a journalist from Dublin's *Hot Press* magazine, Bono asked whether he'd read Ecclesiastes—the Old Testament book that details the futility of godlessness. The question was posed with a smirk, but it obviously contained the key to the album. Yes, these songs were bleak, but wasn't that what a life of unadulterated materialism was like if you took away the disguise?

The track that offered a crack of light was "The Wanderer," which, appropriately, the group had Johnny Cash sing for them. "The song is definitely the antidote to the Zooropa manifesto of uncertainty," said Bono. "Even if the album begins with 'I don't have a compass / I don't have a map,' this track gives one possible solution."

From Answers to Questions
One reason for the apparent unevenness of U2's spiritual life is the

very public way they've had to grow up. If they stumble, it makes the gossip columns. If they talk nonsense, it's fixed in print for the rest of their lives and beyond. The lyrics of U2 tell the story of Bono's interior life, his struggles as well as his victories, his doubts as well as his certainties.

Another reason is the length of time they've spent outside the church. Since leaving the Shalom group in the early 1980s, they have been without a spiritual base and have therefore been deprived of systematic Bible teaching, discipline, fellowship, Communion and worship. This has led to do-it-yourself theology that has gone unchallenged. It has also meant that they no longer see themselves as part of the whole community of Christians, young and old, black and white, fashionable and unfashionable, rich and poor, but as part of an elite who no longer need to follow the New Testament pattern of church life. Bono has claimed that "living by the Spirit" means "this is my life and it's between me and God and no one else"—an outlook that ignores the corporate dimension and leads to what has been called "Lone Ranger Christianity."

What has made U2's career interesting is that they started with answers and much later moved toward questions. It's an irony that hasn't escaped Bono. "Van Morrison started out singing about girls and ended up singing about God," he told *The Sunday Times* in 1992. "With us, I guess it's been the other way round."

Like a Prayer

13

I'm saying that sexuality and spirituality can coexist.
Madonna

When I'm kinky I'm very kinky. When I'm spiritual I'm very spiritual. Like I told you, I'm very schizoid.
Marvin Gaye

I feel so very close to the Lord when I'm that aroused. Never closer.
Prince

A split between the pleasures of the flesh and the pleasures of the spirit was fundamental to the culture of the American South when rock 'n' roll was first recorded. Almost all of the music's originators believed that human love and affection had no place in spiritual music, just as religious devotion had no place in secular music. They could use the performing techniques and the tunes of gospel for show-business ends, but they couldn't use the theological content. There was a firm dividing wall between the sacred and the secular.

The Gnostics of the first century had taught that the body is evil and an impediment to the soul. The aim of an enlightened spiritual person, they said, is to transcend bodily appetites. This teaching was to pollute Christianity over the centuries, manifesting itself both in Protestant "holiness" cults and in the Roman Catholic emphasis on virginity and celibacy as prerequisites for the highest spiritual calling.

Rock 'n' roll was partly a reaction to this kind of split, growing up as it did in the Bible Belt of America under the nurture of young men from strict fundamentalist backgrounds. Gospel was a physical music, but hollerin', dancing and shaking were supposed to be indications of a passion for the divine. It may often have been an expression of sublimated sexuality, but it had to at least look like devotional abandon.

With rock 'n' roll there was no need to pretend. This was music for the body, and the lyrics reflected that. They were about running, dancing, driving, racing, kissing, touching, hugging, loving—everything that gospel music ignored in its pursuit of otherworldly realms.

Many musicians from church backgrounds were sexually confused: so many physical activities were considered taboo that it appeared God had made a mistake by housing their souls in flesh. The choice seemed to be denying the body and being saved or satisfying the body and being damned.

Black writer Eldridge Cleaver saw rock 'n' roll as the means of reuniting the white person's body and mind. Watching white people learning to do the twist in the early 1960s, he observed,

They came from every level of society, from top to bottom, writhing pitifully though gamely about the floor, feeling exhilarating and soothing new sensations, release from some unknown prison in which their bodies had been encased, a sense of freedom they had never known before, a feeling of communion with some mystical root-source of life and vigor, from which sprang a new awareness and enjoyment of the flesh, a new appreciation of the possibilities of their bodies.

Early rock 'n' roll may have united body and mind, but it didn't pay much attention to the spirit. The physical appetites it so naturally celebrated were not subject to any spiritual claims, and one of the results was that rock 'n' roll became a synonym for the life of wretched excess. To live "the rock 'n' roll life" was to push everything to the limit—to "live fast, die young and leave a good-looking corpse," as the popular saying went.

Sinful and Sacred

The issue of sex and religion in rock 'n' roll has became more confusing in the 1980s and 1990s as some performers tried to unite not just secular and sacred, but sinful and sacred. It was one thing to want to see legitimate sexual activity divinely blessed, but quite another to want to mix immorality with spirituality, or to suggest that sin can lead to salvation. What provoked the trend of parading sex toys alongside religious icons, of combining the lewd with the devotional in public performances?

In the drive for holistic lifestyles, people were less inclined to compartmentalize their needs. Religious yearnings and sexual needs were both seen as valid, and few could see any reason that spirituality couldn't be sexy and sexuality couldn't be spiritual.

It was significant that those in the forefront of the new spiritual sexuality in rock 'n' roll grew up in strict churchgoing homes and claimed that they weren't given good models for reconciling sex with religion. Tori Amos, the daughter of a Methodist minister, said that she turned to music because she was always made to feel guilty about passion. "The way I was reared," she said, "the role model for women was the Virgin Mary, the sexless thing." Her songs became a way she could freely express herself, and not surprisingly, issues of religion, sex and guilt emerged in her lyrics.

Madonna

Madonna, who as Madonna Ciccone was raised by devout Catholic parents in Bay City, Michigan, where she was later educated by nuns, used her inner conflicts about sex and religion as the raw material of her work. By acting out the forbidden in the context of the sacred, she believed she was purging herself of guilt feelings. For Madonna, redemption from sin meant redemption from the notion of sin.

"I guess I'm trying to cast off those feelings of shame and sin through my work," she once admitted.

As I discover it myself, so I communicate it to everybody else. My problem with the Catholic Church is that it has always separated sexuality and spirituality. The two are not allowed to coexist. I think they're both a part of humanity, a part of the human essence. A person can be spiritual, can be religious, can be sensual and can be sexual.

I think all of those things make up a human being, but in organized religion they're always trying to separate it. You're made to feel bad if you have sexual feelings, but that's a part of life. I think that making love to a person can be a spiritual experience, a religious experience.

Madonna has long since given up the practice of the faith she was raised in, but she retains her belief in the existence of God and the practice of prayer. Before each concert she and her musicians link hands while she prays to "the Lord" for their needs, and she says she still believes in heaven. "I believe in everything," she told *Rolling Stone* in 1991. "That's what Catholicism teaches you."

Yet she is in "rebellion against the Church and against the laws decreed by my father, which were dictated through the Church." Her way of expressing that rebellion has been to juxtapose sex to religion, appearing half-naked with a crucifix around her neck or straddling an altar while making suggestive gestures with an incense burner on her 1990 tour.

Her most controversial track in this respect was "Like a Prayer," in which sexual ecstasy was described in religious terms. Hearing a lover call her name was like hearing the words of a prayer or the sigh of an angel; orgasm was like an ecstasy that lifted her into the realms of mystery. The choir of gospel singer Andrae Crouch was used to create the church feeling as the couple in the song reached their climax.

All this might have passed without much comment if Madonna

hadn't produced a promotional video where she was seen in a church making love to an animated statue of a Catholic saint while surrounded by burning crosses. It was enough to earn her a Vatican rebuke, and when she toured Italy with her Blond Ambition tour she was forced to cancel two concerts after pressure from the Catholic Church.

"If you are sure I am a sinner, let whoever is without sin cast the first stone," she announced on her arrival in Rome. "I ask you, fair-minded men and women of the Catholic Church—come and see my show and judge it for yourselves. My show is not a conventional rock concert, but a theatrical presentation of my music, and like the theater it poses questions, provokes thought and takes you on an emotional journey."

Actually she enjoyed this sort of response to her work, because it showed that she was hitting where it hurt. She held the Catholic Church responsible for her guilt over her promiscuous sex life, and this was her revenge. If it was effective, she thought, it might play its small part in getting the Vatican eventually to rethink its sexual doctrines, but the more immediate gratification would be that it helped to still the voice of her conscience. The more brazen she became in breaking the rules, the less guilt she would feel about breaking them.

She later explained to *The Sunday Times* that the video was a metaphor, showing that sexuality and spirituality should be brought together. "Making love to a saint you can empassion yourself, you can have love, you can believe in God and be a highly sexual being," she said. "The crosses on fire were symbols of so many things from racism and the Ku Klux Klan to my own rage about religion and Catholicism and the negative connotations I believe it has."

Marvin Gaye

The archetypal artist of sex and religion was Marvin Gaye, son of a Pentecostal preacher, who was taught that sex was for procreation only and who heard his parents refer to intercourse as "the nasty." He was left with feelings of repression that turned him first into an awkward and shy teenager and then into a singer who was constantly trying to make sense of his twin passions—Jesus and sex.

Gaye's method was to dignify his sexual appetite by giving it a religious veneer. His 1973 album *Let's Get It On* was a brave attempt to justify an extramarital affair. "I can't see anything wrong with sex between consenting adults," he wrote in the liner notes; "I think we make far too much of it." In the title song, which he cowrote with Ed Townsend, he begged his lover to overcome any feelings of reticence and flavored his come-ons with gospel language.

You don't have to worry that it's wrong

If the spirit moves you—let me groove you

Let your love come down

Get it on! Do you know I mean it?

I've been sanctified.

His ideal state was one in which unbridled lust could coexist with deep religious conviction. In his personal life he would flip from the pages of pornographic magazines to his copy of the Bible, from the company of prostitutes to the company of preachers.

Gaye's torment was his inability to find peace in this way. Beneath his protestations—"I don't believe in overly moralistic philosophies"—it was obvious that he had failed to convince even himself. In the last year of his life he recorded the track "Sanctified Lady," in which he asked for a woman "who loves Jesus" so that he could "make love all night long." Commented Gaye's biographer, David Ritz, "It was Marvin's attempt to merge the profane with the profound, to integrate his two strongest sources of emotional enthusiasm—God and sex. He knew it was the only way he could ever be happy."

Gaye came to believe he was schizoid—that there was a good Marvin who wanted to serve God and a bad Marvin who was concerned only with self-gratification. He still referred to his pop songs as "dirty" songs, thinking it demeaning that his talent had to be used to stir base emotions, yet he had no assurance of salvation.

Asked by Gavin Martin of *New Musical Express* in 1982 whether he was a Christian, Gaye answered,

> The definition of a Christian is someone who believes in Jesus Christ. An even more accurate definition of a Christian is a person who is a follower of Christ and that entails doing the things that Christ did. So I'd have to think whether I do the things that Christ did and I'd come up pretty good on that score. I'd make a fair score, but it wouldn't be too high. I still consider myself a Christian because I believe in and love Jesus Christ. I'm not an awfully evolved Christian at this point. But we're working on it.

His final hit single was "Sexual Healing," a recognition that he was torn between the repressions of his childhood, his sense of divine calling and the fantasies of the Playboy culture. A year later, after a ferocious domestic argument, he was shot dead by his father in Los Angeles. "I'm torn between many passions, desires and loves," he once admitted. "I'm sad because I know the bottom line, I know what is going to happen to this world."

Prince

Sex has become the religion of our secular age. Sexual images dominate the films, novels, advertisements and songs of the late twentieth century just as religious icons pervaded the art of the Middle Ages. Sexual fulfillment has become as important to us as the eternal safety of the soul was to past ages.

Sex is no longer seen exclusively as an expression of love, but as a means of self-discovery. Through multiple partners you find your true self. In an age starved of true spiritual experience, the loss of ego experienced during a sexual climax is the closest many people get to a feeling of transcendence. As Malcolm Muggeridge once commented, "Sex is the only mysticism materialism offers."

It is as a mystical experience that Prince regards sex. Born in Minneapolis and raised in a Seventh-day Adventist church, he looks for a sexual experience that isn't just OK with God but actually brings him closer to God. He sees the orgasm as an explosion that temporarily blows open the gates of heaven. "I feel so very close to God when I'm that aroused," he once said. "Never closer. Sexual passion and the Good Lord are as high as you can possibly get."

Prince has perplexed audiences with his combination of sexual explicitness (songs about fornication, voyeurism and incest) and religious fervor. He could be as dirty as a pornographer and as evangelistic as a preacher, all in the same show. On one tour he had his audience chanting "God is love," and in his song "The Cross" he pleaded with his listeners not to "die without knowing the cross."

The Christian beliefs that Prince has expressed in interviews—heaven, hell, the devil, the importance of the crucifixion, the fact of Christ's return—appear surprisingly orthodox. What no one seems able to determine, mainly because of his refusal to subject himself to media scrutiny, is how serious he is about it all. "Prince worships two gods," his former bodyguard Chick Huntsbury once said. "He worships religion and sex. He's just a little confused over which one he likes the best." One of his backing singers described him as someone who "likes talking a lot about God, but who sure doesn't lead a very godly life."

It was with the *LoveSexy* album in 1988 that he fused what had previously been two unrelated elements in his work. *LoveSexy,* he tried to convince his audience, was a higher form of sex. It was "the feeling you get when you fall in love, not with a girl or boy, but with the heavens above." In "Glam Slam" he said that what he had "seems to transcend the physical."

What music critic Nelson George has called Prince's "sex as salvation" was most clearly stated in "Anna Stesia," a typical Prince love song ("ravish me / liberate my mind") that suddenly lurches into a verse of penitence ("save me Jesus, I've been a fool") and ends with an appeal for everyone to love God ("girls and boys, love God above"). Through being ravished by Anna Stesia, he has been brought "closer to my higher self / closer to heaven / closer to God."

Of Analogies and Realities

There are obvious parallels between sexual intercourse and spiritual fulfillment. Characteristics of love, devotion, trust, self-disclosure, abandonment and absorption into another are present in both. All religions have used the image of the lover and the beloved to illustrate the union of humankind with the divine.

Depeche Mode explored the analogy in its 1993 album *Songs of Faith and Devotion.* The lyrics were written in the style of contemporary gospel, with references to heaven, angels, mercy, faith, blessings, prayer and sin, but the subject was a sexual relationship that took the writer "home / to glory's throne / by and by" ("I Feel You"). In "One Caress" he claims, "Just one caress from you / And I'm blessed." "Higher Love" rhapsodizes,

I surrender all control

To the desire that consumes me whole

And leads me by the hand to infinity

That lies in wait at the heart of me.

On the album's cover the four members of the group stare somberly out of a black background. In two of the inner photographs they are shown outside a strip club with crude paintings of half-naked women on the walls.

The metaphysical poets, in particular John Donne, explored the sensual dimensions of knowing God in vigorous and sometimes bawdy language. Yet there is a great difference between recognizing analogies between intercourse and spiritual surrender and suggesting that orgasm can actually become a form of spiritual surrender.

This latter teaching was present in ancient Babylon, where male followers of the goddess Ishtar were encouraged to visit sacred prostitutes. The prostitutes, according to Reay Tannahill in her study *Sex in History* (1981), "acted as congenial intermediaries between worshipper and deity." Tantric forms of Hinduism and Buddhism also taught that ritual sex, preferably with a stranger, could bring about bliss and release, because sexual excitement indicated the presence of divine energy. Tannahill says, "It offered a glimpse of the one-ness that might be achieved between the individual soul and the World Soul."

Again, there is a great difference between reclaiming sexuality as a God-given aspect of our humanness and declaring that all sexual impulses are good and worthy of being obeyed.

Madonna has declared that her work is dedicated to the eradication of shame. In particular, she means the shame that came from measuring her life against the Roman Catholic Church's teachings on sexual behavior. "Sexual repression is responsible for a lot of bad behavior," she said. "I'm saying, don't be afraid. It's OK to have this thought and that feeling."

Yet the solution to sexual repression is not to destroy shame. Reticence, modesty and self-control are essential to civilized relations between the sexes. Finding the solution involves canceling real, deserved shame and then dealing with false guilt. In the absence of a God who both judges and forgives, it's impossible to experience the former. In the absence of commonly accepted divine laws, it's impossible to accurately diagnose the latter.

Countdown to Armageddon

14

My heroes? Qadafy, Messenger Elijah, Muhammad, Jesus.
Professor Griff, Public Enemy

The program of the Nation of Islam is the best program for black people to survive within the structures of the United States.
Chuck D, Public Enemy

We're not hippies. We're the brothers from another planet. Outer space, inner consciousness. Me, myself and I.
De La Soul

*N*WA (Niggas With Attitude), with its rappers Dr. Dre, Ice Cube and Eazy-E, purveyed what has become known as "gangsta rap," a rap that detailed ghetto life in ghetto language. Drugs, prostitution, shootouts, one-parent families—this was simply the way things were. They weren't offering a solution.

The most incendiary track of their 1989 debut album *Straight Outta Compton,* whose lyrics contained over two hundred variations of the F-word, was "F— Tha Police." NWA was accused of police baiting and inciting violence. Later that year two fans were stabbed at an NWA concert, and another concert was stopped after fans stormed the stage. The following year, promoters of NWA's American tour forced the members to sign a contract promising that they wouldn't perform the song. This agreement was honored until the final night of their appearance in Detroit, when the police stepped in.

When accused of promoting violence and misogyny, NWA's defense was that they were simply reflecting ghetto life. In 1989 Ice Cube said,

I feel like this: If I'm a kid, I'm getting chastised by my parents, by teachers, by people in the community, authorities, grandmothers. When the kids go out to party, they're sick of getting told what to do. They're sick of having people go down their throats, telling them how to act. So we don't do that. There's no "kids, go do your homework, don't do drugs," We aren't all about that. Kids are smart enough to know what's wrong, so when they party to NWA, they won't hear "don't do this and don't do that," they just hear the stuff they see every day.

A Poverty of Hope

Within a few years gangsta rap had become the predominant form of rap, with acts such as Ice T, Dre, Gravediggaz and the multimillion-selling Snoop Doggy Dogg. These performers aren't writing as social observers; Ice T was once a member of the notorious Crips street gang in Los Angeles, and Snoop Doggy Dogg was arrested in December 1993 and charged with being an accessory to a murder. Both men have had close friends killed in shootouts and stabbings.

Not all rappers yearn for gun muzzles and submissive sexual partners, but there is agreement on the nature of the problem they're dealing with. Rap is ghetto music, and most of its creators are black Americans from inner-city areas marked by a poverty of hope. Previous generations were able to endure hardship because of a conviction that things would one day improve and their children would inherit a better quality of life. Such expectations no longer exist, and ghetto dwellers feel trapped—physically, socially and economically.

Often the most obvious means of escape for young people are gangs that provide a sense of adventure and confer status on their members.

Through robberies members can improve their lifestyle, and through violence they wipe out enemies and so effect social change. Drugs such as crack provide a momentary illusion of freedom.

Because their yearnings are legitimate and because many young American blacks have no hope of ever satisfying these yearnings through legitimate means, few rappers are willing to condemn the gangsterism. They prefer to condemn the conditions that brought it about. This is why rappers says that criticisms of rap's obscenity, violence and misogyny are oppressive.

Ice T says,

Gangs were born out of this chaos—the inner city. When you grow up in South Central [Los Angeles], and you've never had anything in your life you control, you seek control. Gangs offer you ultimate control to do what you want. Just getting that for a minute is very intoxicating. Gang members are out there trying to control their own little world. It's only a tiny little place. It may not look like much to you, but it's like a country to them. It's easy for outsiders to say it's just a little block, but a lot of those kids won't leave that block for years, and in some cases their entire lives. It's theirs. That becomes their whole world. Everybody wants to have power over their world.

The Nation of Islam

The alternatives to gangsta rap are almost all politicoreligious solutions, whether it be the Islam of Public Enemy, the mystical Afrocentrism of X Clan or the gospel message of Hammer and the reborn Run-D.M.C. Of these, it's Islamic fundamentalism that has become most closely associated with rap.

The teachings of the black Muslim movement known as the Nation of Islam have found favor with pioneer rapper Afrika Bambaataa, Rakim (of Eric B and Rakim), Shorty of L.A.'s Da Lench Mob, Ice Cube, A Tribe Called Quest, and past and present members of Public Enemy—Flavor Flav, Chuck D, Terminator X and Professor Griff.

Members of Public Enemy, who have become embroiled in controversy over their more extreme views, are protected on tours by body-
guards supplied by the Fruit of Islam (the Nation of Islam's youth
wing). In their lyrics they sometimes praise Nation of Islam leader
Louis Farrakhan. "Public Enemy is at war," Chuck D once said.
"Black people should be at war to regain their enslaved minds. It's the
war to regain awareness."

The Nation of Islam, which now has mosques or temples in 120
American cities, was founded in Detroit by Wallace D. Fard in 1930.
Farrakhan became its leader in 1975 upon the death of Elijah Muhammad, the man followers believed to have been the most recent "messenger from Allah." In the 1960s the movement came to public attention through the conversion of the world heavyweight boxing
champion Cassius Clay (who consequently changed his name to Muhammad Ali) and the assassination in Harlem of its spokesman, Malcolm X.

Followers of the Nation of Islam are a familiar sight in the American inner city. Traditionally dressed in dark suits with white shirts
and red bow ties, they sell copies of the newspaper *The Final Call,*
which now claims a weekly circulation of half a million. In a 1994
survey of African-Americans, 62 percent said they believed Farrakhan
was good for the black community, and an impressive 82 percent said
he spoke the truth.

Farrakhan's appeal is not difficult to understand: he offers pride,
self-respect, a national identity and, above all, hope. He tells his fellow
blacks that they are not merely equal to whites—which was the Christian approach of Martin Luther King Jr.—but superior, because civilization began in Africa. His call is for blacks to assume their rightful
position in the world. "Being the first people of the earth, we are
destined to be the last," says Farrakhan. "We are the creators and the
makers. The limited civilization of the white man and his rule is now
terminating, never to be brought into existence again."

Farrakhan's speeches, published in a volume titled *Back Where We*

Belong, are an alarming mix of bogus scholarship, black racism and Islamic fundamentalism. He teaches that the white race was created six thousand years ago by a black scientist called Yakub in order to test the mettle of the black race. The white race won, and ever since then the black race has been in bondage. The time has come, Farrakhan says, for blacks to escape from captivity and become the master race again. The Jews, the World Bank and the Club of Rome are among the enemies he singles out.

Beyond the rhetoric, what makes the Nation of Islam appealing is its commitment to social programs and its promotion of personal morality. Under the strict code of Islam there would be no prostitution, drug taking, alcoholism, theft, obscene language or disrespect for parents. "Nothing but Islam will make you a respectable people," argues Farrakhan. "We Muslims are your example, living here in your midst. There is no delinquency in Islam. Are you with us to put our people on top of the world?"

Ice Cube, a supporter of the Nation of Islam although not a member, even condones the harsh punishments carried out by Middle Eastern Islamic states. In an interview with *New Musical Express* he stated that he would support the amputation of thieves' hands and the castration of rapists.

"In Islam, the laws are very strict and there are not too many of them," he said. "Revenge is healthy. It deters people from messing with you. They know that there are consequences. If people know that there is a consequence of messing with black people, they won't be too quick to do it again. We're on the threshold of a revolution in this country."

William Pannell, a professor at Fuller Theological Seminary, suggests that one of the reasons this form of Islam is gaining a hold in urban communities is the lack of moral guidelines in a "do-your-own-thing" society. "Since they're not getting this from government, education, social agencies, or the many churches offering cheap grace, Islamic law becomes very compelling."

Clean living has rarely appealed within rock culture, but then not too many rock musicians have come from communities torn apart by homelessness, drug abuse, violence, unemployment, poverty and AIDS. You can enjoy singing about a "walk on the wild side" when you've received a top education and come from a middle-class home, but not when your friends are being killed on the streets and your family lives in fear.

The Nation of Islam sets up health-care centers and drug-rehabilitation programs and trains former gang members to become community leaders. These results are tangible, and to the downtrodden that makes more sense than finely spun prose. "It put a big change on me," said Afrika Bambaataa when asked for his response to the work done with gang members. "It got me to respect people even though they might not like us because we were Muslims. The Nation of Islam was doing things that America had been trying to do for a while—taking people like junkies and prostitutes from the street and cleaning them up. Rehabilitating them in a way that the jail system wasn't doing."

The media-conscious Farrakhan realizes the significance of rap in spreading the Nation of Islam's message to the young. He has met with leading rappers in his Chicago home. In the acknowledgments of *Back Where We Belong* he made mention of Prince Akeem (a minister of youth who once made a rap album), Queen Latifah, Big Daddy Kane, Skinny Boys and Public Enemy.

Conversions and Backlash
Shorty, from L.A.'s Da Lench Mob, was introduced to the Nation of Islam by Public Enemy. He saw his conversion as a rejection of a negative life in favor of a "righteous" way. He immediately gave up smoking, drinking and chasing women. "I gotta be an example 'cause I feel I could show a lot of people it's easy to change your life," he told Brian Cross in his study of West Coast rap, *It's Not About a Salary*. "People think if they stop smoking and drinking and partying, ain't nobody gonna like me. They gonna think I'm a punk. But doing

that'll show you who's really your friend. They like you square, but that's just bein' who you are from the beginning."

Public Enemy's 1988 album *It Takes a Nation of Millions to Hold Us Back* expertly blended the sound of hard rap with a call to check out the claims of Farrakhan. He was mentioned by name in "Bring the Noise" and "Don't Believe the Hype," and Farrakhan voice clips were used between tracks. The teachings of Islam were implicit in other tracks, as with the warning against drugs in "Night of the Living Baseheads" and the call for women to be reeducated in "She Watch Channel Zero?!"

Chuck D and Professor Griff, then known as Public Enemy's "minister of information," used their interviews to promote the Nation's teachings. Interviews, Chuck D argued, were "a battle for the minds of the readers, for the conquest of media control," and an important part of the group's program. He once claimed that the group was founded "to bring our community leadership to a worldwide audience. . . . Everything is planned. The only reason I was able to make such a good plan is because I was such a rap fan."

Yet it was in such interviews that some of the more unsavory teachings of the Nation of Islam slipped out and caused a backlash from otherwise sympathetic critics. In May 1989 Professor Griff gave an interview to *The Washington Times* in which he accused the Jewish people of the "majority of wickedness which goes on around the globe," including "the genocide of black people" and the financing of "experiments on AIDS with black people in South Africa." Embarrassed by what he'd said, Public Enemy announced that he was no longer a member of the group. He was soon reinstated, however, and in August 1989 a sniper believed to be from the Jewish Defense League was arrested by a New York Police Department SWAT team after he was seen aiming a rifle at Flavor-Flav as the latter entered the group's management offices in SoHo.

In March of the following year, Griff released a solo album called *Pawns in the Game* which was rich in the teachings of the Nation. The

title track made reference to Exodus 21:16: "And he that stealeth a
man, and selleth him, or if he be found in his hand, he shall surely
be put to death" (KJV); the conclusion was that it is justifiable to kill
"slave owners." "Real African People" claimed that blacks who col-
lude with corporate white America are guilty of the "ultimate sin."

In interviews Griff was more cautious than he had once been, but
he clearly still subscribed to the anti-Semitic views put forward by
Farrakhan. "Jews are part of the human family," he conceded to *New
Musical Express* when pressured to justify his statement. "All kind
[sic] people are part of the human family. Jews are humans just like
black people are humans. I have no personal animosity or hatred for
anyone in the human family. Now, for those particular people that
chose to do things contrary to the will of God, that I have a problem
with."

The African nationalism and social programs of the Nation of Islam
are generally more appealing than Islamic religious discipline. It's unlikely that there would have been so many Muslim converts from the
black 'hoods if it weren't for the promise of power in the future.
Farrakhan taps into young blacks' hopes and fears, and Islam gives
him authority and his people discipline. "I'm not a Muslim that prays
and all that," admits Chuck D. "But Islam basically just means that
you submit to the will of God. That's all it means." Ice Cube too has
said he's not ready for the full devotional life expected of a committed
Muslim.

Other Religious Movements
The Five Percent Nation is a more liberal offshoot of the Nation of
Islam, the name originating from its belief that 85 percent of the
people are exploited by the ruling 10 percent, leaving only 5 percent
who are neither exploiters nor exploited. They are the wise, the enlightened. Rap adherents of the Five Percent Nation include Rakin,
Poor Righteous Teachers and Brand Nubian.

Poor Righteous Teachers (the name comes from Elijah Muhammad's description of the enlightened 5 percent) use rap as an educational medium for the black community. The music is "wise, civilized, dip-hip-hop from a black mind" ("Rock Dis Funky Joint") and represents their way of life—"and this be that of Islam." Brand Nubian, on its album *In God We Trust,* have a track titled "Meaning of the 5%," which is a rhythm track run under a speech explaining Elijah Muhammad's teaching.

New York's X Clan, founders of the Afrocentric movement Blackwatch, also consider themselves to be educators rather than entertainers. They want to teach black people about their roots in pre-Christian African religion. "If you dig our music as entertainment, then something is wrong," says founding member Professor X, who adorns himself in ancient Egyptian religious symbols and raps about Isis and Osiris.

It can soothe you, it can make you happy, make you celebrate, and make you think. But that's not entertainment.

People are dancing to us, but there's something being said and I've seen people stop and put their fingers to their head and think real hard about when I'm saying. I thought it was going to be a problem with them digesting. There's so many people out there talking about Africa and they sell out. So here comes X Clan. What's the difference? It's the vibe. Spirits will get into you and say, "Let me check this a little deeper."

Christian Faith and Rap

If, as so many insist, the answer to the problems of America's inner cities lies in a social revolution grounded in religious truths, why isn't there a predominant form of gospel rap? The church has deep roots in the black community, and during the civil rights movement of the 1960s it was gospel music that echoed the hopes of those who shared the dream of Martin Luther King Jr. Why has gospel failed to capture the imaginations of today's young urban blacks, given that the language of religion and strict laws haven't been obstacles for the Nation of Islam?

Christianity faces opposition because it is seen as the religion of the slave masters. A rediscovery of African identity, many believe, necessarily involves a rediscovery of African religion. Louis Farrakhan encourages black mistrust of what he calls "the false religion of Christianity" and states that the white race used religion to deceive everyone it could. "It was through Christianity that they got their authority over the black, brown, yellow and red races," he says. In a similar vein, Ice T says of churchgoing blacks, "They still have the slave mentality. They haven't snapped out of it yet."

There is an accompanying perception that the church has ignored social problems. In "Fishing 4 Religion" Arrested Development portrays a black preacher who tells his congregation that shouting never changed anything and that the Christian way has to do with prayer and devotion, not political activism. This group pictures itself as caught between the church, which they admire for its faith, and the revolutionaries, whom they resist because "it seems like no religion's in there."

Lyric-writer Speech wants to present a spiritual alternative to violent revolution. In "Tennessee" he pleads with the Lord to be his "guiding force and truth" and goes on to say,

Lord, it's obvious we got a relationship
Talkin' to each other every night and day
Although you're superior over me
We talk to each other in a friendship way.

On other tracks, such as "Give a Man a Fish," "Raining Revolution" and "Washed Away," he calls for political change based on personal righteousness:

I feel the rain enhances the revolution
And reminds us of a spiritual solution
And reminds us of a natural yet unnatural solution.

("Raining Revolution")

There have been attempts to create Christian rap, but as with all forms of music made by Christians for Christians, it is a pallid response to the real thing. Rap is a way of life, rooted in the shared hardships of the ghetto, and a credible Christian contribution would have to come from inside. Christian rappers like D.C. Talk and Al S.W.I.F.T. sound as though they're employing rap in order to "reach the kids." Even though they throw in phrases like "on the house," it's evident that they're speaking in a foreign language to convert the natives.

The best-known rappers to have church connections are Hammer (once known as M.C. Hammer) and Run-D.M.C., both of whom claim to have experienced a return to the faith of their childhood after reaching the pinnacles of fame. Run-D.M.C. was the leading rap group in America in 1986, having gone triple platinum with its *Raising Hell* album and a single hit with "Walk This Way." Hammer had a huge hit with "U Can't Touch This" in 1990.

Raised in Oakland, California, Hammer had grown up in the church, and his first group was called the Holy Ghost Boys. "When I had just started out, I would only write about gospel subjects," he told me. "They used to call me a gospel rapper." His commercial music, routinely dismissed by hard-core rappers as a concession to commercial pop, brought him great success; but despite religious tracks like "Son of the King," it wasn't until his *Too Legit to Quit* album that he nailed his colors to the mast.

In the sleeve notes he wrote, "I have felt guilty about my success. I possess all of my material dreams and yet there is a void. God has shown me his mercy and reclaimed me. That brings me joy. But there is hurt and a burden that I feel. I need to help my people." In an obvious rebuttal of the Nation of Islam's teachings, he wrote that the white man is not the biggest threat to the black community. "The biggest threat . . . is the black man. The black man continues to self-destruct." The biggest hit from the album was "Do Not Pass Me By," essentially a gospel song with rap breaks.

After the success of *Raising Hell,* Run-D.M.C. lost momentum. The albums *Tougher Than Leather* and *Back from Hell* were relative failures, and they didn't launch a comeback until *Down with the King* in

1993, an album that showcased a new Run-D.M.C.

In the sleeve notes, Run (Joseph Simmons, brother of Def Jam label owner and rap impresario Russell Simmons) thanked "my Lord and Savior Jesus Christ for guiding me through the hard times"; D.M.C. (Darryl McDaniels) thanked God for all his "blessings"; and Jam Master Jay (Jason Mizell) thanked God for "all the love and good health." This would have seemed routine on a soul album, but for rap the mention of Jesus Christ as "Lord and Savior" was unique. It indicated a conscious change.

It was later revealed that both Run and D.M.C. had converted in 1990 after a period of "depression, substance abuse and personal and professional failure." Jam Master Jay was apparently already a believer. The group began attending the Zoe Baptist Ministry on 103rd Street in New York, sometimes performing during the services. "We were dealing with Christian principles before," Run explained to *Rolling Stone*. "We just didn't have the whole thing."

Techno Tribal & Positively Primal

15

House music is like any religious experience. It's a matter of conversion.
Fraser Clark, Megatripolis

Ideally, our music would help people transcend levels of consciousness.
Will Sin, the Shamen

Along with the new techno scene has come along a lot of exploration in new spirituality.
Phil Hartnoll, Orbital

*T*he scene that has variously been dubbed techno pagan, techno futurist, zippie, tribal and festy-rave crossover represents a fascinating merger of the hedonism of the rave culture and the radical politics and New Age philosophies of such postpunk manifestations as travelers and "crusties." The results have been a dance culture with an interest in shamanism and the power of music to alter consciousness. In many ways it's a conscious return to the age of psychedelic happenings and the drug-induced utopianism of Timothy Leary and his ilk, but this time it's less generational and more computer literate, and it has come into being without the aid of articulate star performers playing guitars at high speed. Techno pagan music is based on keyboards and drum machines and is more likely to be heard on a CD player in a club than on stage in performance.

The term *techno pagan,* dreamt up by Fraser Clark, publisher of the *Encyclopedia Psychedelica* and founder of the Megatripolis Club in London, pinpoints the origins of a subculture that looks to the pre-Christian era for its spiritual ideas and to the twenty-first century for its technology. The "techno" aspect of the style grew out of the house music developed in Chicago at the turn of the 1980s, which has since transmuted into scores of subgenres, including garage house, hardcore, hip house, acid house, tribal, trance, ambient and techno.

Strictly speaking, techno came out of Detroit in the mid-1980s and combined the rhythms of black urban America with the electronics of Europe—in particular of German bands such as Kraftwerk. But a related form was being developed in Chicago at the same time. Acid house used the Roland TBR303 bassline machine and tweaked samples to create a hypnotic effect.

Rave and Ecstasy

In 1988 techno and acid house became the soundtrack for Britain's "Summer of Love," when empty buildings and open spaces were commandeered for giant sound systems and light shows, and crowds of up to five thousand took part in massive all-night raves. The drug of choice for this summer of love, though, was not LSD but Ecstasy, the psychedelic amphetamine MDMA, which suffuses the taker with feelings of well-being, love for others and apparently boundless resources of energy.

Because Ecstasy is a psychedelic, it has many of the same effects as LSD. In his book *E for Ecstasy,* Nicholas Saunders reports, "The combination of the drug with music and dancing together produces an exhilarating trance-like state, perhaps similar to that experienced in tribal rituals or religious ceremonies." Russell Newcombe, delivering a paper at a symposium on Ecstasy in Leeds, England, in November 1992, argued that a rave could be seen as a religious ceremony, with the mixing desk as an altar and the DJs as priests. Raving can be seen, he said, as "worshiping the god of altered consciousness."

In an ideal rave, the drugs and the music would work to the same end: to give individuals in the crowd the illusion of being part of a single pulsating organism. The drug would slowly blur the distinctions of the real and unreal, "me" and "them," while the high-decibel music, with its hypnotic 140-160 beats per minute, reprogrammed the consciousness.

In *E for Ecstasy,* Saunders, a fifty-year-old businessman with a hippie background, described his own first experience of taking Ecstasy at a rave:

> I got into dancing in my usual rather self-conscious way, keeping an eye on what other people were doing and well aware that I was 30 years older than nearly everybody else. Then, imperceptibly, I gradually relaxed, melted into it, and knew I was part of it all. There was no need to be self-conscious; I had no doubt I was accepted; there was nothing I might do that would jar because everyone else was simply being themselves, as though they were celebrating their freedom from the constraints and neuroses of society. Although everyone was separately celebrating their own space, when I looked around I would easily make eye contact—no one was hiding behind a mask. There was virtually no conversation or body contact except for the occasional short hug, but I experienced a feeling of belonging to the group, a kind of uplifting religious experience of unity that I have only felt once before.

Virtual Reality

Techno music also represented a change in attitude toward new technologies. Traditionally rock has revered the raw and the primitive in music, the back-to-basics, and has been suspicious of computers, databanks and synthetic sound, but the new computer-literate generation has no such qualms. The image of the guitar-strumming teenager in front of a wardrobe mirror has for these young people been replaced by that of the young person with a keyboard, samplers and a computer, who without ever having received a music lesson can steal sounds from the rich and famous and create master tapes in the safety of a bedroom. This is typically accompanied by a sense of excitement about new developments in virtual reality, cyberspace and the information highway.

Many of the Silicon Valley pioneers, now in their forties, were hippies in the 1960s and have attached their countercultural idealism to computers. Virtual reality is mind-expanding. The information highway is about access, freedom of speech and world unity. The once-frightening world of wires, buttons and screens, associated with dehumanizing technology by the old counterculture, is now seen as friendly. To catch a taste of what's happening in this area you read not *Rolling Stone* or *Spin* but *Mondo 2000* or *Wired,* where techno performers are interviewed alongside cyberpunk authors, physicists and robotics hackers. Techno sees itself as the soundtrack of tomorrow.

Techno Meets Primitive
The fusion of pagan with techno came via the New Age culture of those who had outgrown the punk era and reverted to a form of hippyism. With their dreadlocks, dirty jeans (crusted with mud, hence "crusties"), Doc Marten boots and vicious-looking dogs, they were best known in Britain for squatting in empty houses, taking part in New Age convoys, celebrating the summer solstice at Stonehenge and being a visible presence at the annual Glastonbury Festival.

In subcultural terms, they were a world apart from the fashion-conscious dancers at raves, but the two groups were drawn together when they both fell foul of the law. The travelers, who had fought running battles with the police to be allowed to gather at Stonehenge, found allies in ravers who had had their events raided. When the Criminal Justice and Public Order Bill was drafted by the British government in 1994, the two forces united in protest. "The older, more politicised traveller scene, with its embattled hippy ideals, found a revitalising energy, and was galvanised by trance music and techno," observed Alix Sharkey in the *Guardian*. "The younger, more hedonistic rave scene crashed head-on into psychedelics, mysticism and the agit-prop politics of counter-culture. The resulting synergistic shock waves are now rumbling through the social order, and cracks are starting to appear."

In the United States, particularly in the areas around San Francisco, there was similar cross-fertilization; much of it was stimulated by British visitors. In the heart of the Haight-Ashbury district, the Tweakin' Records store is dominated by house music, and Gaia Mantra on Mission is reckoned to stock the hippest collection of techno and ambient vinyl in the area. The younger Deadheads (fans who follow the Grateful Dead) see vital connections between techno pagan and what the Grateful Dead did for its audience in the 1960s. Sound systems are now often set up outside Grateful Dead gigs, so that fans have a free rave before the concert begins.

Steve Silberman, coauthor of *Skeleton Key: A Dictionary for Deadheads,* opened a discussion on the connection between Dead music and house music on the Internet. In his opening statement he said,

Both the house music scene and the dead scene are places where diverse groups of people come together to have peak experiences in the presence of Big Deep Music that encourages trance and contemplation, Big Crowds in which the individual can immerse his or her self in a Group mind and an untiring Group Body, entheogens/empathogens which further deepen the collective identity and increase vividness of the Present Moment. Both scenes are "sexy," "religious," eternally youthful, both inclusive and exclusive, somewhat outlaw, techno-shamanistic, mobile. Both scenes are also somewhat skeptical of the other. Both agree, in each their own way, that the "groove is in the heart."

Megatripolis

No one was more excited by this new hybrid than Fraser Clark, whose *Encyclopedia Psychedelica* had long been predicting a new "con-

sciousness craze" that would emerge out of the youth culture before
the end of the twentieth century. As a veteran of the consciousness
craze of the 1960s, Clark was well placed to be a theoretician this time
around. After receiving an honors degree in psychology in 1965, he
traveled the world in search of the hippie dream. In 1993 he opened
Megatripolis, a club that reflected his techno pagan ideal.

In the Cathedral, the main dance floor of Megatripolis, hard-core
techno is pumped out of speakers as lights flash and dry ice drifts.
Market stalls in the corridors sell jewelry, trance music tapes, beads,
smart drinks and face paints. Up a staircase lined with signs advertising everything from environmental campaigns to psychic healing,
there is the Virtualitroom (ambient music and slide shows) and the
Techno-Silence Room (lectures on political and spiritual issues). The
club thereby becomes a means of introducing dancers to esoteric
teachings.

Clark sees techno pagan as helping birth an alternative culture that
will replace what he calls "the Roman Christian Monotheistic Mind
State." "We're rapidly becoming the dominant religion!" he enthused
in an interview with *Mondo 2000*. "The only danger is the Monotheists
who perceive the world going to the devil and would rather put us all
out of our misery."

Archaic Revival and the Shamen

In America the leading techno pagan guru is ethnopharmacologist
Terence McKenna, author of *The Archaic Revival*. McKenna's life has
been devoted to an unorthodox exploration of the effect of hallucinogenic drugs on the evolution of human consciousness. Like Clark, he
regards Christianity as a negative religion that has prevented humankind from investigating higher states of consciousness. His notion of
an "archaic revival" is a return to the drug-induced experiences he
believes were enjoyed by Neolithic people.

"Welcome to the Archaic Revival," he wrote in the introduction to
the book.

Twenty-five years ago I began to grapple with the realization that exploring the "wholly Other" was related to shamanism. Pursuing that insight led me to use plant hallucinogens as a means of probing the mysterious dimension this oldest of humanity's religions has always claimed to be able to access. Of all the techniques used by the shaman to induce Ecstasy and visionary voyaging—fasting, prolonged drumming, breath control, and stressful ordeals—I now feel confident that the use of hallucinogenic plants is the most effective, dependable, and powerful.

It was perhaps inevitable that McKenna would find himself drawn to the emerging techno pagan culture. It had the audience and the electroshamans, while he had the anthropological explanations. Just as Timothy Leary had explained the experiences of acid trippers in the language of Tibetan Buddhism, so McKenna would explain the experiences of mashed ravers in terms of shamanistic flights of Ecstasy and "visionary voyaging."

His most effective link with the dance scene came when he met the British indie group Shamen after delivering a lecture at London's Institute of Contemporary Arts in 1991. The Shamen was founded by two former psychiatric nurses, Will Sinnot (known as Will Sin) and Colin Angus, who—as the group name suggests—were interested in making music that "helped people transcend levels of consciousness." Disenchanted with the conventional rock scene, they created a moving club called Synergy, to which they invited their favorite DJs and where they explored laser technology in their own live act. In this environment they tried to perfect a dance music that would be mind-altering.

"With our past interest in psychedelics and both of us having been involved in psychiatry, we are interested in that," Sinnot told *New Musical Express* in 1990. "Neither of us believe you can actually simulate a trip . . . but you can get a reaction akin to these things." (Sinnot was to drown in 1991 after making a video for the single "Move Any Mountain.")

The Shamen's research into shamanism naturally led them to

McKenna's work. After hearing him speak, they suggested interviewing him about some of their favorite topics and using an edited version of his answers as the vocal on a track on their new album *Boss Drum*. In fact, the whole recording was to be deeply influenced by McKenna's theories, the "boss drum" of the title referring to "the drum which is central to the whole shamanistic quest," according to Angus.

The album was effectively a manifesto for techno paganism. The title song urged the listener to activate the eternal rhythm for "tomorrow's tribe" and to make that "vital reconnection to the goddess mind." This revolution of consciousness is described in the song as "Healing rhythmic synergy / Techno tribal and positively primal / Shamanic anarchistic archaic revival." Another track on the album, "Ebeneezer Goode," was a thinly disguised celebration of Ecstasy; after the song was released as a single in Britain, Ecstasy became the "White Rabbit" of the rave generation. Everyone knew what the lyrics referred to, yet the words weren't specific enough to warrant being banned from the airwaves.

"Re: Evolution" was essentially McKenna's solo track, with the Shamen playing an electronic rhythm track behind an eight-minute tape of him talking about shamanism, psychedelic drugs and his belief that rave culture is a harbinger of an archaic revival. His statement on rave music is worth quoting in full:

> The emphasis in house music and rave culture on physiologically compatible rhythms and this sort of thing is really a rediscovery of the art of natural magic with sound. That sound properly understood, especially percussive sound, can actually change neurological states, and large groups of people getting of this kind of music are creating a telepathic community of bonding which will hopefully be strong enough then to carry the vision out into the mainstream of society. I think the youth culture that is emerging in the nineties is an end of the millennium culture that is actually summing up Western Civilization and pointing us in an entirely different direction, that we are going to arrive in the third millennium

in the middle of an archaic revival which will mean a revival of these physiologically enlivening musical signatures, a new art, a new social vision, a new relationship to feminism, to nature, to ego. All of these things are taking hold, and not a moment too soon.

Chant and Religious Symbols
Just as the acid gurus of the 1960s had believed drugs, music and ancient religion would usher in a new age of more highly evolved humans, so too the Techno Pagans believe that we are soon to witness a huge leap forward in which their music will play a significant part. "Psychedelics help to whittle the ego down to size," says Colin Angus. "The ego has got to be eliminated somehow from the human psychological structure before we can get to the next millennium. . . . The ego is definitely one of the big boundaries that we've got to dissolve and get by before we can go forward."

Although not all techno pagans are as articulate as McKenna, Fraser and Angus, they join in acknowledging that people are seeking more from their music. "Along with the new techno scene has come a lot of exploration in new spirituality," admits Phil Hartnoll of the British group Orbital. "It seems as though everyone has got crystals hanging around their necks." In an interview with *Mondo 2000* Hartnoll mused about the power of Ecstasy to "make you feel your spirit," the return to primitive tribal trance music and the possibility of coming up with sound frequencies that induce out-of-body experiences. German DJ Sven Vath says that performing is for him a "religious experience" and explains that his role is to "give people pictures and fantasies. I do instrumental music because I'm a dancer and it gives enough space for everyone to let their fantasy just flow and go."

Ambient music, often designed for chill-out rooms, has created a market for ethereal sounds that evoke feelings associated with the spiritual. Romanian musician and composer Michael Cretu surprised the industry in 1991 with the first Enigma album, *MCMXC a.D.,* which mixed dance rhythms, world music and Gregorian chants to guide listeners into the world of "spirit and meditation." The album sold over twelve million copies in twenty-five countries, two million of them in America.

Cretu gave his mainly instrumental tracks religious-sounding titles ("The Rivers of Belief," "Way to Eternity," "Hallelujah") and had his wife, Sandra Lauer, breathlessly intone lines like "Let the rhythm be your guiding light." The album's cover featured a hologram of a hooded figure beside a cross, standing on a mountaintop bathed in light. All this gave the impression of a very "spiritual" work, although the album's snippets of speech advised that our innermost desires are divine and must be obeyed.

The Cross of Changes, the second Enigma album, was less dance-oriented but perpetuated the same teaching of self-reliance wrapped in religious language. Cretu, who rarely speaks to the media or explains his work, did admit to *The New York Times* that the most significant influence on the album was his study of numerology.

It was possibly *MCMXC a.D.*'s massive sales that stimulated interest in Gregorian chant as a form of ambient music. These unaccompanied vocals in Latin, with origins possibly as far back as the sixth century, are increasingly recommended in New Age music catalogs as aids to meditation. In 1994 a double album, *Canto Gregoriano,* recorded over twenty years ago by Benedictine monks from a monastery in Santo Domingo de Silos in Spain, became a surprise bestseller, climbing into the top ten in America, Australia, New Zealand, South America and Europe and selling over four million copies.

Market research in Spain, where the album was first released, found that 60 percent of the sales were to people in the sixteen-to-twenty-five age group. In Britain tracks were being played at raves as "chill-out" music. Said Father Clemente Serna, the abbot of Santa Domingo de Silos, "The modern world is not satisfying people's spiritual needs. There is a real need for profound change."

The Quest Continues

Few would doubt that the 1990s are witnessing a renewal of interest in religious experience, from books on encounters with angels to the mysticism of the new physics. The approach of the year 2000 is heightening expectations of rapid social change, while the environmental crisis is forcing people to accept that the survival of humankind exists in discovering a right relationship between human beings and nature.

Rock 'n' roll anticipated these changes in the 1960s and is encouraging them today. Many of the religious notions that seemed like fads thirty years ago have returned with greater impact now that the former hippies are in positions of power. It's significant that the paganizing of the techno scene has come largely through the efforts of men in their forties, who first took acid in the 1960s.

The search for redemption in rock 'n' roll has concentrated overwhelmingly in altered consciousness brought about by a combination of loud music and psychedelic drugs. Even when the drugs are left behind, the bias is toward pantheistic beliefs, where the goal is to get lost in the cosmic whole. This was true of the original psychedelic era, and it's true of the techno pagan scene today. It was also true of the bulk of what has happened in between, from experiments with mantras in India to the search for modern-day shamanism.

It can feel exciting to be caught up in ideas that have found their time, but the most important question to ask is not "What's hot?" or even "What works?" but "What is true?" Those who take drugs or fall under the spell of repetitive music undoubtedly feel temporarily changed, but how can they be sure that this is a "spiritual" change? Might it not just be the actions of brain chemicals on the synapses? And even if we were to accept that something spiritual has occurred, how can we be sure that it is good, that it isn't a spiritual deception?

These experiences, because they are not subject to any tried and tested revelation from God, don't adequately answer the basic questions that religion has always asked: Where do I come from? Why am I here? How should I live? Where am I going? New York dance recording artist Moby, who makes no secret of being what he calls "a lover of Jesus," believes that a lot of what passes for "spirituality" on the contemporary dance scene is a result of naiveté and of the desire to dress up old-fashioned hedonism in more acceptable terms. "People talk about 'shamanism' and 'paganism' when what they're really into is taking a lot of drugs," he says. "They don't want to say, 'I'm partying,' so they say, 'I'm a Techno Pagan,' but except for people like Colin Angus of the Shamen, there are very few who have any understanding of what paganism is."

There will continue to be a search for redemption in rock 'n' roll, if only because the creation of music seems to provoke musicians into asking questions about the ultimate source of creativity. Van Morrison remains convinced that music originates in the spiritual realm. "Music is spiritual," he says. "The music business is not."

"I think musicians tend to be spiritually orientated because a mystery takes place," suggests Pete Townshend. "Why does a certain chord give me a buzz? Why does that combination of notes have that effect? As soon as you ask the question, you're on a path."

Sources

Books

Anderson, Christopher. *Madonna Unauthorized.* New York: Simon & Schuster, 1991.

Aranza, Jacob. *Backward Masking Unmasked.* Shreveport, La.: Huntington House, 1983.

Baba, Meher. *The Mastery of Consciousness.* Twickenham, U.K.: Eel Pie, 1977.

Barrett, Leonard E. *The Rastafarians.* London: Heinemann Educational, 1977.

————. *The Sun and the Drum.* London: Heinemann, 1976.

Blackwell, Lois S. *The Wings of a Dove: The Story of Gospel Music in America.* Donning, 1978.

Blanchard, John. *Pop Goes the Gospel.* Welwyn, U.K.: Evangelical Press, 1983.

Booth, Stanley. *Dance with the Devil.* New York: Random House, 1984.

Braden, William. *The Private Sea: LSD and the Search for God.* New York: Bantam, 1968.

Braun, Michael. *Love Me Do: The Beatles' Progress.* London: Penguin, 1964.

Bugliosi, Vincent. *Helter Skelter.* New York: Bantam, 1975.

Burt, Jesse, and Duane Blackwell. *The History of Gospel Music.* Nashville: K and S, 1971.

Cash, W. I. *The Mind of the South.* New York: Vintage, 1941.

Cashmore, Ernest. *Rastaman.* London: Allen and Unwin, 1979.

Cavendish, Richard. *The Black Arts.* London: Routledge & Kegan Paul, 1967.

Charles, Ray, and David Ritz. *Brother Ray.* London: Futura, 1982.

Charters, Samuel. *Robert Johnson.* New York: Oak, 1973.

Coon, Caroline. *1988.* London: Orbach and Chambers, 1977.

Dalton, David. *The Rolling Stones: The First Twenty Years.* London: Thames and Hudson, 1981.

Davis, Stephen. *Bob Marley*. London: Panther, 1984.

———. *Hammer of the Gods*. London: Sidgwick and Jackson, 1985.

Davis, Stephen, and Peter Simon. *Reggae Bloodlines*. New York: Anchor, 1977.

Dundy, Elaine. *Elvis and Gladys*. London: Weidenfeld and Nicolson, 1985.

Farrakhan, Louis. *Back Where We Belong*. Philadelphia: PC International, 1989.

Ferguson, Marilyn. *The Aquarian Conspiracy*. London: Routledge & Kegan Paul, 1981.

Geldof, Bob. *Is That It?* London: Sidgwick and Jackson, 1986.

Genovese, Eugene. *Roll Jordan Roll*. New York: Vintage, 1976.

Gleason, Ralph J. *The Jefferson Airplane and the San Francisco Sound*. New York: Ballantine, 1969.

Goldman, Albert. *Elvis*. London: Allen Lane, 1981.

Goldrosen, John. *Buddy Holly*. London: Panther, 1979.

Goswami, Satsvarupa Dasa. *Prabhupada*. Los Angeles: Bhaktivedanta Book Trust, 1983.

Green, John. *Dakota Days*. London: Comet, 1984.

Harrison, George. *I Me Mine*. London: W. H. Allen, 1982.

Harrison, Hank. *The Dead*. Milbrae, Calif.: Celestial-Arts, 1980.

Heilbut, Tony. *The Gospel Sound*. New York: Simon & Schuster, 1971.

Hirshey, Gerri. *Nowhere to Run*. New York: Times Books, 1984.

Hoare, Ian, ed. *The Soul Book*. London: Methuen, 1975.

Hopkins, Jerry, and Daniel Sugarman. *No One Gets Out of Here Alive*. New York: Warner, 1980.

Hoskyns, Barney. *Prince: Imp of the Perverse*. London: Virgin, 1988.

Jahn, Mike. *Jim Morrison and the Doors*. New York: Grosset and Dunlap, 1969.

Johnson, James Weldon, ed. *The Book of American Negro Spirituals*. New York: Viking, 1925.

Keil, Charles. *Urban Blues*. Chicago: University of Chicago Press, 1966.

Larson, Bob. *The Day Music Died*. Carol Stream, Ill.: Creation House, 1971.

———. *Rock and the Church*. Carol Stream, Ill.: Creation House, 1971.

Leary, Timothy. *Flashbacks*. London: Heinemann, 1983.

———. *The Politics of Ecstasy*. London: Paladin, 1970.

Leech, Kenneth. *Youthquake*. London: Abacus, 1976.

Lennon, Cynthia. *A Twist of Lennon*. London: Star, 1977.

Lewis, Myra, and Murray Silver. *Great Balls of Fire*. London: Virgin, 1982.

McEwan, Joe. *Sam Cooke: The Man Who Invented Soul*. New York: Sure Books, 1977.

McKenna, Terence. *The Archaic Revival*. San Francisco: HarperCollins, 1991.

———. *Food of the Gods.* New York: Bantam, 1992.

Marcus, Greil. *Mystery Train.* New York: E. P. Dutton, 1976.

Marsh, Dave. *Born to Run.* New York: Doubleday/Dolphin, 1979.

Masters, R. E. L., and Jean Houston. *The Varieties of Psychedelic Experience.* London: Anthony Blond, 1966.

Mehta, Gita. *Karma Cola.* London: Cape, 1980.

Michaels, Ross. *George Harrison.* New York: Flash Books, 1977.

Michell, John. *A View over Atlantis.* London: Abacus, 1973.

Mylett, Howard. *Jimmy Page: Tangents Within a Framework.* London: Omnibus, 1983.

O'Connor, Flannery. *Mystery and Manners.* New York: Farrar Straus Giroux, 1961.

———. *Wise Blood.* New York: Farrar Straus Giroux, 1949.

Reich, Charles, and Jann Wenner. *Garcia: A Signpost to New Space.* San Francisco: Straight Arrow, 1972.

Ritz, David. *Divided Soul.* London: Michael Joseph, 1985.

Rolling Stone editors. *The Ballad of John and Yoko.* London: Michael Joseph, 1982.

Rose, Tricia. *Black Noise.* Hanover, N.H.: Wesleyan University Press, 1994.

Roszak, Theodore. *Unfinished Animal.* New York: Harper & Row, 1975.

Rubin, Jerry. *Growing Up at Thirty-seven.* New York: M. Evans, 1976.

Sanchez, Tony. *Up and Down with the Rolling Stones.* New York: Morrow, 1979.

Sanders, Ed. *The Family.* London: Rupert Hart-Davis, 1972.

Saunders, Nicholas. *E for Ecstasy.* London: Author, 1993. .

Scott, Cyril. *Music: Its Secret Influence Throughout the Ages.* London: Rider, 1943.

Search for Liberation. Worcester, U.K.: Bhaktivedanta Book Trust, 1981.

Shapiro, Harry. *Waiting for the Man.* London: Quartet, 1988.

Spencer, John Michael, ed. *The Theology of American Popular Music.* Durham, N.C.: Duke University Press, 1989.

Spitz, Robert Stephen. *Barefoot in Babylon.* New York: Viking, 1979.

Stanley, Lawrence, ed. *Rap: The Lyrics.* New York: Viking Penguin, 1992.

Starkie, Enid. *Arthur Rimbaud.* London: Faber and Faber, 1961.

Swaggart, Jimmy. *To Cross a River.* Plainfield, N.J.: Logos International, 1977.

Symonds, John. *The Great Beast: The Life and Magick of Aleister Crowley.* London: Macdonald, 1971.

T, Ice. *The Ice Opinion.* New York: St. Martin's, 1994.

Tame, David. *The Secret Power of Music.* Wellingborough, U.K.: Turnstone, 1984.

Taylor, Derek. *It Was Twenty Years Ago Today.* London: Bantam, 1987.

Tendler, Stewart, and David May. The Brotherhood of Eternal Love. London: Panther, 1984.

Toop, David. *Rap Attack 2.* London: Serpent's Tail, 1991.

Tosches, Nick. *Hellfire: The Jerry Lee Lewis Story.* New York: Dell, 1982.

Vermorel, Fred, and Judy Vermorel. *The Sex Pistols.* London: Star Books, 1978.

Wenner, Jann. *Lennon Remembers.* San Francisco: Straight Arrow, 1970.

White, Charles. *The Life and Times of Little Richard.* London: Pan, 1985.

White, Timothy. *Catch a Fire.* London: Elm Tree, 1983.

Wolfe, Tom. *The Electric Kool-Aid Acid Test.* New York: Bantam, 1969.

Yogananda, Paramhansa. *Autobiography of a Yogi.* London: Rider, 1969.

Yogi, Maharishi Mahesh. *The Science of Being and Art of Living.* London: International SRM, 1966.

Zanetta, Tony, and Henry Edwards. *Stardust.* London: Michael Joseph, 1986.

Articles

Aldridge, Alan. "A Good Guru's Guide to the Beatles' Sinister Songbook." *Observer Magazine,* November 26, 1967.

Aronowitz, Al. "The Return of the Beatles." *Saturday Evening Post,* August 8, 1964.

Beard, Steve. "Peace, Love and Understanding Cyberspace." *Arena,* August 1994.

"The Beatles, the Maharishi and the Meaning of Life." *Intro,* 1967.

Bentley, Bill. "T-Bone Burnett: Born Again, but Still Looking." *L.A. Weekly,* August 8, 1980.

Blake, John. "Zeppelin Black Magic Mystery." *Evening Standard,* 1980.

Block, Adam. "Pure Bono." *Mother Jones,* May 1989.

Bono. Interview by Max Bell. *The Face,* November 1988.

———. Interview by David Breskin. *Rolling Stone,* October 8, 1987.

———. Interview by Liam Mackey. *Hot Press,* December 1988/January 1989.

Burroughs, William. "Rock Magic." *Crawdaddy,* June 1975.

Cain, Barry. "Johnny Knows He's Not Mad." *Record Mirror,* December 11, 1976.

Charone, Barbara. "Life in the Fast Lane." *Sounds,* January 8, 1977.

Collin, Matthew. "Turn On, Tune In, Sort It Out." *Observer Life,* December 5, 1993.

Cook, Richard. "The Altar'd Boys." *New Musical Express,* March 19, 1983.

———. "A Dreamboat Named Desire." *New Musical Express,* February 27, 1982.

Coon, Caroline. "Rotten to the Core." *Melody Maker,* November 27, 1976.

Cromelin, Richard. "A Herbal Meditation with Bob Marley." *Rolling Stone,*

September 11, 1975.

Crowe, Cameron. "Zeppelin Rising Slowly." *Rolling Stone,* August 12, 1976.

Dalton, Stephen. "Synergy for the Devil." *New Musical Express,* September 20, 1990.

Denton, A. Robert. "The Relationship of Drugs to Contemporary Religion." *Journal of the American Scientific Affiliation,* September 1973.

Dobkin de Rios, Marlene, and Frederick Katz. "Some Relationships Between Music and Hallucinogenic Ritual." *Ethos,* 1974.

Downing, David. "I Was Hoping It Was a Lie." *Let It Rock,* February 1973.

Dunn, Cyril. "You Don't Know You're in There but You Know You've Been." *Observer Magazine,* January 14, 1968.

Egginton, Joyce. "Drug Cult Ends in Ritual Murder." *Observer,* July 15, 1984.

Errigo, Angie. "Ask the Answer Man." *Creem,* February 1978.

Farren, Mick. "The Titanic Sails at Dawn." *New Musical Express,* January 1976.

Felton, David, and David Dalton. "The Most Dangerous Man in the World." *Rolling Stone,* June 25, 1970.

Flanagan, Bill. "U2: If by Land, If by Sea." *Musician,* September 1992.

Fletcher, Tony. "Satanic Rock: Southern Death Cult." *Sky,* January 1992.

Fong-Torres, Ben. "The Resurrection of Santana." *Rolling Stone,* December 7, 1972.

Fox, Marisa. "Too Big for His Bitches." *New Musical Express,* August 18, 1990.

Gans, David. "Just Plain Folks." *Record,* January 1984.

Gilmore, Mikal. "Baptism by Earth Wind & Fire." *Rolling Stone,* January 26, 1978.

————. "T-Bone Burnett's Moral Messages." *Rolling Stone,* November 11, 1982.

Goodwin, Christopher. "By Any Means Necessary." *The Sunday Times* (London), August 7, 1994.

Goodwin, Michael. "Marley, the Maytals and the Reggae Armageddon." *Rolling Stone,* September 11, 1975.

Graham, Bill. "U2 Could Be a Headline." *Hot Press,* March 8, 1979.

Gritter, Headley. "The Magic of Bob Marley." *Record Review,* April 1980.

Haas, Charlie. "Still Grateful After All These Years." *New West,* December 17, 1979.

Hall, Dave. "The Endless Enigma." *Jam Entertainment News,* June 10, 1994.

Harrison, George. Interview. *Melody Maker,* September 2-9, 1967.

Hewitt, Paolo. "Clued Up Clan." *New Musical Express,* April 21, 1990.

Higginbotham, Andrew. "Warfare, Lies and the Art of the Devil." *Select,* 1992.

Hilburn, Robert. "I Learned Jesus Is Real and I Wanted That." *Los Angeles*

Times, November 25, 1980.

Hobbs, Mary Anne. "When Bush Comes to Shove." *New Musical Express,* August 8, 1992.

Holden, Stephen. "Enigmatic Man." *The New York Times,* February 9, 1994.

Holdenfield, Chris. "An Endless Party at Glastonbury." *Rolling Stone,* July 22, 1971.

Hoskyns, Barney. "Flags and Penance." *New Musical Express,* June 22, 1985.

Howes, Keith. "Patti Smith." *Gay News,* 1978.

Hunter, James. "There Are Riders Approaching." *Record,* December 1983.

Jackson, David. "Al Green Changes Hearts and Minds." *The Village Voice,* January 29, 1979.

Jackson, Joe. "Even Better Than Surreal Thing!" *Hot Press,* 1993.

Jerome, Jim. "Jerry Lee Lewis Has Been Through Hell." *People,* 1979.

"Jimmy Page." *Circus,* October 13, 1973.

Jolly, Mark. "Zippies on the Super Highway." *Independent on Sunday,* July 24, 1994.

Jones, Nick. "Beatle George and Where He's At." *Melody Maker,* December 16, 1967.

———. "People Put You on a Pedestal . . ." *Melody Maker,* December 30, 1967.

Jurnovoy, Joyce. "Always Taking a Risk." *Cue,* March 20, 1976.

Karlen, Neal. "Prince Talks." *Rolling Stone,* September 12, 1985.

Kerridge, Roy. "Fall of the Rastamen." *Spectator,* January 19, 1985.

Lidz, Theodore, and Albert Rothenberg. "Psychedelism: Dionysius Reborn." Department of Psychiatry, Yale University (New Haven, Conn.).

Lindsay, Robert. "New Age Invades American Way of Life." *International Herald Tribune,* October 3, 1986.

Logan, Nick. "How Jeremy Spencer Saw the End of the World." *New Musical Express,* April 24, 1971.

McClellan, Jim. "The Shamen: Are They for Real?" *The Face,* December 1992.

McCrystal, Cal. "In the Land of the Mad." *The Sunday Times* (London), August 2, 1970.

McEnery, Paul. "Technology of the Soul." *Mondo 2000,* no. 12, 1994.

McKenna, Kristine. "A Monster Called Sting." *Rolling Stone,* September 1, 1983.

McLaren, Malcolm. Interview by Krystina Kitsis. *ZG,* no. 7.

Madonna. Interview by Andrew Neil. *The Sunday Times Magazine,* October 18-25, 1992.

Marcus, Greil. "Al Green Makes Us Feel So Fine." *Rolling Stone,* February 23, 1978.

———. "Amazing Chutzpah." *New West,* 1979.

Marsh, Dave. "Can Patti Smith Walk on Water?" *Rolling Stone,* April 20, 1978.

Martin, Gavin. "Call Us Unforgettable." *New Musical Express,* October 27, 1984.

————. "King of the Celtic Fringe." *New Musical Express,* February 14, 1981.

————. "Out of the Twilight and into the Daylight." *New Musical Express,* December 6, 1980.

————. "The Predator's Decision Is Final." *New Musical Express,* December 5, 1992.

————. "Sad to Be Gaye." *New Musical Express,* October 28, 1989.

Mondo, Connie. "Bringing It All Back House." *Mondo 2000,* no. 7, 1993.

Morris, Mixmaster. "Ambient San Francisco." *i-D,* August 1994.

O'Grady, Lorrain. "Carlos and John: They Share a Guru and a Band." *Rolling Stone,* October 11, 1973.

O'Hagan, Sean. "Bono." *Arena,* Winter 1992.

————. "Bono Drag." *The Face,* April 1992.

Paphides, Peter. "Mysterious Ways." *Melody Maker,* July 3, 1993.

Perry, Neil. "Death Metal: Evil Under the Sun." *Select,* January 1992.

"Psychedelic: The New In-Word." *Melody Maker,* December 16, 1967.

Rambali, Paul. "Rock 'n' Roll Scoundrels." *New Musical Express,* August 19, 1980.

Rayns, Tony. "The Elusive Lucifer." *Monthly Film Bulletin,* 1982.

Richards, Keith. Interview by Robert Greenfield. *Rolling Stone,* August 19, 1971.

Roberts, Dave. "The Lost Boys." *Alpha,* February 1992.

Roberts, John Storm. "Earth Wind & Fire—Mystagogic Funk." *High Fidelity,* January 1979.

Townshend, Pete. Interview by Rick Sanders and David Dalton. *Rolling Stone,* June 14, 1969.

Sawyer, Miranda. "Apocalypse Now." *Select,* October 1992.

Shaar Murray, Charles. "With God on His Side." *New Musical Express,* August 25, 1979.

Sharkey, Alix. "New Tribes England." *Guardian Weekend,* December 11, 1993.

————. "What a Long Weird Trip It's Been." *Independent,* November 17, 1993.

Smith, Patti. Interview by Penny Green. October 1973.

Spencer, Neil. "Third World Superstar." *Observer Magazine,* April 17, 1977.

Stokes, Dermot. "Listen to the Lion." *Hot Press,* 1982.

Sweeting, Adam. "Gods Will Be Gods." *Melody Maker,* July 30, 1983.

Tapia, Andrés. "Churches Wary of Inner-City Islamic Inroads." *Christianity*

Today, January 10, 1994.

Thrills, Adrian. "Cactus World Views." *New Musical Express,* March 14, 1987.

Toop, David. "Techniques of Ecstasy." *The Wire,* 1993.

Toure. "Run-D.M.C.: Back on the Throne." *Rolling Stone,* July 8, 1993.

Turner, Robin. "With the Beatles Meditating in India." *Daily Express,* February 20, 1968.

Walker, Martin. "King, Ace, Joker." *Guardian,* September 8, 1973.

Watts, Mick. "Cat Stevens." *Melody Maker,* 1974.

_____ . "A Most Peculiar Man." *Melody Maker,* December 25, 1971.

Werbin, Stu. "Live from the Asteroid Belt." *Rolling Stone,* October 26, 1972.

Wells, Steven. "100 Per Cent Prof." *New Musical Express,* 1990.

_____ . "Some Muthas Do 'Ave 'Em." *New Musical Express,* June 2, 1990.

Wiederhorn, Jon. "The Bono God Hoo-Haa Band." *Melody Maker,* March 21, 1992.

Wilby, Peter. "The Logic of Charles Manson." *Observer,* July 22, 1973.

Wilson, James. "LSD and Me by Paul McCartney." *Daily Mirror,* June 19, 1967.

Wiseman, Rich. "Santana Comes Home." *Rolling Stone,* May 6, 1976.

Woodard, Josef. "John McLaughlin's Life in the Emerald Beyond." *Musician,* 1987.

Wooding, Dan. "Dylan by His Pastor." *Buzz,* 1981.

Young, Charles M. "Visions of Patti." *Rolling Stone,* July 27, 1978.

Index

Aarseth, Oystein, *99*
AC/DC, *98, 100*
Achtung Baby album
  (U2), *184, 185*
acid casualties, *64*
Acid House, *210*
"Acrobat" (U2), *184*
Afrocentrism, *199, 205*
After the Fire, *176*
"After the Thrill Is Gone"
  (Eagles), *111*
Akeem, Prince, *202*
Al S.W.I.F.T., *207*
Alarm, the, *172*
Alexander, J. W., *44*
"All You Need Is Love"
  (Beatles), *107, 116*
Alpha Band, *170*
Alpha magazine, *183*
Altamont concert, *106-7*
Amazing Grace album, *40*
"Ambush in the Night"
  (Marley), *135*
American Recordings
  album (Johnny Cash),
  173
Amos, Tori, *189*
"Anarchy in the UK" (Sex

Pistols), *178*
ancient knowledge, *116-17*
Anderson, Jon, *13, 114,
  116*
Anderson, Kip, *47*
Anderson, Queen C., *33*
Anger, Kenneth, *90-93*
Angus, Colin, *215-16, 217,
  220*
"Anna Stesia" (Prince),
  194
anti-Semitism, *203-4*
"Anyway Anyhow
  Anywhere" (the Who),
  15, 76
archaic revival, *214*
Arrested Development,
  206
Assemblies of God, *19, 20,
  21, 22*
astral traveling, *116, 118*
"Astral Weeks" (Van
  Morrison), *122*
Astral Weeks album, *121-
  22*
Augustine, St., *8*
Avalon Sunset album
  (Van Morrison) *124*

Baba, Meher, *76-78, 82,
  84*
Babaji, Sri Mahavatara,
  70
"Babyface" (U2), *185*
Back from Hell album
  (Run-D.M.C.), *207*
"backward masking," *162*
"Badlands" (Springsteen),
  153
Baez, Joan, *178*
Bahia music, *152*
Bailey, Alice, *123*
Bailey, David, *86*
Bailey, Philip, *160*
Balin, Marty, *52*
"Ballad of a Thin Man"
  (Dylan), *166*
Bambaata, Afrika, *199,
  202*
Band, the, *104*
Band Aid, *156-57*
Banton, Buju, *136*
Barrett, Leonard, *135, 136*
Baxter, J. R., publisher,
  29
Bay City Rollers, *115*
"Be Thou My Vision"

(Van Morrison), *124*

"Be with Me, Jesus" (Soul Stirrers), *48*

Beach Boys, *69, 81, 114*

"The Beast in Me" (Nick Lowe), *173*

Beatles, *12, 15, 52-53, 57, 60, 63, 116, 143;* and Maharishi Mahesh Yogi, *68-69, 73, 78, 80, 82;* and Swami Prabhupada, *80, 82;* breakup, *107*

Beautiful Vision album (Van Morrison), *123*

Beggars Banquet album (Rolling Stones), *90*

The Belle Album (Al Green), *50*

Benton, Glen, *99*

Berry, Chuck, *19, 74, 154, 161*

Bible, *21, 41, 128, 130, 145, 152, 176, 177*

Big Brother and the Holding Company, *79*

Big Circumstances album (Cockburn), *173*

"Bird on a Wire" (Leonard Cohen), *173*

Bisher, Furman, *29*

Black, Bill, *32*

Black Magic, *94-95; see also* occult

Black Muslims, *199*

Black Sabbath, *98, 100, 160*

Black Swan, *101*

Black Widow, *98*

Blackwatch, *205*

Blackwood, Cecil, *31*

Blackwood, R. W., *31*

Blackwood Brothers, *29, 30, 31*

Blake, William, *97, 122, 123, 125*

Blanchard, John, *160*

"Blessed Jesus Hold My Hand" (Presley and others), *32*

Blond Ambition album (Madonna), *191*

"Blue Suede Shoes" (Perkins), *32*

Bluenotes, *48*

Bond, Graham, *97, 101, 142*

Boney M, *130*

Bonham, John, *101*

Bono (Paul Hewson), *11, 13, 173, 175, 176-86*

Boomtown Rats, *157*

Boone, Pat, *11*

"Born to Run" (Springsteen), *154*

Born to Run album, *153*

"Boss Drum" (Shamen), *216*

Boss Drum album, *216*

Bowie, David, *93*

Boy album (U2), *178*

Boy George, *12, 13*

Braden, William, *60*

Brahma, *71*

Brahman (absolute consciousness), *72, 74-75*

"Brahman" (Quintessence), *75*

Brand Nubian, *12, 204, 205*

Brewster, W. Herbert, *32, 33*

"Bridge Over Troubled Water" (Simon and Garfunkel), *48*

"Bring the Noise" (Public Enemy), *203*

Broonzy, Big Bill, *39*

Brotherhood of Eternal Love, *62*

Brown, Dennis, *136*

Brown, James, *38, 39, 45, 46, 47*

Browne, Jackson, *110, 111*

Brownlee, Archie, *38*

Bruce, Lenny, *168*

Buddhism, *123, 126, 195*

Bulgakov, Mikhail, *90*

Burden, Eric, *54, 60*

Burke, Solomon, *47*

Burnett, T-Bone, *159, 170-72*

Burning Spear (Winston Rodney), *132, 133, 136*

Burzum, *99, 100*

Butler, Don, *30-31*

Byrds, the, *160*

Byrne, David, *13, 150-51;* film *The House of Life, 152*

Candomble, *152*

Canto Gregoriano album (Enigma), *218*

Capleton, *136*

Cash, Johnny, *31, 34, 35, 160, 173, 174, 185*

Cash, W. J., *34*

Cass, Mama, *101*

Cassidy, David, *115*

Cavendish, Richard, *95*

Celtic Frost, *98*

Celtic lore, *123*

"A Change Is Gonna Come" (Sam Cooke), *45*

"Change My Way of Thinking" (Dylan), *166*

charismatic Christianity, *176*

Charles, Ray, *19, 37, 38, 39, 42, 43, 46*

Charters, Samuel, *101*

Chesterton, G. K., *171*

Chicago Seven, *115*

Children of God cult, *112*

Chinmoy, Sri, *70, 81, 82, 84*

Christianity, *12, 13, 14, 15, 123, 159-74, 175, 182,*

_183, 205-8_
Chuck D, _197, 199, 203, 204_
Church of Christ, _22_
Circles in the Stream album (Cockburn), _173_
Clapton, Eric, _55, 61, 87, 129, 140_
Clark, Fraser, _209, 210, 213, 214_
Clarke Sisters, _172_
Clash, the, _142, 143, 144_
Clayton, Adam, _176, 182_
Cleaver, Eldridge, _188_
Cloven Hoof, _98, 99_
Cochran, Eddie, _74_
Cockburn, Bruce, _173_
Cocker, Joe, _104_
COGICS, _44_
Cohen, Allen Y., _65_
Cohen, Leonard, _173_
"Cold Sweat" (James Brown), _46_
Cole, Nat King, _38_
"Come Together" (Lennon), _59_
computers and music, _209, 210, 211_
Cook, Paul, _141_
Cooke, Sam, _39, 43-45_
Coon, Caroline, _141, 142_
Coryell, Larry, _81_
Costello, Elvis, _170_
Counting Crows, _170_
Cowper, William, _184_
Crash Test Dummies, _14_
Cream, _61, 87_
Cretu, Michael, _217, 218_
Crickets, _28_
"Criminals" (Burnett), _172_
Crips, _198_
Crosby, Stills & Nash, _106, 109_
Cross, Brian, _202_
The Cross of Changes album (Enigma), _218_

Crouch, Andrae, _44, 190_
Crowley, Aleister, _91, 92, 93, 94, 95, 97, 119_
"Crucifixion" (Deicide), _99_
Crumpler, Denver, _30_
Culture Club, _13_
"Cupid" (Sam Cooke), _44_
cyberspace, _212_
"Cypress Avenue" (Van Morrison), _122_

Da Lench Mob, _199, 202_
Dalton, David, _89_
"Dance for the One" (Quintessence), _75_
Dangerous album (Michael Jackson), _12_
Dark Horse album (George Harrison), _81_
Darkness on the Edge of Town album (Springsteen), _153_
Darkthrone, _98_
Davis, Sammy, Jr., _31_
Davis, Stephen, _97, 133_
D. C. Talk, _207_
De La Soul, _197_
Deacon Blue, _172_
Deadheads, _213_
death metal music, _98, 99_
Def Jam label, _208_
Deicide, _98, 99_
Dene, Terry, _177_
Depeche Mode, _195_
Desperado album (Eagles), _111_
devil, _22, 23, 24, 25, 26, 85-102; see also_ occult
Disc, 75
Disc and Music Echo, 69
"Disguises" (the Who), _77_
Disraeli Gears album (Cream), _61_
Dive Deep album (Quintessence), _75_

Dixie Hummingbirds, _38_
D.M.C. _see_ Run-D.M.C.
"Do Not Pass Me By" (Hammer), _207_
Dobkin de Rios, M., _61_
Donne, John, _122, 195_
Donovan, _11, 55, 68, 73_
"Don't Believe the Hype" (Public Enemy), _203_
Doors, the, _12, 96, 114_
The Doors (film), _146_
Dorsey, Thomas A., _37, 42, 43, 49, 51_
"Down by the Riverside" (Presley and others), _32_
"Down There by the Train" (Waits), _173_
Down with the King album (Run-D.M.C.), _207_
Downing, David, _109_
Dozier, Lamont, _19_
Dr. Dre, _197_
Dre, _198_
drugs, _34, 54-65, 87, 199, 214; see also_ Ecstasy; ganja; heroin; LSD
Dylan, Bob, _12, 13, 15, 16, 109, 114, 129, 136, 139, 144, 159, 165-70, 171, 177, 178_

Eagles, _110, 111, 160_
Earth, Wind and Fire, _121, 160_
"East at Easter" (Simple Minds), _148_
Eazy-E, _197_
"Ebenezer Goode" (Shamen), _216_
Ecclesiastes, _111, 185_
Echo and the Bunnymen, _146, 147_
Ecstasy (drug MDMA), _210, 211, 216_
Ed Sullivan Show, 143

Edge, the (Dave Evans), *175, 176, 177, 180*
Edwin Hawkins Singers, *80*
Egyptian book of the Dead, 121
Egyptology, *120-21, 205*
Eliot, T. S., *171*
Emperor, *98*
Encyclopedia Psychedelica (Clark), *210, 213*
Enigma, *217*
Eno, Brian, *13, 150-51, 183*
Equinox bookstore, *94*
Eric B and Rakim, *199*
Esmond, Paul, *165*
Ethiopia, *128, 131, 132*
evangelism, Christian, *160*
Evans, Dave, *see* Edge
"Every Grain of Sand" (Dylan), *168*
"Everybody Needs Somebody to Love" (Burke), *47*
"Exodus" (Marley), *128-29, 136*

"F- tha Police" (NWA), *197*
The Face magazine, *182*
Faithfull, Marianne, *91*
Fakir, Abdul, *37*
Famous Flames, *45*
Fard, Wallace D., *200*
Farrakhan, Louis, *200, 201, 202, 203, 204*
Farren, Mick, *140, 141, 142*
festy-rave crossover, *209*
The Final Call newspaper, *200*
"Fire" (U2), *181*
"Fire and Rain" (James Taylor), *163*

"Fishing 4 Religion" (Arrested Development), *206*
Five Blind Boys of Alabama, *38*
Five Per Cent Nation, *204*
Flavor Flav, *199, 203*
Fleetwood Mac, *112*
flower power, *63*
"The Fly" (U2), *184*
Franklin, Aretha, *39, 40*
Franklin, Bertha, *45*
Franklin, C. L., *40*
Fraser, Robert, *91*
Friends album (Beach Boys), *81*
Fruit of Islam, *200*
Full of Fire album (Al Green), *50*

Gaia Mantra store, *213*
Gamble, Kenneth, *48*
gangsta rap, *197-99*
ganja drug, *132, 133-35*
Gano, Gordon, *159, 172*
Garcia, Jerry, *56, 60, 87, 119*
Garrett, Peter, *172*
Garvey, Marcus, *128, 131*
Gaye, Marvin, *16, 39-40, 47, 114, 187, 191-93;* death, *193*
Geldof, Bob, *156-58*
Genovese, Eugene D., *41, 46*
George, Nelson, *194*
"Get Up, Stand Up" (Marley), *128*
Gibbs, Christopher, *91*
Gift from a Flower to a Garden album (Donovan), *68*
Gimme Shelter film, *107*
Ginsberg, Allen, *79-80, 166, 170*
Girard, Chuck, *163*

"Give a Man a Fish" (Speech), *206*
"Give It Up or Turn It Loose" (James Brown), *46*
"Give Peace a Chance" (Lennon), *59, 80*
Giza pyramids, *120*
"Glam Slam" (Prince), *194*
Glastonbury Festival, *121, 174, 212*
"Gloria" (U2), *180*
Goats Head Soup (Rolling Stones), *160*
"God Save the Queen" (Sex Pistols), *141*
Godard, Jean-Luc, *90*
"Gods Will Be Gods" (Echo and the Bunnymen), *147*
Godspell, 163
Going for the One album (Jon Anderson), *116*
Gold Gate Quartet, *38*
Goldberg, Steven, *166*
Goldrosen, John, *28*
gospel music, *15, 21, 28-36, 37-51, 187, 205;* secularized, *37, 43, 44*
Gospel Music Association, *30-31*
Gospel Road album (Johnny Cash), *173*
"Gotta Serve Somebody" (Dylan), *169*
Graham, Bill, *157*
Graham, Billy, *35, 177*
Grant, Norman, *133, 134*
Grateful Dead, *56, 59, 61, 62, 79, 104, 114, 118-20, 213*
Gravediggaz, *198*
"Great Balls of Fire" (Jerry Lee Lewis), *23, 25*
Green, Al, *13, 16, 49-51*

Green, Peter, *112*
Greenbaum, Norman, *163*
Greenbelt Festival, *172*
Griff, Professor, *197, 199, 203-4*
Guardian newspaper, *213*
Guralnick, Peter, *39*
Guthrie, Arlo, *170*
Guthrie, Woody, *170*

Haile Selassie (Ras Tafari), *131, 137*
Haley, Bill, *162*
"Hallelujah" (Enigma), *218*
"Hallelujah I Love Her So" (Ray Charles), *46*
hallucinogenics, *87*
Hamill, James E., *19-20, 22*
Hammer (M. C. Hammer), *199, 207*
Hare Krishna, *79-80, 82, 83*
"Hare Krishna Mantra," *80*
Harmoneers, *30*
Harris, R. H., *45*
Harrison, George, *53, 54, 56, 57, 62, 64, 66, 68, 70, 71, 72, 73, 80*
Hart, Mickey, *119*
Hartnoll, Phil, *209, 217*
Hatha yoga, *126*
"Have You Seen Your Mother, Baby" (Rolling Stones), *85*
Hawkwind, *121*
"Heartbreak Hotel" (Presley), *143*
"Heaven Up There" (Echo and the Bunnymen), *147*
"Hefner and Disney" (Burnett), *171*
Heilbut, Anthony, *43*
Hell, Richard, *142, 151*

"Hellhound on My Trail" (Robert Johnson), *89*
Hendrix, Jimi, *55, 59, 60, 67, 104, 114, 117-18, 144, 178;* death, *107*
Henley, Don, *110*
heroin, *97, 105, 144, 163*
Heron, Mike, *55*
Hess, Jake, *29, 30*
Hesse, Herman, *Siddhartha, 67*
Heston, Charlton, *31*
Hewson, Paul, *see* Bono
Hibbert, Toots, *127*
"Higher Hell" (Echo and the Bunnymen), *147*
"Higher Love" (Depeche Mode), *195*
Highway 61 Revisited (Dylan), *166*
"Highway to Hell" (AC/DC), *98*
Hinduism, *12, 56, 58, 66-84, 123, 195*
Hoare, Ian, *49*
Hoffman, Eric, *99*
Holland-Dozier-Holland, *19*
Holly, Buddy, *19, 28*
Holy Magick, *97, 142*
Hopkins, Jerry and Danny Sugarman, *146*
horror metal bands, *98*
Hot Press magazine, *175, 185*
"Hotel California" (Eagles), *111*
Hotel California album, *110*
The House of Life film, *152*
"House of Mirrors" (Burnett), *171*
"How Great Thou Art" (Presley), *21*
"How I Got Over"

(Mahalia Jackson), *32*
Howell, Leonard, *128*
Huff, Leon, *48*
Human Be-In, *59*
"Human Touch" (Springsteen), *155*
Human Touch album, *155*
Humbard, Rex, *21*
Huntsbury, Chick, *194*
Huxley, Aldous, *The Doors of Perception, 73*
Hyles, Arnold, *30*
Hymns to the Silence album (Van Morrison), *124*

"I Am the Walrus" (Lennon), *55*
"I Believe in You" (Dylan), *167, 169*
"I Can't Explain" (the Who), *76*
I Ching, *113*
"I Feel You" (Depeche Mode), *195*
"I Found Out" (Lennon), *83*
"I Still Haven't Found What I'm Looking For" (U2), *181*
Ice Cube, *197, 198, 199, 201, 204*
Ice T, *198, 199, 206*
Iggy Pop, *178*
"I'm a Boy" (the Who), *77*
Immortal, *98*
In Another Land album (Larry Norman), *164*
In God We Trust album (Brand Nubian), *205*
"In League with Satan" (Venom), *99*
In Search of the Lost Chord album (Moody Blues), *75*

"In the Garden" (Dylan),
 169
*Inarticulate Speech of the
 Heart* album (Van
 Morrison), *123*
Incredible String Band, *55*
India, and religion, *12, 66,
 67; see also* Hinduism
information highway, *212*
International Times, 70, 92
Invaders of the Heart, *14*
Isaacs, Gregory, *136*
Ishtar, goddess, *195*
ISKCON (International
 Society for Krishna
 Consciousness), *79, 80,
 84*
Islam, *12, 113, 199-202,
 204*
Islam, Yusef (Cat
 Stevens), *113*
Island Records, *75*
*It Takes a Nation of
 Millions to Hold Us
 Back* album (Public
 Enemy), *203*
"It's a Man's Man's Man's
 World" (James Brown),
 47
"I've Been Born Again"
 (Johnnie Taylor), *47*
"I've Got a Woman" (Ray
 Charles), *37, 43*

Jackson, Jesse, *40*
Jackson, Mahalia, *28, 32,
 38, 124*
Jackson, Michael, *12, 13*
Jagger, Mick, *13, 28, 48,
 54, 69, 73, 103, 107;* and
 dark forces, *85, 86, 88,
 90, 92-93*
Jam Master Jay (Jason
 Mizell), *208*
"Jamming" (Marley), *136*
Jefferson Airplane, *59, 60,*

 79, 106
Jehovah's Witnesses, *13*
Jesus Christ, *24, 125, 173,
 177;* name used in songs,
 124, 163, 164, 172
*Jesus Christ Superstar,
 163*
Jesus Loves You, *12*
Jesus rock, *162, 163*
Jeter, Claude, *38, 48*
Jethro Tull, *161*
Jews, *13, 203, 204*
John, Elton, *115, 139*
John Wesley Hardin
 album (Dylan), *166*
Johnson, Linton Kwesi,
 137
Johnson, Robert, *89, 101*
Jones, Brian, *54, 69, 73,
 86, 88, 91, 115;* death,
 107
Jones, Gloria, *44*
Jones, Johnny "The
 Hurricane," *45-46*
Jones, Steve, *141*
Joplin, Janis, *67, 106, 107*
Jordanaires, *32*
The Joshua Tree album
 (U2), *151, 184, 185*
Journeys Out of the Body
 album (Naegele), *126*
Joy Division, *146*
Joy Will Find a Way
 album (Cockburn), *173*
Judaism, *13*
"Just a Closer Walk with
 Thee" (Van Morrison),
 124
"Just a Little Talk with
 Jesus" (Presley and
 others), *32*
"Just Over the Hill"
 (Mahalia Jackson), *32*

Kane, Big Daddy, *202*
Kasso, Richard, *100*

Katz, F., *61*
"Keep on Pushing"
 (Curtis Mayfield), *49*
Kenton, Stan, *29*
Kerouac, Jack, *170*
Kerr, Jim, *147, 148*
Kesey, Ken, *60*
King, B. B., *33*
King, Ben E., *47*
King, Martin Luther, Jr.,
 40, 202, 205
King Diamond, *99*
Kisser, Cynthia, *100*
Kraftwerk, *210*
Krishna, *12, 13, 71, 79, 80,
 81, 82, 83*
Krishnamurti, Jiddu, *123*
Kristofferson, Kris, *173*
Kriya yoga, *83*

LA Weekly, 171
Larkin, *126*
Larson, Bob, *160, 161*
Latifah, Queen, *202*
Lauer, Sandra, *218*
Leadon, Bernie, *111, 160*
League of Spiritual
 Discovery, *58, 62*
"Lean on Me" (Bill
 Withers), *47*
Leary, Timothy, *54, 57-59,
 62, 64, 66, 67, 73, 75, 103*
Led Zeppelin, *93, 97, 101*
Led Zeppelin III album,
 95
Lee, Tommy, *99*
"Legend of a Mind"
 (Moody Blues), *59, 75*
Lennon, Cynthia, *72*
Lennon, John, *11, 13, 53,
 54, 55, 56, 57, 59, 64, 78,
 80, 82, 83, 84, 103, 107,
 159, 178;* after the
 Beatles, *109*
Lesh, Phil, *120*
Let's Get It On album

(Marvin Gaye), *192*
Lewis, C. S., *171*
Lewis, Jerry Lee, *13, 17, 19, 20, 21-27, 31, 34, 35, 160*
Ley-lines, *117*
Liberace, *29*
"Like a Prayer" (Madonna), *190*
"Like a Song" (U2), *181*
Lindsey, Hal, *136*
Lister, Hovie, *29*
Little Richard, *12, 19, 21, 27-28, 35, 144, 160, 161*
Live Aid, *156, 157*
Living in the Material World album (George Harrison), *81*
"Living Proof" (Springsteen), *155-56*
Lone Justice, *172*
Lords of the New Church, *146*
Los Lobos, *170*
Louvin Brothers, *28*
"Lovable" (Sam Cooke), *44*
Love, and drugs, *63-64, 108*
Love, Mike, *69, 73*
Love Devotion Surrender (McLaughlin and Santana), *81*
"Love Minus Zero" (Dylan), *166*
Love Song, *163*
Love Wars album (Womack and Womack), *48*
LoveSexy album (Prince), *194*
Lowe, Nick, *173*
LSD, *52, 54-65, 66, 67, 68, 72-73, 85, 86-87, 104, 105, 106, 112, 113, 116, 126*

Lucky Town album (Springsteen), *155*
Lyles, Bill, *31*

McCartney, Paul, *52, 53, 54, 55, 60, 63, 67, 70, 73, 82, 116;* after the Beatles, *109*
McCrystal, Cal, *98*
McCulloch, Ian, *147, 148*
McDaniels, Darryl, *208*
McEwen, Joe, *44*
McGuinn, Roger, *55, 160, 170*
McGuire, Barry, *160*
McKee, Maria, *172*
McKenna, Terence, *12, 214, 215, 216, 217*
McKenzie, Scott, *64, 105*
McLaren, Malcolm, *138, 141, 142, 143, 144*
McLaughlin, John, *70, 81*
McPhatter, Clyde, *39*
"Madame George" (Van Morrison), *122*
"Madison Avenue" (Burnett), *171*
Madonna, *187, 189-91, 196*
magic and Rastas, *134-35; see also* occult; voodoo
Maharishi Mahesh Yogi, *68-69, 73-74, 78-79, 80, 81, 82*
Mahasaya, Sri Lahiri, *70*
Mahavishnu Orchestra, *70*
Malcolm X, *200*
The Man Who Sold the World album (David Bowie), *93*
Manamarhashi, *70*
Mansfield, David, *170*
"Mansion on the Hill" (Springsteen), *155*
Manson, Charles, *101, 108*
Marcus, Greil, *35-36, 50,*

167
"Marcus Garvey" (Burning Spear), *132*
Marley, Bob, *12, 14, 127, 128, 129, 130, 133-36, 138*
Marsh, Dave, *145*
Martin, Gavin, *193*
Martin, George, *53-54*
"Mary Don't You Weep" (Jeter), *48*
Masters and Houston, *The Varieties of Psychedelic Experience, 55, 63, 87*
Matlock, Glen, *141, 144*
Matthews, Randy, *163*
May, Brother Joe, *27*
maya (world of illusion), *72*
Mayfield, Curtis, *39, 49*
Mayhem, *99*
MCMXC a.D., *217-18*
"Me and the Devil Blues" (Robert Johnson), *89*
"Meaning of the 5%" (Brand Nubian), *205*
medicine men, *134-35, 136*
Megatripolis Club, London, *209, 210, 213-14*
Mehta, Gita, *68*
Melodians, *130*
Melody Maker, 62, 141, 183
Melvin, Harold, *48*
Merry Pranksters, *60*
mescaline, *73, 86*
Michell, John, *91, 117, 120*
Midnight Oil, *172*
Miles, Barry (Indica Bookshop), *57, 69, 176*
"Milkcow Blues Boogie" (Presley), *21*
Mitchell, Joni, *105*

Mizell, Jason, *208*

Moby, *13, 220*

Monde 2000 magazine, *212, 214, 217*

Monterey International Pop Festival 1967, *63*

Moody Blues, *59, 75*

Moon, Keith, *140*

Moore, Scotty, *32*

Morbid Angel, *98*

Morrison, Jim, *12, 15, 55, 96-97, 101, 115, 144, 146;* death, *107*

Morrison, Van, *8, 12, 13, 16, 114, 121-26, 139, 186, 220*

Mother Jones magazine, *182*

"Mother's Little Helper" (Jagger), *54*

Motley Crue, *99*

"Move Any Mountain" (Shamen), *215*

"Move On Up" (Mayfield), *49*

"Move On Up a Little Higher" (Mahalia Jackson), *32*

"Mrs. Robinson" (Paul Simon), *163*

Muggeridge, Malcolm, *69, 193*

Muhammad, Elijah, *200, 205*

Muldaur, Maria, *172*

Mullen, Larry, *176*

Murray, Charles Shaar, *168*

Muslims, *see* Islam

"My Beautiful Reward" (Springsteen), *155*

"My Father's House" (Springsteen), *154*

"My God Is Real" (Jerry Lee Lewis), *23*

My Life in the Bush of

Ghosts album (Eno and Byrne), *151*

"My Sweet Lord" (George Harrison), *80*

"My White Devil" (Echo and the Bunnymen), *147*

Myers, Larry, *165*

"Mysterious Ways" (U2), *184-85*

Mystery Train album (Marcus), *35*

mysticism, *114-26*

Naegele, David, *126*

Nash, Graham, *62*

Nashville Skyline album (Dylan), *110*

Nation of Islam, *199-202, 208, 204, 207*

Navajo Indians, *61*

Nebraska album (Springsteen), *154*

Nee, Watchman, *180*

Never Mind the Bollocks (Sex Pistols), *143*

New Age/New Consciousness, *14, 115-17, 120, 125-26, 209, 212*

"New Gold Dream" (Simple Minds), *149*

"A New Kind of Man" (Van Morrison), *125*

New Morning album (Dylan), *110*

New Musical Express, 124, 140, 168, 176, 193, 201, 204, 215

New West magazine, *167*

"New Year's Day" (U2), *181*

New York Times, 145, 218

Newcombe, Russell, *210*

Newton-John, Olivia, *161*

"Night" (Springsteen), *154*

"Night of the Living Baseheads" (Public

Enemy), *203*

"19th Nervous Breakdown" (Rolling Stones), *87*

No Guru, No Method, No Teacher (Van Morrison), *123*

"No Woman, No Cry" (Marley), *136*

Norman, Larry, *164-65*

"Nowhere Man" (Lennon), *54*

Nubian, Brand, *12, 204*

"Numb" (U2), *185*

NWA (Niggas With Attitude), *197-98*

"O Happy Day" (gospel), *80*

Oak Ridge Quartet, *29*

Oates, John, *161*

Obituary, *98*

occult, *86-102, 117*

O'Connor, Flannery, *24, 154, 171*

O'Connor, Sinead, *14*

October album (U2), *179, 181, 183*

Oh Mercy album (Dylan), *169*

Ojas, *126*

"The Old Time Camp Meeting of the Air" (W. Herbert Brewster), *33*

Oldham, Andrew "Loog," *86*

"On the Firing Line" (Soul Stirrers), *45*

"One Caress" (Depeche Mode), *195*

"Only Sixteen" (Sam Cooke), *44*

Only Visiting This Planet album (Larry Norman), *164*

Orbison, Roy, *13, 22*

Orbital, *217*

Osbourne, Ozzy, *98, 100*

Osmond, Humphrey, *86*

Osmonds, the, *115*

Pace, Charles, *94*

Page, Jimmy, *84, 93-95, 97, 101-2*

"Paint It Black" (Rolling Stones), *85*

Pallenberg, Anita, *86, 91, 97*

Palmer, Robert, *22*

Pannell, William, *201*

Parker, Charlie, *76*

Pawns in the Game album (Professor Griff), *203*

"Peace in the Valley" (Presley and others), *32, 33, 43*

Pentecostals, *18, 28*

People magazine, *24*

Perkins, Carl, *32, 35*

Peter, Paul and Mary, *160*

Peters, Mike, *172*

Philadelphia International Records (Philly label), *48*

Phillips, John, *85, 101*

Phillips, Sam, *24*

Piano Red, *29*

Pickering, Stephen, *166*

Pickett, Wilson, *39*

"Pictures of Lily" (the Who), *77*

Pinder, Mike, *75*

Pink Floyd, *161*

Plant, Robert, *94*

"Please, Please, Please" (James Brown), *46*

Poor Righteous Teachers, *204-5*

Prabhupada, Swami, *79-80, 82, 84*

"Precious Angel" (Dylan), *167*

"Precious Lord" (Dorsey), *43*

Presley, Elvis, *12, 17, 19-21, 22, 28, 29, 31, 32, 33, 34-36*

Preston, Billy, *44*

The Pretender (Jackson Browne), *111*

Prince, *161, 187, 193-94*

Professor X, *205*

"Prove It All Night" (Springsteen), *153*

Psalms, *130-31, 177*

psychedelic drugs, *see* Ecstasy; LSD

Psychedelic Experience (Leary), *57*

Psychedelic Reader (Leary), *57*

Public Enemy, *12, 197, 199, 200, 203*

punk music, *138-46*

"Punky Reggae Party" (Marley), *139*

"Purple Haze" (U2), *185*

pyramids, Giza, *120*

Quadrophenia (the Who), *78*

Queen, *139*

"Quicksand" (David Bowie), *93*

Quicksilver Messenger Service, *59, 79*

Quintessence, *74-75*

Qur'an, *113, 150*

ragga music, *136*

Rainbow Bridge concert (Hendrix), *118*

Rainey, Ma, *42*

"Raining Revolution" (Speech), *206*

Raising Hell album (Run-D.M.C.), *207*

Rakim, *199, 204*

Ramones, the, *142, 151*

Rangers Quartet, *30*

Ranks, Shabba, *136*

rap, *197-99, 202, 203, 205, 206-8*

Raschke, Carl A., *126*

Rastafarianism, *12, 127-37, 138-39*

Rattle and Hum album (U2), *178*

rave culture, *209, 211, 215-17*

Rawls, Lou, *39*

"Real African People" (Professor Griff), *204*

Redding, Otis, *39*

redemption, *14, 18, 33, 83, 103, 129, 152, 160, 168, 190*

"Redemption" (Johnny Cash), *173-74*

Reed, Lou, *178*

"Re:Evolution" (Shamen), *216*

reggae, *129, 132, 133, 136, 137*

Release (agency), *142*

Renaldo and Clara (Dylan film), *170*

Resurrection Band, *163*

Revelation, book of, *130*

Revolver album (Beatles), *57*

Rhodes, Bernie, *142*

Richard, Cliff, *11, 124, 160, 177*

Richards, Keith, *54, 85, 97, 129, 144;* and the occult, *86, 88, 90, 91*

Rimbaud, Arthur, *144, 145*

Ritz, David, *192*

"Rivers of Babylon" (Melodians/Boney M.), *130*

"The Rivers of Belief"

(Enigma), *218*
Roberts, Dave, *183*
"Rock Dis Funky Joint"
   (Poor Righteous
   Teachers), *205*
Rodney, Winston
   (Burning Spear), *132,
   133, 136*
Roll Jordan Roll
   (Genovese), *41, 46*
Rolling Stone magazine,
   *24, 48, 78, 86, 109, 145,
   171, 172, 190, 208*
Rolling Stones, *69, 106,
   114;* and dark forces, *86-
   92, 160-61*
Rolling Thunder Tour,
   170
Roman Catholicism, *148,
   149, 150, 157, 188, 190-
   91, 196*
Ross, Ricky, *172*
Rotten, Johnny, *129, 138,
   141, 142*
Roxy Music, *151*
Rubin, Jerry, *115-16*
Ruffin, David, *39*
Run-D.M.C., *199, 207-8*
Rundgren, Todd, *121*

"San Francisco" (Scott
   McKenzie), *64, 105*
*San Francisco Tribune,
   167*
"Sanctified Lady"
   (Marvin Gaye), *192*
"Sanctify Yourself"
   (Simple Minds), *148*
Sanders, Alex, *98*
Santana, *81-82, 104*
Santana, Carlos, *81*
Sarasivati, Brahmananda
   (Guru Dev), *74*
Satan, *see* devil
*Saturday Evening Post,
   53, 69*

Saunders, Nicholas, *210*
"Saved" (Dylan), *167*
Saved album, *166, 167,
   168, 169, 171*
"Say It Loud—I'm Black
   and I'm Proud" (James
   Brown), *46*
Scientology, *123*
Scott, Cyril, *124*
Scully, Tim, *62*
Sebastian, John, *105*
"The Secret Heart of Mu-
   sic" conference, *123*
"The Seeker" (the Who),
   59
Self-Realization
   Fellowship, *69*
Sergeant Pepper album
   (Beatles), *59, 62, 64, 68,
   70, 71, 92*
Serna, Father Clemente,
   218
sex, *21, 23, 34, 47, 161-62,
   187-96*
Sex Pistols, *138, 139, 141-
   42, 143, 144, 178*
"Sexual Healing" (Marvin
   Gaye), *193*
Sexual Healing album, *47*
"Sexy Sadie" (Lennon), *78*
"Shake Off the Ghosts"
   (Simple Minds), *148*
Shalom, *186*
shamanism, *58, 115, 144,
   145, 209, 215, 216, 219*
Shamen, *12, 215-16*
Shankar, Ravi, *67, 71, 72*
Sharkey, Alix, *213*
"She Gives Me Religion"
   (Van Morrison), *122*
"She Watch Channel
   Zero?!" (Public Enemy),
   203
Sheep, *163*
Shepard, Sam, *184*
Shiva, *71*

Shorty, *199, 202*
Shot of Love album
   (Dylan), *168, 169*
Shout at the Devil album
   (Motley Crue), *99*
"Shut It Tight" (Burnett),
   172
Siddhartha (Hesse), *67*
Silber, Irwin, *166*
Silberman, Steve, *213*
Simmons, Joseph, *208*
Simmons, Russell, *208*
Simon and Garfunkel, *48,
   163-64*
Simple Minds, *146, 147-49*
sin, *145*
Sin(not), Will, *209, 215*
Sinatra, Frank, *29, 31*
Situationism, *143*
Skelton, Red, *31*
Skinny Boys, *202*
Slade, *115*
"Slavery Days" (Burning
   Spear), *132*
Slayer, *98*
Slow Train Coming
   album (Dylan), *165, 166,
   167, 168, 169, 171, 177*
Smith, Patti, *16, 138, 144-
   45, 178*
Snoop Doggy Dogg, *198*
So Long Ago the Garden
   album (Larry Norman),
   164
Social Deviants, *142*
Soles, Steven, *170*
"Solid Rock" (Dylan), *167*
soma drug, *58*
"Somebody Up There
   Likes You" (Simple
   Minds), *148*
"Son of the King"
   (Hammer), *207*
Songfellows, *31, 37*
*Songs of Faith and
   Devotion* album

(Depeche Mode), *195*
soul music, *48-49*
Soul Stirrers, *38, 44, 45*
Southern California Community Choir, *40*
"Sparkle in the Rain" (Simple Minds), *149*
Speech, *206*
Spencer, Jeremy, *112*
"Spirit in the Sky" (Greenbaum), *163*
spiritual, Negro, *41*
Spiritual Regeneration Movement, *68*
Springsteen, Bruce, *8, 14, 35, 76, 152-56*
"Sri Ram Chant" (Quintessence), *75*
Stamps, the, *31*
Stamps, V. O., publisher, *29*
"Stand By Me" (Ben E. King), *47*
Starkie, Enid, *145*
Starr, Ringo, *73, 82*
Statesmen Quartet, *29, 30*
Stealing Fire album (Cockburn), *173*
Stevens, Cat, *55, 103, 113*
Stewart, Rod, *115, 139*
Sting (Gordon Sumner), *13, 147, 149-50, 157*
Stone, Oliver, *146*
Stookey, Paul, *160*
Stowe, Harriet Beecher, *41*
Straight Outta Compton album (NWA), *197*
"Stranger in a Strange Land" (U2), *181*
Stranglers, *146*
"Substitute" (the Who), *76, 77*
"Summer of Love" raves, *210*
Sumner, J. D., *20, 29, 31,*

34
Sun Records, *21, 31*
"Sunday Bloody Sunday" (U2), *181*
The Sunday Times, 186, 191
Swaggart, Jimmy Lee, *23, 26*
Swan Silvertones, *38, 48*
Syamasundara, *80*
"Sympathy for the Devil" (Rolling Stones), *90, 106*
Synergy club, *215*

"Take It to the Limit" (Eagles), *111*
Tales from Topographic Oceans album (Jon Anderson), *116*
Talking Heads, *151*
Tame, David, *124*
Tannahill, Reay, *195-96*
tantric Hinduism and Buddhism, *195*
Tardy, John, *98*
Taylor, Derek, *53*
Taylor, James, *163*
Taylor, Johnnie, *40, 44, 47*
techno dance, *13*
techno futurist, *209*
techno pagan, *209-20*
Tenetehara Indians, *61*
"Tennessee" (Speech), *206*
Terminator X, *199*
Tharpe, Sister Rosetta, *27*
"That's All Right" (Presley), *31*
Their Satanic Majesties Request album (Rolling Stones), *85*
"There Is a Holy City," *41*
"This Little Girl of Mine" (Ray Charles), *43*
"This Little Light of Mine" (gospel), *43*

"Thunder Road" (Springsteen), *154*
The Tibetan Book of the Dead, 54, 67
"Tired of Being Alone" (Al Green), *50*
To Cross a River (Swaggart), *23*
Tommy album (the Who), *15, 77, 164*
"Tomorrow Never Knows" (Beatles), *56*
Too Legit to Quit album (Hammer), *207*
Tosh, Peter, *136*
Tougher Than Leather album (Run-D.M.C.), 207
Townsend, Ed, *192*
Townshend, Pete, *13, 54, 66, 72, 74, 75-78, 84, 107, 164, 220*
trance musicians, *115, 118, 126*
The Trance Tapes (Ojas), *126*
trances, induced by rock 'n' roll, *162*
Transcendental Meditation, *69, 73-74*
"Trenchtown Rock" (Marley), *135*
tribal, *209*
A Tribe Called Quest, *199*
"True Love Ways" (Buddy Holly), *28*
Tucker, Ira, *38*
Tucker, Ken, *171*
Turner, Nik, *121*
"Tutti Fruitti" (Little Richard), *21*
Tweakin' Records store, *213*
Twinkle Brothers, *133*
"Twistin' the Night Away" (Sam Cooke), *44*

"U Can't Touch This"
(Hammer), 207
U2, 151, 172, 175-86
Ultrakill! magazine, 100
Under the Red Sky album
(Dylan), 169
The Unforgettable Fire
album (U2), 151
Universal Remnant
Church of God, 27
USA Today, 169

Vath, Sven, 217
Vaughan, J. D., publisher,
29
Vedic scriptures, 58
Venom, 98, 99
"A Very Cellular Song"
(Mike Heron), 55
Vicious, Sid, 144
Vikernes, Varg, 99-100
Violent Femmes, 172
Virgin Mary, 189
virtual reality, 212
voodoo, 26, 27

Wailers, 136
Waits, Tom, 173
"Wake Up Everybody"
(Harold Melvin), 48
"Walk This Way" (Run-
D.M.C.), 207
"The Wanderer" (U2), 185
War album (U2), 181
"Washed Away" (Speech),
206
Washington Times, 203
Watson, Lyall, 120
Watts, Alan, 73
"Way to Eternity"
(Enigma), 218
Weir, Bob, 120

"Welcome to Hell"
(Venom), 99
Wexler, Jerry, 17, 38
"What I'd Say" (Ray
Charles), 39
"When Will I Ever Learn
to Live in God" (Van
Morrison), 124
"Whenever God Shines
His Light" (Van
Morrison), 124
Whitaker, Jess, 38
White, Maurice, 121
"White Rabbit" (Jefferson
Airplane), 60
"White Rabbit" (Shamen),
216
Who, the, 59, 67, 75, 77,
104, 107, 114
"Who Killed Davy
Moore?" (Dylan), 114
"A Whole Lotta Shakin"
(Jerry Lee Lewis), 26
"Why Don't You Look
into Jesus?" (Larry
Norman), 164
"Why Me" (Presley), 21
"Why Me, Lord"
(Kristofferson), 173
"Why Should the Devil
Have All the Good Mu-
sic?" (Larry Norman),
164
Williams, Deniece, 172
Williams, Marion, 33
Wilson, Brian, 52, 55, 101
Wilson, Colin, 125
Winwood, Steve, 54, 60
Wired magazine, 212
"With a Shout" (U2), 181
"With God on Our Side"
(Dylan), 114

Withers, Bill, 47
"Without a Woman" (Kip
Anderson), 47
Wobble, Jah, 14
Womack, Bobby, 44
Womack, Cecil, 48-49
"Wonderful" (gospel), 44
"Wonderful World" (Sam
Cooke), 44
"Won't Get Fooled
Again" (the Who), 107
"Woodstock" (Joni
Mitchell), 105
Woodstock festival 1969,
104-6

X Clan, 199, 205
Xitintoday album
(Hawkwind), 121

Yes, 116
Yogananda, Paramhansa,
69, 70, 83, 116
"You Better Leave That
Liar Alone" (gospel), 43
"You Better Leave That
Woman Alone" (Ray
Charles), 43
"You've Got the Power"
(James Brown), 46
Yukteswar, Sri, 70

Zaehner, R. C., 1, 108
Zappa, Frank, 161
Zen Buddhism, 13, 166
zippie, 209
Zooropa concerts and
album (U2), 182, 183,
185